Frommer's®

PORTABLE
California
Wine Country

5th Edition

by Erika Lenkert

Here's what critics say about Frommer's:

"Amazingly easy to use. Very portable, very complete."

—*Booklist*

"Detailed, accurate, and easy-to-read information for all price ranges."

—*Glamour Magazine*

WILEY

Wiley Publishing, Inc.

Published by:

WILEY PUBLISHING, INC.

111 River St.
Hoboken, NJ 07030-5774

ISBN-13: 978-0-471-78739-6
ISBN-10: 0-471-78739-6

Editor: Caroline Sieg
Production Editor: Katie Robinson
Photo Editor: Richard Fox
Cartographer: Roberta Stockwell
Production by Wiley Indianapolis Composition Services

For information on our other products and services or to obtain technical support, please contact our Customer Care Department within the U.S. at 800/762-2974, outside the U.S. at 317/572-3993 or fax 317/572-4002.

Wiley also publishes its books in a variety of electronic formats. Some content that appears in print may not be available in electronic formats.

Manufactured in the United States of America

5   4   3

Contents

List of Maps

ABOUT THE AUTHOR

Native San Franciscan **Erika Lenkert** fled the dot-community to find respite and great food and wine in Napa Valley. When she's not writing about food, wine, and travel for the likes of *Four Seasons Magazine* or *InStyle*, or promoting her book *The Last-Minute Party Girl: Fashionable, Fearless, and Foolishly Simple Entertaining*, she's in search of Wine Country pleasures to share with Frommer's readers. She also remains subservient to her owners—two Siamese cats and most recently, her new daughter Viva.

In addition to this guide, Erika authors and co-authors a number of other Frommer's guides to California, including *Frommer's California*, *Frommer's San Francisco*, and *Frommer's Memorable Walks in San Francisco*.

SPECIAL THANKS

Erika would like to thank Lyla Max for not only tirelessly pouring over these pages to help confirm their accuracy, but also for providing excellent newborn advice, reassurance, and friendship—free of charge.

AN INVITATION TO THE READER

In researching this book, we discovered many wonderful places—hotels, restaurants, shops, and more. We're sure you'll find others. Please tell us about them, so we can share the information with your fellow travelers in upcoming editions. If you were disappointed with a recommendation, we'd love to know that, too. Please write to:

> *Frommer's Portable California Wine Country*, 5th Edition
> Wiley Publishing, Inc. • 111 River St. • Hoboken, NJ 07030-5774

AN ADDITIONAL NOTE

Please be advised that travel information is subject to change at any time—and this is especially true of prices. We therefore suggest that you write or call ahead for confirmation when making your travel plans. The authors, editors, and publisher cannot be held responsible for the experiences of readers while traveling. Your safety is important to us, however, so we encourage you to stay alert and be aware of your surroundings. Keep a close eye on cameras, purses, and wallets, all favorite targets of thieves and pickpockets.

FROMMER'S STAR RATINGS, ICONS & ABBREVIATIONS

Every hotel, restaurant, and attraction listing in this guide has been ranked for quality, value, service, amenities, and special features using a **star-rating system.** In country, state, and regional guides, we also rate towns and regions to help you narrow down your choices and budget your time accordingly. Hotels and restaurants are rated on a scale of zero (recommended) to three stars (exceptional). Attractions, shopping, nightlife, towns, and regions are rated according to the following scale: zero stars (recommended), one star (highly recommended), two stars (very highly recommended), and three stars (must-see).

In addition to the star-rating system, we also use **seven feature icons** that point you to the great deals, in-the-know advice, and unique experiences that separate travelers from tourists. Throughout the book, look for:

Finds	Special finds—those places only insiders know about
Fun Fact	Fun facts—details that make travelers more informed and their trips more fun
Kids	Best bets for kids and advice for the whole family
Moments	Special moments—those experiences that memories are made of
Overrated	Places or experiences not worth your time or money
Tips	Insider tips—great ways to save time and money
Value	Great values—where to get the best deals

The following **abbreviations** are used for credit cards:

AE	American Express	DISC	Discover	V	Visa
DC	Diners Club	MC	MasterCard		

FROMMERS.COM

Now that you have the guidebook to a great trip, visit our website at **www.frommers.com** for travel information on more than 3,000 destinations. With features updated regularly, we give you instant access to the most current trip-planning information available. At Frommers.com, you'll also find the best prices on airfares, accommodations, and car rentals—and you can even book travel online through our travel booking partners. At Frommers.com, you'll also find the following:

- Online updates to our most popular guidebooks
- Vacation sweepstakes and contest giveaways
- Newsletter highlighting the hottest travel trends
- Online travel message boards with featured travel discussions

The Best of the Wine Country

Whether you're on a budget or blowing your annual bonus, there's no way around it: A Wine Country experience epitomizes indulgence. Literally all that's expected of you is to eat, drink, relax—and then do it all over again. The rest—wine tastings, spa treatments, hot-air balloon rides, canoe trips, horseback tours—is mere icing on an already idyllic cake. In fact, you don't even have to like wine to love the Wine Country; anyone who enjoys lounging in a hammock on a warm summer's day will succumb because the Wine Country is just that: the country. The verdant expanses of rolling hills patterned with grape-garnished trellises, hued with mustard and wildflowers, and dotted with farmers plowing the soil and vintners tending to their vines is country life at its picture-perfect best.

Of course, there's a whole lot more: wineries both great and small producing some of the world's finest wines, nationally renowned chefs serving exceptional cuisine, luxury resorts, boutique shopping, and soothing mineral hot springs. Yes, the world may be falling apart elsewhere, but not here—for this eternal Eden of indulgence is where you go when you feel the need to be pampered, when it's time to whip out the charge card for that $200 dinner or bottle of cabernet sauvignon and say, "Frankly, my dear, I don't give a damn."

1 The Best Wineries

IN NAPA VALLEY

- **Artesa** (Carneros, Napa Valley): Sure they've got a huge wine portfolio that includes a slew of tasty pinot noirs, but what makes Artesa one of my all-time favorite places to send visitors is the winery itself. Built into the Carneros hillside with stellar views of the San Pablo Bay and beyond, from the outside it seems like an underground fortress topped with super-cool fountains. From within it's an airy, modern space with plenty of elbowroom. Plainly put, it's just too darned cool. See p. 54.

- **Clos Pegase** (Calistoga, Napa Valley): Viewing the art at this temple to wine is as much the point as tasting the wines themselves. Renowned architect Michael Graves designed this incredible oasis, which integrates an impressive modern art collection—including a sculpture garden—with a state-of-the-art winemaking facility that features 20,000 square feet of aging caves. See p. 73.

- **Domaine Chandon** (Yountville, Napa Valley): Founded by Moët et Chandon, the valley's most renowned sparkling winery has all the grandeur of a world-class French champagne house. Strolling with a glass of bubbly in hand through this estate's beautifully manicured rose gardens—complete with pond and sculpture—is a quintessential Wine Country experience. If you just can't bear to leave, no worries. Just pull up a chair in their fancy French dining room or in the more casual salon or patio and relish the pastoral splendor. See p. 58.

- **The Hess Collection** (Napa, Napa Valley): Half the fun is winding your way to this beautiful and secluded hillside winery, which is as much about contemporary art as it is about fermented grape juice. Spectacular gallery spaces show off their stunning collection and the gift shop is one of the most tasteful in the valley. It's a gorgeous place. See p. 56.

- **Joseph Phelps Vineyards** (St. Helena, Napa Valley): Intimate, comprehensive tours and knockout tastings make this one of my favorite wineries to visit. An air of seriousness hangs heavier than harvest grapes when you first arrive, but the mood lightens as your knowledgeable guide explains the ins and outs of winemaking and you begin to taste five to six varietals. These range from sauvignon blanc to what's bound to be terrific cabernet. (*Wine Spectator* regularly awards Phelps's cabernets and blended reds with scores in the high 90s, and aficionados have been known to come close to brawling over bottles of the coveted Insignia cabernet.) Don't forget to reserve ahead; tours and tastings are by appointment only. See p. 68.

- **Schramsberg** (Calistoga, Napa Valley): Old hand-carved caves complete with cobwebs, echoes, and loads of ambience; a comprehensive walk through sparkling wine production; and a grand finale tasting around a round table in a private room make this a great stop for those looking for a little entertainment with their education. See p. 72.

- **Swanson Vineyards & Winery** (Rutherford, Napa Valley): No other winery offers such a luxurious, relaxed, and fun tasting as this sexy little reservations-only stop. Join the select few guests at a round table, taste delicious wines, and nibble on bonbons while you make new friends and learn about the famed Rutherford dust. Now that's living. See p. 61.

IN SONOMA VALLEY

- **The Benziger Family Winery** (Glen Ellen, Sonoma Valley): As soon as you arrive here, you'll know you're at a family-run winery—in fact, you'll feel instantly like part of the Benziger clan. This low-volume, high-quality winery offers an exceptional self-guided tour, a 40-minute tram tour through its pastoral grounds, $5 tastings, and many excellent, reasonably priced wines. See p. 130.

- **Gloria Ferrer Champagne Caves** (Carneros District, Sonoma Valley): Gloria is the grande dame of Sonoma Valley's sparkling wine producers. On a sunny day, it's impossible not to enjoy sipping a glass of brut on the terrace of this palatial estate as you take in the magnificent views of the vineyards and valley below. If you're unfamiliar with the *méthode champenoise,* make time for the 30-minute tour, which takes you past the fermenting tanks and the bustling bottling line and into the dark caves brimming with rack after rack of fermenting wine. See p. 126.

- **Gundlach Bundschu Winery** (Sonoma, Sonoma Valley): Gundlach Bundschu is the quintessential Sonoma winery: nonchalant about appearance, obsessed with wine. Oenophiles in the know covet GB's reds, particularly the zinfandels, which are remarkably inexpensive for such well-crafted wines. Tours include a trip into the 430-foot cave. GB also has the best picnic grounds in the valley. See p. 127.

IN NORTHERN SONOMA

- **Bella Vineyards & Wine Caves** (Dry Creek Valley, Northern Sonoma): Even if this boutique winery weren't producing exceptional zinfandels, it'd still be a top stop for me since the place is so enchanting. Even the drive (down a one-lane road to its end) is an adventure, but the real payoff is the adorable barn fronted by century-old olive trees and the *très chic* cave where tasting can be enjoyed at café tables under hip dangling lamps. It's relaxed glamour worth seeing for yourself. See p. 173.

- **Ferrari-Carano Vineyards & Winery** (Healdsburg, Northern Sonoma): With the most stunning landscaping in Northern Sonoma, this winery includes an Asian-inspired garden, a profusion of blooms (especially in spring), vast vineyard views, and sips of some pretty tasty wine. See p. 172.

- **Preston of Dry Creek** (Healdsburg, Northern Sonoma): Absolutely charming is the best way to describe this family-owned winery. A must-stop on any Northern Sonoma itinerary, it's got everything you could wish for in a country winery: beautiful grounds with an abundance of flora (and picnic tables!), a friendly tasting room in a cheery Victorian farmhouse setting, a large selection of wines to sip and buy, estate-grown organic produce, homemade bread, and even a bocce ball court. See p. 173.

2 The Best Winery Tours for First-Timers

IN NAPA VALLEY

- **Domaine Chandon** (Yountville, Napa Valley): Not only are the grounds sublime, but the comprehensive tour walks you through the high-tech facilities and the entire bubbly-making process, from the history of the winery to the cellars, riddling room, and bottling line. Tours are free and reservations aren't necessary, but if you want to taste, it'll cost you: $9 to $14 for a full glass (sorry, no free sips). Come during high season, though, and you can supplement your bubbly with a few appetizers and kick back on the garden-front patio. See p. 58.
- **Robert Mondavi Winery** (Oakville, Napa Valley): As one of the most prominent wineries in the valley, it's only appropriate that Robert Mondavi would offer a guided tour for every sort of wine taster. The basic 1-hour comprehensive production tour covers all aspects of the winemaking process and gives you a look at the destemmer-crusher, the tank room where fermentation is done, the bottling room, and the vineyard, all accompanied by a top-notch narrative—the guides are great at making sure you know what you're looking at. Make your reservations in advance, if possible; these tours are not offered daily and get booked up, especially in high season. See p. 60.
- **St. Supéry Winery** (Rutherford, Napa Valley): This straightforward winery is a great place for first-time tasters to learn more about oenology. The nifty self-guided tour comes complete with "SmellaVision," an interactive display that teaches you how to identify different wine aromas and attributes; there's also a demonstration vineyard that you can wander through to learn about growing techniques. See p. 62.
- **Frank Family Vineyards** (Calistoga, Napa Valley): Although this isn't a remotely comprehensive tour, it is the least intimidating.

Staff members run one of the friendliest wineries in the valley, which includes taking the time to explain *anything* you want to know about wine. They also serve you all the bubbly you want and have a back room featuring still wines. See p. 72.

- **Schramsberg** (Calistoga, Napa Valley): The label that U.S. presidents serve when toasting with dignitaries from around the globe also serves up the Wine Country's best introduction to the *méthode champenoise* process of making sparkling wine. The excellent tour at Schramsberg is comprehensive and non-threatening, and it's an experience you won't soon forget; the highlight is the visit to the 2½ miles of hand-carved champagne caves—you'll feel like you've landed in the middle of a *Tom Sawyer* adventure. And the tasting room is positively gothic. Be sure to book a spot on a tour in advance, as tours fill up quickly. See p. 72.

- **Sterling Vineyards** (Calistoga, Napa Valley): This dazzling-white, Mediterranean-style winery, perched high above the rest of the valley atop a rocky knoll (you'll arrive via aerial tram), offers one of the most comprehensive self-guided tours in the entire Wine Country. It's great for getting to know the entire winemaking process at your own pace. See p. 73.

IN SONOMA VALLEY

- **The Benziger Family Winery** (Glen Ellen, Sonoma Valley): *Wine Spectator* magazine hailed this family-run winery as having "the most comprehensive tour in the wine industry." The exceptional self-guided tour, which includes a free 40-minute tram ride through the estate vineyards, is both informative and fun. Tram tickets are a hot commodity, so be sure to plan ahead for this one. See p. 130.

3 The Best Experiences Beyond the Wineries

- **Hot-Air Ballooning over Napa's Vineyards:** Admit it: Floating over lush green pastures in a hot-air balloon is something you've always dreamed of but never gotten around to actually doing. Here's your best chance: Napa Valley is the busiest hot-air balloon "flight corridor" in the *world*—and what more romantic place to sail up, up, and away? For recommendations on the best Napa hot-air balloon companies, see "More to See & Do," in chapter 4.

- **Spreading out Your Picnic Blanket for a Gourmet Alfresco Feast:** You've been with the crowds all day—sitting with them in traffic and sipping elbow-to-elbow in the tasting rooms. If the thought of joining the masses for a meal after all that seems about as romantic and relaxing as a New York subway ride, cancel your restaurant reservations and pack a picnic instead. Both Napa and Sonoma have some of the most spectacular picnic spots on the planet, not to mention incredible artisan food products and excellent places to fill your basket. See "Where to Stock Up for a Picnic & Where to Enjoy It," in chapter 4 for details on picnicking in Napa, and see "Where to Stock Up for a Picnic & Where to Enjoy It," in chapters 5 and 6 for details on picnicking in Sonoma.

- **Pampering Yourself at a Spa:** The Wine Country is the perfect place to relax—so what better place to indulge in a tension-relieving massage, a purifying facial, or a rejuvenating body wrap? My favorite spots to spa it are St. Helena's **White Sulphur Springs Inn & Spa** (② 707/967-8366), **Health Spa Napa Valley** (② 707/967-8800), the **Fairmont Sonoma Mission Inn & Spa** (② 800/257-7544), and **Hotel Healdsburg** (② 707/431-2800). See chapter 4 for details on Napa spas, chapter 5 for Sonoma, and chapter 6 for Hotel Healdsburg.

- **Horseback Riding through the Wine Country:** If you like horses, consider seeing the countryside from the saddle. **Napa Valley Trail Rides and Sonoma Cattle Company** (② 707/255-2900) will lead any level of rider on a leisurely ride through beautiful Skyline Park in Napa. Or contact **Triple Creek Horse Outfit** (② 707/933-1600), which orchestrates rides in both Napa's Bothe-Napa Valley State Park and Sonoma's Jack London State Historical Park. The season runs from April through October. See "More to See & Do," in chapters 4 and 5.

- **Touring Sonoma's Wineries on Two Wheels:** With quiet, gently sloping country roads and lots of bucolic scenery, Sonoma is perfect for cycling. Local bike tours will rent you a bike, take you on one of their organized excursions to wineries, provide a gourmet lunch featuring local foodstuffs, and also carry any wine you purchase and even help with shipping it home. See "More to See & Do," in chapter 4 and "Touring Sonoma Valley by Bike," in chapter 5.

- **Getting Your Thrills in the Skies:** If you're the thrill-seeking type, catch a panoramic ride in an authentic 1940 Boeing-built

Stearman biplane with **Vintage Aircraft Company** (✆ 707/
938-2444), whose planes depart from the south end of
Sonoma Valley. See "More to See & Do," in chapter 5.

4 The Best Luxury Hotels & Inns

- **Auberge du Soleil** (Rutherford, Napa Valley; ✆ 800/
  348-5406): This spectacular Relais & Châteaux member is
  one of my absolute favorite luxury destinations on the planet.
  (And yes, I've seen a lot of 'em.) Quiet, indulgent, and luxuriously romantic rooms are large enough to get lost in—and
  you'll want to once you try out the fireplace, whirlpool tub,
  and private balcony overlooking the valley. Tack on an incredible spa with valley views from the hot tub and their restaurant's terrace, and it's pure heaven. If you've got the cash, this
  is the way to go, except, perhaps, if you can book a room at its
  newer sister Property, **Calistoga Ranch** (Calistoga, Napa Valley; ✆ 707/254-2800). Park yourself on your private deck at
  one of their uberluxury cabins within a pristine canyon; exit
  only to treat yourself at their spectacular indoor-outdoor spa,
  delicious private restaurant overlooking Lake Lommel, or pool
  and you'll be hard pressed to leave. See p. 91 and p. 97.
- **Meadowood Napa Valley** (St. Helena, Napa Valley; ✆ 800/
  458-8080): I love Meadowood, too, but it offers a more resort-
  like experience. Tucked away in its own private wooded valley,
  it's a favorite retreat for Hollywood celebs and corporate CEOs
  who can hide out in freestanding New England–style cottages,
  spend days hiking the private trails or playing golf, tennis, or
  croquet, and follow up with a trip to the health spa and
  whirlpool. For those who love full-service luxury with all the
  fixin's, there's no better option. Indeed it's perfect anytime of
  year, but I find the most magical time to come is the holidays
  when the resort is quieter and romantically lit with white
  Christmas lights. See p. 93.
- **Cottage Grove Inn** (Calistoga, Napa Valley; ✆ 800/
  799-2284): This romantic cluster of cottages is my top pick
  for doing the Calistoga spa scene in comfort and style. Each
  one-room cottage is ultracompact, but it makes a lot out of a
  little and comes complete with a wood-burning fireplace,
  homey furnishings (perfect for curling up in front of the fire),
  cozy quilts, and an enormous bathroom with a skylight and a
  deep, two-person Jacuzzi tub. But if you want the perks that

come with a hotel, go for one of the suites with the outdoor hot tubs at the nearby Mount View Hotel & Spa. See p. 98.

- **Fairmont Sonoma Mission Inn & Spa** (Sonoma, Sonoma Valley; ✆ **800/257-7544**): A popular retreat for the wealthy and the well known, this multimillion-dollar resort is Sonoma Valley's most luxurious (and big-business) resort. A gargantuan spa and workout area and its naturally heated artesian springs are the place's coups de grâce. Sauna, steam room, whirlpool, outdoor exercise pool, weight room, a whole menu of spa treatments— you can pamper yourself in myriad ways, and retire to your superluxe suite when the day is done. Alas, the rooms are extremely expensive, but, hey, this is Wine Country. Get used to it. See p. 140.

- **Gaige House Inn** (Glen Ellen, Sonoma Valley; ✆ **800/935-0237**): Truth be told, I've never stayed in a better B&B— ever, anywhere, period. Here's what you have to look forward to: gorgeous plantation-inspired decor with tasteful worldly accents, the best robes ever designed, unbelievable nightly appetizers that inspired an invitation to the James Beard house for the chef, late-night cookie-plate raids, and professionalism associated with fine hotels. In a nutshell, it's first-class service, an abundance of amenities, luxurious rooms outfitted with top-quality goods—everything you'd expect from an outrageously expensive resort, but with a homey, tailored, and intimate atmosphere. See p. 147.

- **Kenwood Inn & Spa** (Kenwood, Sonoma Valley; ✆ **800/353-6966**): Romantics, look no further. Here, the honey-colored, Tuscan-style buildings, flower-filled flagstone courtyard, and pastoral views of vineyard-covered hills are enough to make any northern Italian homesick. The lavishly done rooms come with just about every extra you could want (except TV, which would interfere with the tranquil ambience). The full-service spa is small but to die for, and the staff is friendly and helpful. See p. 149.

5 The Best Moderately Priced Accommodations

- **Wine Country Inn** (St. Helena, Napa Valley; ✆ 888/465-4608): This attractive wood-and-stone hideaway, complete with a French-style mansard roof and turret, offers lovingly and individually decorated rooms and copious amounts of hospitality. It's also very well priced, considering the outrageous rates usually charged in St. Helena. One of the inn's best features is its attractively landscaped outdoor pool (heated year-round); in fact, the whole charming place overlooks a pastoral landscape of Napa Valley vineyards. See p. 96.

- **White Sulphur Springs Inn & Spa** (St. Helena, Napa Valley; © 800/593-8873): This woodsy escape is a short winding drive away from downtown St. Helena. Established in 1852 and set among 330 acres of creeks, waterfalls, hot springs, redwood, madrone, and fir trees, White Sulphur Springs claims to be the oldest resort in California; it's geared toward nature-nugget types, who will appreciate both the cozily rustic cabins and the pristine surroundings. A full menu of spa treatments, outdoor pool and natural hot springs, and a holistic vibe round out the relaxation. See p. 96.

- **El Dorado Hotel** (Sonoma, Sonoma Valley; © 800/289-3031): Designed by the same folks who put together Napa's exclusive Auberge du Soleil, this place on Sonoma's historic square may look like a 19th-century Wild West relic from the outside, but inside, it's midrange 20th-century deluxe. French windows offer lovely views of the courtyard, which features a heated lap pool, and the ground floor houses one of the area's best restaurants. See p. 144.

- **Glenelly Inn and Cottages** (Glen Ellen, Sonoma Valley; © 707/996-6720): With verdant views of Sonoma's oak-studded hillsides, this former 1916 railroad inn is drenched in serenity, and it has everything you'd expect from a Wine Country retreat. Bright, immaculate rooms have old-fashioned clawfoot tubs and Scandinavian down comforters, a hearty country breakfast is served beside the large cobblestone fireplace, and there's a long veranda where you can curl up in a comfy wicker chair to admire the idyllically bucolic view. See p. 149.

6 The Best Restaurants

- **Bistro Don Giovanni** (Napa, Napa Valley; © 707/224-3300): My favorite casual restaurant in the valley, this has a consistent combination of perfect thin-crust pizzas (margarita and the seasonal fig, prosciutto, and balsamic are spectacular), soul-satisfying pastas (anything with duck ragout!), wood-oven specialties, friendly service, and an excellent bar dining and drinking scene. Perch yourself at the bar, order a glass of wine or a cocktail from fabulous bartenders Aaron or

Ben, and you're likely to strike up a jolly conversation with a local—perhaps even me! See p. 102.

- **Bouchon** (Yountville, Napa Valley; ℂ 707/944-8037): This locals' favorite tops even my charts—after Bistro Don Giovanni, that is. The sleek and festive French bistro atmosphere and outstanding classics such as steak frites, a towering bibb lettuce salad, and steamed mussels in white wine broth. Beyond lunch and dinner, it's an excellent late-night stop, when they serve a limited menu and attract restaurant staff at the bar. See p. 110.

- **The French Laundry** (Yountville, Napa Valley; ℂ 707/ 944-2380): If you've got the cash, are a serious food lover, and can get a reservation, you have no choice but to dine here and find out for yourself why chef/owner Thomas Keller's restaurant continues to be hailed as the best restaurant in the world. Dinner at this intimate restaurant is an all-night affair complete with truffle shavings, dramatic presentations, and swirling and sniffing. When it's finally over, you won't believe how many different delicacies found their way out of the kitchen and into your heart. See p. 108.

- **Terra** (St. Helena, Napa Valley; ℂ 707/963-8931): As far as fine dining goes, Terra is my number-one choice, period. Within a historic fieldstone restaurant, James Beard Award–winning chef Hiro Sone creates incredibly sophisticated, vibrant, and refined cuisine that deftly shows his French, Italian, and Japanese culinary training as well as his appreciation for the best of local seasonal ingredients. Sone's wife— pastry chef and front-of-the-house gal Lissa Doumani— ensures each eve is delicious, from the polished service to the to die for desserts. Take my word for it: If you're going to splurge, Terra is a must-try.

- **ZuZu** (Napa, Napa Valley; ℂ 707/224-8555): If you've had it with French and Italian fare and Wine Country–themed dining rooms, race directly to this neighborhood haunt. Shockingly affordable and serving a worldly array of Mediterranean-inspired "small plates," it's a snack-lover's nirvana. I'm addicted to the single-serving paella, yummy and intriguing by-the-glass wines, and friendly attitude here. See p. 108.

- **Cafe La Haye** (Sonoma, Sonoma Valley; ℂ 707/935-5994): One of my personal favorites. This small, sophisticated Sonoma cafe is a must-stop on your Wine Country dining binge. You'll enjoy the simple yet savory dishes emanating from the tiny open kitchen as well as a friendly waitstaff, attractive art, and absurdly reasonable prices. See p. 152.

- **Depot Hotel–Cucina Rustica Restaurant** (Sonoma, Sonoma Valley; © 707/938-2980): This much welcome addition to downtown Sonoma ups the culinary ante of an area that's surprisingly sparse on destination dining rooms. Drop in to sample Mediterranean-inspired cuisine by chef Ryan Fancher, who brings some tricks he learned while cooking at Napa's famous The French Laundry. See p. 152.

- **The Girl & the Fig** (Sonoma, Sonoma Valley; © 707/938-3634): The cuisine at this modern, attractive cafe is nouveau-country with French nuances—and, yes, usually figs: They appear in such creations as the winter fig salad made with arugula, pecans, dried figs; and Laura Chenel goat cheese with a fig-and-port vinaigrette and a hearty pork chop with fig compote, roasted fennel, mashed potatoes, and pork jus. Of course there are lots of options minus the figs, too. Tourists and locals pack the place (and its lovely back patio) nightly, so reserve ahead. See p. 153.

- **Meritage** (Sonoma, Sonoma Valley; © 707/938-9430): Chef Carlo Cavallo put his heart and soul into this exciting Sonoma mainstay that combines the best of Southern French and Northern Italian cuisines. What's not to like about wild boar chops in a white truffle sauce, handmade roasted pumpkin tortelloni, and napoleon of escargot in a champagne-and-wild-thyme sauce—all at surprisingly reasonable prices? Check it out. See p. 154.

- **Cyrus** (Healdsburg, Northern Sonoma; © 707/433-3311): One of Northern California's most elegant and opulent dining experiences can be yours with a reservation at this restaurant designed to reminisce the small fine-dining establishments of Bordeaux, France. Blow the budget and start by ordering from the caviar cart and the champagne cart, then let genius chef Doug Keane work his culinary magic. Definitely save room for dessert. Those offered here achieve real star status. See p. 188.

- **Jimtown Store** (Alexander Valley, Northern Sonoma; © 707/433-1212) Part general store, part gastronome's dream deli and cafe, this roadside attraction is downright adorable, from its old-school looks and toy and candy collection to its exceptional edibles, from sandwiches to housemade spreads (definitely get the fig and olive tapenade) to pastas and cookies. See p. 191.

2

The Wine Country Experience

by John Thoreen

Seeing the Wine Country can be an enormously pleasant day trip. However, investing at least a full day in each valley will reward you with multiple hedonistic dividends—and put you near the head of the class in understanding the ultrapremium wines of California. The pages that follow give you a head start on your trip by introducing you to Napa Valley, Sonoma Valley, and Northern Sonoma County and the exciting world of winemaking.

1 Introducing Napa Valley & Sonoma Valley

San Francisco is often seen as a charming yet congested metropolis. In contrast, the two rural valleys just an hour to the north, Sonoma and Napa, and Northern Sonoma farther north by a half hour, offer a delightfully calming and rustic retreat. In the Wine Country, the focus is mainly on gastronomy: adventures with wine and food, augmented by a setting of charming villages and towns, sunny afternoons, striking mountain landscapes, carefully presented works of art and architecture, and seas of the world's tidiest vineyards.

The mix of sophistication and rusticity can be peculiar: Dusty pickups park outside some of the finest restaurants in the country. Vintners clad in denim jackets carry bottles of first-growth Bordeaux Chateaux into local bistros. Barns both small and large are more likely to house wine barrels than bales of hay. Many of the homes that pepper the region, tucked back among the vines or perched on hillsides, appear in the pages of *Architectural Digest.* And these are small towns!

Although Napa and Sonoma counties view each other as competitors, and although you can sense a difference in attitude traveling from one region to the other, together as the Wine Country they differ from any other region in California. This uniqueness is based on several factors: a tumultuous geology comprised of 50 or 60 perfectly poor soils; a colorful yet disjointed historical record; a climate unique to growing world-class grapes; legions of entrepreneurs who have often misunderstood the wine business; resilient farmers who once grew wheat and prunes before switching to grapes; and you, one of more than 5 million folks who visit each year. (Some years ago, a journalist claimed that Napa is second only to Disneyland as a tourist attraction—an exaggeration that has been perpetuated ever since.)

QUALITY, NOT QUANTITY   In the odd jargon of marketing, "premium" refers to wines that sell for under $7, "superpremium" wines run between $7 and $14, and "ultrapremiums" cost $15 and up. The majority of California's premium wines come not from Napa and Sonoma, but from the state's vast Central Valley. Still, most of America thinks of Napa and Sonoma as the Wine Country. In fact, the seemingly endless spread of vines in Napa and Sonoma comprise only a small part of California's total vineyard acreage. Because the yields per acre here are much lower than in the Central Valley, Sonoma produces only about 7% of the wine made in the state; Napa only around 5%. In short, the Wine Country north of San Francisco gained its fame not from quantity, but from quality.

Though the Wine Country's total acreage is small, the intensity of its winemaking activity is remarkable. Sonoma claims to be home to more than 150 wine producers, Napa Valley to more than 250, which places almost *half* of California's 900-plus wine producers in just two relatively small regions. Even more remarkable is the fact that many of the hot boutique labels selling for $50 or more per bottle are housed as "tenants" in larger wineries and are not counted as wineries per se. When you combine the wineries you can visit with those that thrive as "labels," Napa and Sonoma are probably home to 60% or 70% of the ultrapremium labels in California. Thus, when you visit the Wine Country, you're sure to experience many of the very best wines that California has to offer.

THE KEY: GEOGRAPHY

Why does the Wine Country produce such a disproportionate amount of the ultrapremiums in the state? What makes the wines of Sonoma and Napa so good? Mother Nature can take most of the credit: The local climate and geology are the primary factors in the region's winemaking success. Beyond these fortuitous geographical features, the flow of history and twists of politics also come into play, though to a much lesser degree. If not for the ocean, the mountain ranges, the earthquakes, and the volcanoes, the valleys of Napa and Sonoma would never have been formed.

Heading into the Wine Country from San Francisco, you traverse a range of Mediterranean-like climates. Each differs significantly based on its distance from the ocean or San Francisco Bay, and on its proximity to the small mountain ranges that parallel the coast and block the passage of cold ocean air inland. Grapes love this particular climate, as do numerous other crops, ranging from olives, walnuts, apples, and citrus fruits to wild herbs such as fennel, bay, sage, and mustard.

The climatic differences in the Wine Country are subtle, yet significant. Although the Wine Country will never know such weather extremes as the snows of Buffalo, New York, or the humidity of Washington, D.C., everyone who lives here knows that Napa, the city, is cooler by 10 or more degrees on a warm summer day than Calistoga, 20 miles to the north. Because the south end of the Wine Country—referred to as the Carneros District—is cooled by the breeze off the bay, it works best for chardonnay and pinot noir, delicate grapes of Burgundy that cannot thrive in hot climates. Farther north, around Kenwood in Sonoma and St. Helena in Napa, the warmer climate suits Bordeaux grapes such as cabernet sauvignon, merlot, and sauvignon blanc.

THE IMPORTANCE OF PLACE: APPELLATIONS   In both Sonoma and Napa, the latest refinements occurring in the wine world involve discovering a "sense of place" for each style of wine. This critical understanding of soils and slopes happened years ago in Bordeaux, Burgundy, Chianti, and other classic wine-growing regions. Those areas' legally recognized, specific place names say, "This soil planted to this grape on this hillside makes a distinctive style of wine." The United States started such a system only recently. As a result, "Napa" was recognized as an appellation, a "named place," in 1981; the area designated "Sonoma" received its approval in 1983. Finer distinctions have sliced these larger regions into smaller pieces, each of which makes further claims to unique qualities in its wines. Today, Sonoma has 11 subappellations; Napa has 10. Thus, you might see a wine label that reads: "Kenwood Vineyards, Cabernet Sauvignon, Sonoma County, Sonoma Valley," the terms becoming increasingly more specific about the source of the grapes. In Napa it might be "Saintsbury, Pinot Noir, Napa Valley, Carneros."

Over years, players in the local wine scene have debated the merits of appellations and subappellations. One school says that the words *Napa* and *Sonoma* carry tremendous goodwill and that diluting them with numerous new terms will only confuse the consumer, who's often confused enough already about wine. The visionaries argue that as long as "Napa" and "Sonoma" appear on the label, additional specifics will only help the wine drinker. Only time will tell in this latest twist in the history and politics of the Wine Country.

A LOOK AT THE PAST

Sonoma and Napa were latecomers to the California vineyard scene. Around 1780, Franciscan missionaries, establishing the first of their 21 missions in California, planted the first vineyard in the state near San Diego. The first commercial vineyards were established in Los Angeles around 1825. Around the same time, the 21st and last Franciscan mission, Mission San Francisco Solano, planted its vines near present-day Sonoma; the same vines became the first commercial vineyard in the region about 15 years later, when the missions became secularized. Napa saw its first vineyards in 1838, but it had yet to produce commercial wine until 1858, when Charles Krug made a few gallons for John Patchett.

Los Angeles continued to dominate California's wine industry until the 1870s, when Sonoma took over the leadership in total acres around 1875. In turn, Napa replaced Sonoma in acreage a decade later. Not only did Napa and Sonoma grow in size, but also tasters noticed that their wines were demonstrably superior simply because the climates of Sonoma and Napa were (and still are) distinctly cooler than those in the Los Angeles region.

Somewhat sadly, in terms of today's viticultural and winemaking successes, the delightfully colorful history of wine of early California is rather short-lived. In one sense, the wine business in California is only 45 years old. Unlike Europe and other New World wine-growing regions, which have enjoyed continuous generations of winemaking, California had a terrible break in its development—Prohibition—and had to start all over again.

Most of California's wineries shut down during Prohibition, though a few remained in operation to produce wine for sacramental and medicinal purposes. But in the years of temperance, the United States all but lost whatever palate it had acquired for dry table wines. For 35 years after Prohibition, more than half the wine consumed in this country was dessert (or "fortified") wine, so-called ports and sherries, which contain 18% to 20% alcohol and loads of sugar.

Of course, this perversion of good taste has since been reversed, but oddly so. Each wine generation has been dramatically shorter than its predecessor: The first lasted almost 100 years (1825–1919), the second (after the break for Prohibition) only 30 years (1934–65), and the third just 15 years (1966–80). From hereon, the path swerves from winemaking to growing grapes, and necessarily slows down, as the Wine Country has—albeit cautiously—hit its stride.

THE FIRST GENERATION (1825–1919)   This fascinating period in winemaking involves the entangling of a variety of ethnic groups over several generations: Spanish Fathers, Native Americans, European immigrants (the first settlers in Napa and Sonoma were mostly Germanic, followed later by Italians and French), and Chinese (the main labor force; even today you can see the miles of stone walls they built and visit caves they carved out with picks). One of the major struggles of this generation involved breaking away from the grape variety used by the missions (and therefore called *Mission*), but only a few growers possessed such vision: Count Agoston Haraszthy at Buena Vista, T. Belden Crane and Charles Krug in St. Helena, Jacob Schram at Schramsberg (a historical monument that is now making champagne), and later, Gustaf Niebaum at Inglenook (now Rubicon Estate).

Between 1870 and 1890, Sonoma and Napa wines won medals with some frequency in international competitions; most of the region's wines, however, were not even bottled at the wineries but rather sold in bulk to merchants, who often blended them badly. Not infrequently, they were even labeled with European names for sale on the East Coast! Regardless, these years laid a solid basis for a regional wine industry: In 1889, Sonoma could claim around 100 wineries, Napa around 140.

Unbeknownst to winemakers, however, a disaster was in the works. A plant louse the size of a pinhead, *Phylloxera vastatrix*, began attacking vineyards in the 1880s. As a result, Napa lost roughly 75% of its acreage in the 1890s.

THE LOOMING SHADOW OF PROHIBITION   The business managed to hold its own after the turn of the century, only to encounter a far more formidable foe—the cries of Carrie Nation and the Temperance Movement, whose Prohibition stance had been gaining ground with the moral majority in the last decades of the 19th century. Even in Napa, the Anti-Saloon League made inroads with voters as early as 1912, 7 years before Prohibition became a national fact. During this dry era, the number of wineries dwindled from 600 to a few remaining stragglers. (Ironically, the grape acreage *exploded* to satisfy the need for home winemakers across the country who could legally make 200 gal. per household. Unfortunately, the thick-skinned grape varieties that ship well in railcars do not make fine wine.)

THE SECOND GENERATION (1934–65) Whoopee! After years of speakeasies, bathtub gin, and phony sherry, Americans could legally drink real wine!

Well, not at first. The few hundred entrepreneurs who rushed in to make a killing in wine found that they had essentially no market and quickly went bankrupt. Americans had almost no interest in dry European-style table wines. A few producers who had made wine during the last years of Prohibition and aged it throughout the Prohibition period had some success. Growers such as Louis Martini and Cesare Mondavi had survived and flourished by shipping their grapes to home winemakers (legal during Prohibition), and were ready to start promoting their California wines in the late 1930s and early 1940s.

In trying to revive the wine business, one of the major battles was fought over varietal labeling—the labeling system we now take for granted that makes the name of the grape variety (cabernet sauvignon, chardonnay, and so on) the most important word on the label after the name of the producer. All through the 19th century and fully into the 1960s, huge volumes of wine were called burgundy, chablis, chianti, Rhine wine, and such, referring wistfully to some vague growing region or type of grape, and usually delivering wine that only accidentally resembled the stated product. One grower argued vociferously against the new labeling because if the law passed, he would have to actually put some Riesling grapes in his wine labeled "Riesling." To him, Riesling was just a style or a marketing tool. Who cared if it actually tasted like Riesling?

It was a pretty grim era for American winemaking in general, and California's Wine Country wasn't faring well. In 1937 Napa had 37 wineries and Sonoma was flush with 91. Collecting accurate statistics about the era is a challenge, but apparently the number of Napa wineries decreased from 47 in 1945 to 25 in 1960. According to one source, only 12 wineries of those 25 made enough wine to sell outside Napa County; the same source reports that Sonoma's count had dwindled to 7 wineries in 1950 and grew only to 9 by 1960. If these numbers are even close to reality, it's clear that recovery from Prohibition was painfully slow, backsliding a few times along the way.

Nonetheless, a handful of well-grounded wineries sailed through this sluggish period, and a few of their wines can still be appreciated today. Most came from Napa, including Inglenook, Beaulieu, Beringer, Christian Brothers, and Louis Martini. Sonoma, in contrast, had a stronger bulk winemaking tradition and a more casual attitude about the role of wine in the good life. (Subsequently, long-winded arguments have been—and probably always will be—held about the casual Italian-Sonoma approach versus the more Northern European, image-conscious, award-bent, Napa approach.)

Ironically, in recent years, Sonoma has been touting its ability to garner more gold medals than Napa. Whatever the significance of a wall festooned with ribbons and awards, Sonoma has certainly caught up with Napa when it comes to making fine wines.

THE THIRD GENERATION (1966–80)   It's impossible to draw hard lines in the flow of time, but no other single event marks the modern era of winemaking like Robert Mondavi's 1966 move away from Charles Krug, a family-owned winery since 1943, to found his own winery in Oakville. Joe Heitz had launched his own label in 1961; in Sonoma in 1959, James Zellerbach at tiny Hanzell had revived traditional Burgundian winemaking techniques. At around the same time, Peter Newton acquired the first land holdings for Sterling Vineyards. Unlike his peers in the field, Mondavi combined a push toward new winemaking technology, with an aggressive marketing flair that has grown ever since and now extends to several brands and international alliances.

Compared to previous generations of winemakers, third-generation vintners looked like grade-schoolers, a bunch of kids (many of whom were graduates of U. C. Davis or Fresno State) in playgrounds filled with new toys: stainless-steel tanks, small oak barrels, a panoply of yeast cultures to ferment their wines, new vineyards planted to the best grape varieties, and, in several senses, the freedom to play and experiment. In 1972 and 1973, a remarkable cluster of wineries came on the Napa scene: Chateau Montelena, Clos du Val, Burgess Cellars, Mt. Veeder Vineyards, Silver Oak, Caymus, Diamond Creek, Stag's Leap Wine Cellars, Carneros Creek, Franciscan, Silver Oak, Trefethen, Clos du Val, Stonegate, Joseph Phelps, and Domaine Chandon. These seasoned players now share a quarter of a century of winemaking experience—and the beginnings of a legacy.

In Sonoma Valley, Kenwood, Chateau St. Jean, and St. Francis all sprang up in the early 1970s. For these wineries, and the many that followed, the 1970s can be considered the decade when winemakers discovered their styles of wine. With all the new winemaking equipment and new vineyards, styles changed almost annually: one year a crisp, appley chardonnay with moderate oak; the next, a very fleshy, soft wine dominated by a heavy oak bouquet; the third year, a third style. The poor consumer took a wild ride through these years, but as winemakers matured, their styles stabilized.

Napa and Sonoma had often compared their wines with international benchmarks, and favorably so. The French pooh-poohed the comparison; that is, until an English wine merchant staged a tasting in Paris in 1976. There, French wine experts on French soil gave top places in a blind tasting to the chardonnay from Chateau Montelena, as well as the cabernet from Stag's Leap Wine Cellars. The results shocked France and tickled the California Wine Country. At last, they were approaching the big leagues.

THE FOURTH GENERATION (1980–PRESENT)   The most recent phases of change in the Wine Country have been marked by signs of caution—both in the vineyard and in the marketplace—mingled with a few fantastic vintages. Since 1990, we have lived in a golden age of good vintages and astonishing sales, especially for more expensive wines, ranging from $50 to $150 per bottle. Throughout the 1980s and 1990s, the number of new labels grew steadily, as if there were no problems and never will be. Wine has always created optimists.

Wine sales leveled off in the early 1980s, when both Napa and Sonoma vintners discovered that *Phylloxera,* scourge louse of the 1880s and 1890s, had returned, requiring replanting of most of the acreage in both counties. (Actually, *Phylloxera* was never really exterminated; it's permanently in the soil. Rather, the solution to fix the problem went awry.) The prospects of pulling out 70% to 80% of the vines hit growers and wineries hard, both emotionally and financially. A vineyard is a long-term investment, taking 10 to 15 years to mature and lasting 40 to 50 years—if nature, always a temperamental partner, behaves. Add to that the staggering costs—$20,000 to $25,000 per acre to plant a vineyard—and you'd best tell your banker you need another $2,000 per year per acre just to cover farming costs before you get a full crop in 4 or 5 years. Most growers worked out the financing, and by the late 1990s, more than half of the replanting had been finished. Now, with thousands of acres coming on stream, a few voices talk about overproduction. Welcome to the ever-cyclical wine business.

Although Napa and Sonoma make both white wines and red wines extremely well, the 1990s saw a breakthrough in the styling of reds, a higher-level style change than those of the 1970s and early 1980s. Using a couple of techniques that you'll likely hear discussed on tours (for example, "presoaking" and "extended maceration"), winemakers are coming up with richly flavored wines that are supple and approachable, even when young. One enthusiast of the new style, Dennis Johns, formerly at St. Clement Vineyards and now owner of White Cottage Wines, says he wants his red wines to be "sweet, round, and juicy, even in the barrel." Don't look for these wines to have true sweetness. Rather, they have a very fine grade of tannin, which in the past could make wines so puckery they went down like liquid nails. If a decade ago you were ever turned off by red wines, it's time to retaste—and hopefully, enjoy.

2 Winemaking 101

In the flush of today's golden age of California's Wine Country, one might forget that California, let alone Napa and Sonoma, did not invent wine. Credit for this discovery goes to a woman who probably lived around 7,000 years ago: At least one cultural anthropologist suggests that a cave-dwelling woman brought into her cave clusters of wild grapes and put them in a concavity on a rock ledge. Her child, or children, walked over them a few times (or, worse, sat on them), breaking open many berries. The busy cave keeper neglected the grapes for a few days. When she finally noticed the pool of juice (caves *are* dark, after all), it was frothing and giving off strange, but not unpleasant, aromas. It's hard to imagine why she would cup the juice in her hand and drink it, but she did—and it affected her most strangely. Let's assume it was pleasantly tasty, if not a little bit too sweet. In any case, she'd discovered wine—and Sonoma and Napa, as well as the rest of the world, owe her a debt of gratitude.

Amazingly, her techniques saw only a few improvements in the next millennia. First, winemakers learned that wine must be stored in sealed containers—clay amphorae or wooden barrels—or it spoils, turning into vinegar. Second, cool storage also prevents spoilage, hence the use of caves and cellars. The wines of the Greeks and Romans were probably as good, or as bad, as those made by monks in the Middle Ages and only a bit improved by secular winemakers from the Renaissance to the Industrial Revolution.

The science called *oenology,* which has given the world the highest overall quality of wine ever, was developed after Louis Pasteur's work with fermentation and bacteriology around 150 years ago. Only in the past few generations have winemakers acquired very technical training and earned PhDs in viticulture (the science of grape growing) in a concentrated effort to understand wine and vineyards.

Even with this recent development of science applied to wine, the catchphrase today for many winemakers in Sonoma and Napa is, "I want the wine to make itself." The desired image is winemaker as midwife, whose role is merely to assist the mother (grape) in a very natural process—not much different from the cave dweller and her young assistants. It sounds so simple: Harvest ripe grapes, put the juice from the grapes in a container with some yeast, watch the juice ferment into wine, clarify and age the new wine, and drink!

Obviously, making wine is much more complex than that. From arguing about the very meaning of the word *ripe* to controlling the ferment in order to affect flavors and textures of the wine, the contemporary "natural" winemaker must incorporate his or her knowledge of fermentation, microbiology, and even such vagaries as the proper barrel (French, American, or Hungarian oak) for aging. These winemakers enjoy the powerful position of being able to make wine simply, naturally, and without spoilage simply because they know, scientifically, what can go wrong. Our cave dweller didn't have a clue.

On your tours of wineries, you'll hear differing stories about the "right" way to make wine, for each vintner harbors strong opinions—almost like a creed—on his or her wine styling. Be prepared for some inconsistencies; ferreting them out can be half the fun. To help you sort through the claims, here's a brief but broad sketch of the ABCs for making white wines, red wines, and sparkling wines.

WHITE WINES   For white wines, the winemaker wants only the juice from the grapes. (For red wines, both the juice and skins of the grapes are essential; using the white winemaking technique, you can make a *white* wine from a *red-skinned grape.*) Grapes are picked either by hand or by machine and brought to the winery as quickly as possible. Just as a sliced apple turns brown when left on the kitchen counter, grapes oxidize—and can even start fermenting—if they are not processed quickly. At some wineries, the clusters go through a "destemmer-crusher," which pops the berries off their stems and breaks them open (not really crushing them). The resulting mixture of juices, pulp, and seeds—called *must*—is pumped to a press. At other wineries, the whole clusters are put directly into a press (a widely used technique called, logically, *whole-cluster pressing*).

Most presses these days use an inflatable membrane, like a balloon, and gently use air pressure to separate the skins from the juice, which is then pumped into fermenting vessels. In the recent past, most white wines were fermented in stainless-steel tanks fitted with cooling jackets. Cool, even cold, fermentations preserve the natural fruitiness of white grapes. More recently, many Napa and Sonoma producers have begun using small wooden barrels for fermentation of white wines, especially chardonnay. This practice reverts to old-style French winemaking techniques and is believed to capture fragrances, flavors, and textures not possible in stainless steel. Barrel fermentation is labor intensive (each barrel holds only 45–50 gal. for fermentation), and the barrels are expensive ($600–$700 each for French barrels, $250–$300 for American barrels).

After white wines are fermented, they are clarified, aged (if appropriate), and bottled, usually before the next harvest. For the simpler white wines—chenin blanc, Riesling, and some sauvignon blancs—bottling occurs in the late winter or early spring. Most sauvignon blancs and chardonnays go into the bottle during the summer after the harvest. Very few white wines, usually chardonnays, take the slow track and enjoy 15 to 18 months of aging in small barrels with prolonged aging on the *lees,* the sediments from the primary fermentation. Those treatments are unusual, but they produce chardonnays that are richly flavored, complex, and expensive.

RED WINES   The chief difference between white wines and red wines lies simply in the red pigment that's lodged in the skins of the wine grapes. So while for white wines the juice is quickly pressed away from the skins, for rosés and reds the pressing happens after the right amount of "skin contact." That can be anywhere from 6 hours—yielding a rosé or very light red—to 6 weeks, producing a red that has extracted all the pigment from the skins and additionally refined the tannin that naturally occurs in grape skins and seeds.

Almost all red wines are aged in barrels or casks for at least several months, occasionally for as long as 3 years. In the past, casks in California were usually made from redwood and were quite large (5,000–25,000 gal.). Only a few wineries still use redwood today. Most of the wooden containers—collectively called *cooperage*—are barrels now made of American or French oak, and they hold roughly 60 gallons each.

The aging of red wines plays an important role in their eventual style because several aspects of the wine change while in wood. First, the wine picks up oak fragrances and flavors. (Yes, it is possible to "overoak" a wine.) Second, the wine, which comes out of the fermenter murky with suspended yeast cells and bits of skin, clarifies as the particulate material settles to the bottom of the barrel. Third, the texture of the wine changes as the puckery tannins interact and round off, making the wine more supple. Deciding just when each wine in the cellar is ready to bottle challenges the winemaker every year. And, to make the whole process even more challenging, every year is different.

Unlike white wines, which are usually ready to drink shortly after bottling, many of the best red wines improve with aging in the bottle. Napa and Sonoma cabernet sauvignons, for example, often reach a plateau (try not to think "peak") of best drinking condition that ranges from 7 to 12 years after the vintage, the year that appears on the label. However, there are no rigid rules. Some self-proclaimed cabernet freaks prefer their reds rather rough and ready. Only by tasting, tasting, tasting will you find your own comfort zone. Such a trial!

SPARKLING WINE & CHAMPAGNE   In Sonoma and Napa, sparkling wine plays the role of a serious specialty—serious enough to have drawn major investments from four of the best-known French houses from Champagne as well as two from Spain, in addition to 10 or 12 local producers.

Whether the bubbly wine in the fancily dressed bottle is called "sparkling wine" or "champagne" (it *is* legal for wineries in America to call their product "champagne," though it galls the French, pun intended), the key to the pervasive high quality of all these wineries lies in their using the *méthode champenoise* as their production technique. In Champagne, it takes the form of step-by-step regulations that, for the most part, codify practices learned by trial and error for making the best wine. Those regulations have no force in California, but the best producers follow most of them and put the words *méthode champenoise* on their labels. For quality assurance, those are the words to look for (as opposed to *bulk* or *Charmat* process).

There is no better way to understand the fascinatingly intricate "champagne method" than to see it firsthand, to walk through the process with a knowledgeable guide. The harvest begins in August in Napa and Sonoma, with the picking of pinot noir, chardonnay, pinot blanc, and pinot meunier, the grape varieties of champagne. The grapes are picked a bit underripe by "still" (nonbubbly) wine standards, both to retain crispness and to avoid excessive body and flavors. The grapes are then pressed and the juice is fermented into plain—austere, in fact—still white wines. That takes 2 weeks. By November and December, the new wines (each variety and vineyard kept as a separate lot) are clear, or "bright."

Now the winemakers *really* go to work, because they need to blend the new wines in preparation for a second fermentation—this one taking place right in the bottle, the very bottle that eventually comes to your table. That's how you get the bubbles.

The second fermentation takes 4 to 6 weeks. After that, you have primitive champagne, with 90 to 100 pounds per square inch of carbon dioxide (CO_2) in each bottle. And you also have a yeasty sediment in each bottle—a bit of a mess that must be cleaned up eventually. But for now—and perhaps for as long as 3 to 7 years—it's a benign mess. Yeast plays two virtuous roles in making sparkling wine: First, it produces the bubbles; second, as the dead yeast cells decompose over time, they release flavor products that give sparkling wines made by *méthode champenoise* their special fragrances and flavors. The amount and depth of flavor varies widely from producer to producer. Each house has its own style, light or heavy, and tries to replicate it each year. That's why people say, "I'm a Mumm drinker," or "I'm a fan of Krug."

Making fine sparkling wine, and making it well, constitutes the ultimate winemaking challenge. The general rule among winemakers is that great white wines and great red wines are derived mostly from their place of origin: the right grape planted in the right soil and right climate. Sparkling wine involves artifice and finesse at every step, making it all the more remarkable that we drink it so casually, at times even carelessly. But the producers wouldn't have it any other way—if only we would drink more of it!

GROWING GRAPES

Somehow winemaking seems much more glamorous than growing grapes. Growing grapes is farming; it's dusty and hard manual labor. In contrast, winemaking is almost ethereal (except for rolling and stacking barrels and hosing grape skins out of the press).

In truth, most winemakers in Sonoma and Napa spend more time in the vineyards than at the winery. It took 20 or 30 years to learn that quality starts, absolutely, in the vineyard, and that the winemaker can do nothing to compensate for bad fruit. There's simply so much to learn about winemaking that decisions can be revised, even reversed, annually; not so with vineyard decisions.

MODERN GROWING AS GARDENING   In the early 1980s, just as winemakers had worked their way up the learning curve for winemaking and as winery owners had turned to acquiring vineyards as the next source of quality control, everyone in the Wine Country learned that the *Phylloxera vastatrix,* a soil-based plant louse, would be wiping out most of the vineyards, just as it had done a century earlier, first in Europe and then in California (for more on this, see "A Look at the Past" earlier in this chapter). The "fix" was to plant rootstocks that resisted *Phylloxera* and to graft desirable grape varieties above the soil; this worked for several decades.

Unfortunately, it seems that the choice for the principal rootstock was somewhat vulnerable, or *Phylloxera* mutated and developed new appetites, or perhaps a combination of both occurred. Since the mid-1980s, replanting has been a major focus, almost a preoccupation. In hindsight, *Phylloxera* might be seen as a small (but enormously expensive) blessing. It has indeed refocused our attention on the soil; it's no exaggeration to say that today much of the excitement in Napa and Sonoma lies in the vineyards. And we're showing that farming there isn't agribusiness; rather, it could almost be called microfarming. Warren Winiarski, founder of Stag's Leap Wine Cellars, eloquently insists that for himself and the others in Napa, grape growing is not agriculture, it's horticulture—that is, gardening.

As you drive through Sonoma and Napa, you pass hundreds of experimental "gardens." If you look closely at the shape of the vines, the density of the planting, the height of the trellis system, and even the orientation to the compass, you'll perceive a playground in the earth just as the winemakers of the 1970s had a playground of fancy winemaking toys. It's too early to assess the results of this replanting, but the "silver lining" attitude common to farming sees higher grape quality than ever and, thus, higher wine quality.

THE CYCLE OF THE SEASONS   Because you are likely to visit the Wine Country for a day or two in one particular season, you might want to know how the Wine Country looks in other seasons. Although the climate is benign, the changes from season to season still have a drama about them. In the winter, the rainy season in Mediterranean climates, the nights can be cold, dropping to 30° or 40°F (-1° or 4°C), but a sunny winter day sees highs in the 60s (high teens Celsius)—picnic weather if you're wearing a light sweater.

Winter in the Wine Country also can be confused with spring elsewhere. Camellias might bloom on New Year's Day, azaleas shortly thereafter, along with the blue and yellow acacias. From December through April, the vines are dormant, stark outlines of trunks and arms, but the valley floors and hillside are lush green with common weeds and a few seeded ground covers. One of the common weeds is mustard: In good years, you'll find acres and acres of bright-yellow mustard, celebrated each spring with the Napa Valley Mustard Festival.

The vines burst from dormancy in mid-March for the earliest varieties (chardonnay, pinot noir, gewürztraminer) and in April for the later blooming varieties (cabernet sauvignon, zinfandel). The growth is rapid—sometimes almost an inch a day. Until mid-May, there's a danger of frost. By late May and early June, the new shoots, called *canes,* have grown 3 or 4 feet in length; flower clusters start to blossom. The success of the *bloom and set,* as it's called, makes for some nervous moments: Uncontrollable elements such as hot weather and rain can compromise the crop. But, especially compared with the vagaries of weather in continental Europe, the benign Mediterranean weather in the Wine Country goes sour only occasionally.

In midsummer, usually around late July, the first signs of color show up in red grape varieties, a pretty blush at first that in a couple of weeks becomes a deep purple, a sure sign that the grapes are ripening. White grapes change from a lime green to a golden green as they ripen. They get delectably sweeter and sweeter, until the winemaker decides they are ripe for the picking.

From August through October, you'll probably see every available hand in the Wine Country harvesting the grapes. For a single vineyard it takes only a day—perhaps just a few hours—to pick the grapes, since they need to be as fresh and cool as possible. After the grapes are harvested, the vines hopefully have the chance to grow for a few more weeks, storing energy in the form of carbohydrates that will sustain them to the next spring.

After cold nights in November and December, the first winter rains knock and blow the vibrant-colored leaves off the vines, which then go dormant until March and April, when they start the cycle again.

THE LIFE OF THE VINE   Unless soil problems or vineyard pests intervene, a vineyard should have a commercial life of 30 to 40 years. In Sonoma, a number of producing vineyards are approaching the

100-year mark, and although the quantity of the harvest falls off in old vines, the quality seems to improve. As the Italian proverb goes, "You plant a vineyard for your son; you plant an olive grove for your grandson." Regardless of the latest technological advances in viticulture, vineyards will not be rushed—which gives much-needed consolation to grape growers, and a sense of permanence to the Wine Country.

3 How to Wine Taste Like a Pro

Stopping at tasting rooms to sample the goods, otherwise known as *wine tasting,* ranks as one of the top rituals in Wine Country touring. It provides pleasure and a chance to learn why the wines of Sonoma and Napa rank high among the wines of the world.

Precautionary notes would say "taste moderately," for there are literally 200 or so tasting rooms, and the virtues in wine take time to notice. Most of the attendants in tasting rooms know that, generally speaking, Americans drink very little wine (10% of the population drinks more than 85% of the wine consumed). Because we're all on a very pleasant learning curve, you can discover wine at many levels. If you should encounter a winery staffer with "attitude" (unfortunately, it happens), don't buy *any* of that wine and simply move on to the next stop.

The time-honored techniques for tasting wine involve three steps: a good look, a good smell, and a good sip of each wine. You'll learn about wine most quickly if you compare them, ideally side by side. Almost any comparison will reveal features of wines you might not see by tasting one wine at a time. You might think of it as the wines talking to one another. ("I'm smoother than you are." "I'm way more puckery than all of you.") By listening to these little conversations, you can discover just how smooth or how puckery you want your wines to be. Tasting rooms in Napa and Sonoma have their own regimens, usually offering a series of wines. When it seems appropriate, and when the tasting room is not too busy, ask your host if you can do some comparisons.

THE VISUALS OF WINE

Take a moment to look at the wine for its clarity and for its hue. With just a couple glances, you'll see that red wines reveal many shades of red: ruby, garnet, purple, and variations. White wines also differ in hue, from white gold to straw to dark gold, sometimes laced with a light green. For the most part, wines ought to be clear, even brilliant, though a few unfiltered wines now bear a light haze as a badge of courage that says, "I was not heavily filtered." (Filtration for clarification is standard practice and benign if not overdone.)

Color can be a sign of a wine's condition, of its health, even of its age. White wines that show any browning might be going "over the hill" and have a musty, baked smell. Red wines that show a lot of rusty red might also be past their prime, and reds that show a lot of purple are probably young.

THE AROMAS & BOUQUETS OF WINE

Some wine professionals will tell you the olfactory aspect of wine is more important than the taste. Saner heads remind you that wine is a *beverage,* not a perfume; it comes home to rest in the mouth. It's true that our noses work better as tools of perception than our mouths. We can smell several thousand scents but can taste only four: sweet, sour, bitter, and salty. But it's also true that we smell the wine (via the retro nasal passages) when it passes through our mouths.

A decently shaped wineglass will direct a lot of aromas to your nose. Swirling the glass helps excite the fragrances. Comparing the "noses" of two or three wines can be very revealing, but possibly a bit frustrating, too: You "see" differences with your nose but might stumble when you try to describe them. The words are on the tip of your tongue, if they're there at all. What comes to mind may seem silly: apple, coconut, cherries, mushrooms, dirt, cheese, and the like.

If this is the case, then you've hit the Wall of Wine Tasting: vocabulary. It's not easy to describe the fragrances and flavors in wine. We are mostly reduced to similes and metaphors, to comparing wines with more familiar substances. A lot of wine writing is inadvertently humorous; some of it qualifies as bad poetry. That's neither your fault *nor* the fault of the wine. You must simply get over the inadequacies of language to describe wine—and get on with your tasting. Have fun with your verbal fantasies!

Despite all the ambiguity in wine descriptors, the words *aroma* and *bouquet* do possess widely recognized, distinct meanings (though on the street we use them almost interchangeably). **Aroma** points to the characteristic smell of the various grape varieties, which can be quite distinct. Just as you would probably not confuse a pippin apple with a golden delicious, when you are familiar with sauvignon blanc, it will not remind you of chardonnay. **Bouquet,** in the academy of wine, refers to fragrances that come from sources other than the grapes, such as the vanillalike fragrance of French oak.

During your trip to the Wine Country, you can learn the basics of aroma simply by comparing a sauvignon blanc side by side with a chardonnay. Or, in terms of bouquet, you can try a younger cabernet beside an older cabernet. Not every tasting room will be able to arrange all the comparisons, but you will find many opportunities.

THE TASTES OF WINE

Tasting wine—literally putting it through your mouth—can be seen as something quite different from *drinking* other beverages. (Of course, we can drink wine, too. Indeed, *most* of the time we should just drink wine.) Tasting, as opposed to drinking, has built-in dynamics. In fact, it helps to focus on the wine moving through the mouth: something that happens in a measured sequence, like listening to a musical phrase. It's not like taking a snapshot—"Click, I've got it."

One of the legendary tasters in California at the turn of the century, Henry Lachman, merchant and international judge of wines, wrote a monograph in which he discussed each sip of wine as having "a first taste, a second taste, and the goodbye." That's a cute way of dealing with the physiology of our mouths: In the front of the mouth, we taste for **sweetness** and feel the **body** of the wine; in the middle, we find **acidity** and the **flavors** of the grape; and in the back, we sense the **finish** or "goodbye," which can be long or short, supple or astringent. Imagine a tasting as having checkpoints in your mouth: front, middle, and back.

In the abstract, wine dynamics sound odd. With practice, however, especially as you compare the tastes of two or three wines, they become obvious, and the observational skills become quite easy to pick up. After you see how a wine can be full and lush in the front of your mouth, then turn fresh and tasty, and finally linger nicely (or fail to linger), it remains for you to decide what **shapes** you prefer in your wines. Red wines in particular show fairly clear shapes. One of the additional challenges in tasting red wines lies in knowing that the shape changes with age. Rough, puckery young red wines can age into supple, subtly flavorful, pleasing liquids.

Which red wines will age well and over what period of time is, again, something you can learn by comparison. It's best done by arranging a *vertical tasting:* several vintages of the same wine. (*Horizontal tastings* are several producers tasted from the same vintage.) Even three to five wines from vintages spread over, say, 10 years will give you a good idea of how much age you want to have on your red wines. Tasting rooms often have "reserve" wines or "library" wines that you can acquire for tasting.

Tastings of several wines—either vertical or horizontal tastings—make for marvelous evenings of gourmandizing when you return home. Have a few friends over to taste the wines blind (without labels visible). Get everyone's preference. Then sit down to dinner and finish them off, with the labels in full view. Inevitably, opinions will change, often in amusing reversals.

It's up to you to decide how seriously you want to engage the Wine Country. If it's a first visit, consider it an introduction. You can't do it all in a single visit, of course, which is all the more reason to schedule a return trip.

Finally, two important tips for a healthy day in the Wine Country: Be moderate in your wine tasting and generous in drinking water. Cheers!

3

Planning Your Trip to the Wine Country

The pages that follow tell you everything you need to know to plan your trip—how to get there, the best times to go, how much you can expect to spend, strategies for touring the region, and more.

1 Visitor Information

There's so much to see and do in the Wine Country that it's best to familiarize yourself with what's available before you start your trip. A good place to begin your research is **http://winecountry.com**, which offers details on lodging, dining, activities, wineries, and more for all California's wine regions. Both Napa and Sonoma offer informative visitor guides that provide information on everything each valley has to offer, and you can get details on Northern Sonoma by contacting the area's individual visitor bureaus.

The slick, comprehensive *Napa Valley Guide* includes listings and photos of hotels, restaurants, and hundreds of wineries, as well as hours of operation, tasting fees, and picnicking information. The **Napa Valley Conference and Visitors Bureau (NVCVB)**, 1310 Napa Town Center, Napa, CA 94559 (© **707/226-7459;** www. napavalley.com), offers a $10 package that includes this guide plus a bunch of brochures, a map, a document called *Four Perfect Days in the Wine Country Itinerary,* and hot-air balloon discount coupons. If you want less to recycle, ask for just the *Napa Valley Guide,* which sells for $5.95. If you don't want to pay the bucks for the official publications, point your browser to www.napavalley.com, the NVCVB's official site, which has lots of the same information for free.

Like the town itself, the *Sonoma Valley Visitors Guide* is far less fancy—no glossy photos and far less information than Napa Valley's slick guide. But the free pocket-size booklet does offer important lodging, winery, and restaurant details, all of which is available from the **Sonoma Valley Visitors Bureau,** 453 1st St. E., Sonoma, CA 95476 (© **707/996-1090;** www.sonomavalley.com).

Northern Sonoma is a tougher grape to crush, so to speak. Since there's no single source for in-depth information on all the towns and growing regions, you'll need to consult various sources depending on where you intend to spend most of your time. But a good place to start is with the **Sonoma County Tourism Bureau** (© 800/5-SONOMA or 707/576-6662). Give them a call or visit their website at www.sonomacounty.com. There you will find basic information on attractions within each region, a lodging guide, a way to request a free visitor's guide, contact information for the region's various visitors bureaus, and more. Keep in mind that only member businesses will be mentioned on the site and there are many, many more worthy attractions. You can also request a visitor's guide by mail by sending a written request to Visitor's Guide, 520 Mendocino Ave., Suite 210, Santa Rosa, CA 95401.

More details can be found about Santa Rosa by contacting the **Santa Rosa Convention & Visitors Bureau** 9 4th St., Santa Rosa, CA 95401 (© **707/577-8674** or 800/404-7673) for information about the city and its suburbs.

The most concentrated area of wine country attractions is in and around Healdsburg. Thankfully, they have an excellent resource: the **Healdsburg Chamber of Commerce & Visitors Bureau** 217 Healdsburg Ave., Healdsburg, CA 95448 (© **707/433-6935** or 800/648-9922 [CA only]). Visit their sophisticated website (www. healdsburg.org) for extensive information, or call or drop by their visitor center at 217 Healdsburg Ave., at the southern entrance to downtown Healdsburg.

2 When to Go

THE SEASONS   The beauty of the Wine Country is striking at any time of the year, but it's most memorable in **September** and **October,** when the grapes are being pressed and the wineries are in full production. Another great time to come is **spring,** when the mustard flowers are in full bloom and the tourist season is just starting; at this time of year, you'll find less traffic, fewer crowds at the wineries and restaurants, and better deals on hotel rooms. Although **winter** promises the best budget rates and few crowds, it often comes with chilly days and the threat of rain; the valleys, although still lovely, become less quintessentially picturesque as miles of bare vines lay dormant over the cold months. Want to visit in **summer?** Say hello to hot weather and lots of traffic.

Tips **Packing Tips**

If you're visiting the Wine Country between December and March, be sure to pack an umbrella and a pair of durable walking shoes. The rainy season isn't usually fierce, but it is wet.

Wine Country fashion is part city, part country, with an emphasis on comfort. Sensible shoes are key—especially when you're wine tasting because you're likely to tromp through vineyards, gravel, and on occasion, mud. At restaurants, attire ranges from jeans and T-shirts at the more-casual eateries to jacket and tie at the few fancy stops such as The French Laundry. In general, somewhere in between is best when you're stepping out.

THE CLIMATE   Although the valleys claim a year-round average temperature of 70°F (21°C), if you come with a suitcase packed with T-shirts and shorts during the winter holiday season, you're likely to shiver your way to the nearest department store to stock up on warm clothes. In summer, if you rent a car without air-conditioning, you're liable to want to make a pit stop at every hotel swimming pool you pass. And don't let that morning fog and those early cool temperatures fool you; on most days, come noon, that big ol' ball of flames in the sky sends down plenty of heat waves to bless the vineyards and your picnic spot. For the most comfortable experience no matter what time of year, dress in layers and keep in mind that the temperature can drop dramatically at night.

Average Seasonal Temperatures

	Spring (Mar–May)	Summer (June–Aug)	Fall (Sept–Nov)	Winter (Dec–Feb)
Average highs (in °F)	78	92	85	72
Average highs (in °C)	26	33	29	22
Average lows (in °F)	64	81	74	61
Average lows (in °C)	18	27	23	16

3 Money Matters
WHAT THINGS COST IN THE WINE COUNTRY
One thing's for sure: Wine Country ain't cheap. Over the course of a few years, Northern California's newly wealthy poured into the

Festivities to Plan Your Trip Around: The Wine Country's Best Annual Events

Napa Valley Mustard Festival kicks off tourist season starting in February with a celebration of the mustard blossoms that coat the valley and mountains in rich-yellow petals. This is 6 weeks' worth of activities ranging from a crowded, formal, and very fun gourmet gala featuring local restaurants, wineries, and artists at the CIA Greystone to a wine auction, golf benefit, recipe and photography competition, and plenty of food and wine celebrations. For information, call © 707/259-9020, point your browser to www.mustard festival.org, or write to P.O. Box 3603, Yountville, CA 94599.

Right before heavy tourist season kicks off, Healdsburg tempts the oneophile taste buds with a barrel tasting weekend at nearly 100 wineries along the **Russian River Wine Road.** And if you happen to fall in love with a wine you taste, you can secure your share of bottles—at discounted prices—long before they even exist, never mind sell out. (It's called buying *futures.*) Heads up: It's free if you bring your own wine glass, $5 if you need to purchase one to tote from winery to winery. For information visit www.wineroad.com or call © 800/723-6336.

The **Napa Valley Wine Auction,** held each June, is the area's most renowned—and exclusive—event. The annual charity affair brings close to 2,000 deep-pocketed wine aficionados to the Napa area to schmooze and spend serious cash. But don't pack your bags yet: Tickets to the event are $2,500 per couple—and they sell out every year. For information, call © 707/963-3388.

region, encouraging absurdly jacked-up hotel prices and a fight to have the opportunity to pay them.

Hotels ask an average of more than $180 a night in Napa Valley (things aren't much cheaper in the less touristy towns of Sonoma), and there's only room for negotiation during the slow season (Nov–Mar) and often mid-week only. On a busy weekend, a charmless motel or a basic B&B can easily get $180 a night for a room—and hotels often require a two-night minimum.

Another big June attraction is the 10-day **Healdsburg Jazz Festival.** Venues range from vineyards to restaurants to intimate theaters, and headliners sell out quickly. Admission prices vary. Tickets can be purchased via websites, mail, fax, or at the venue. For more information please go to www.healdsburgjazzfestival.com or call © 707/433-4644.

One of my favorite festivals in Sonoma Valley is the **Heart of the Valley Barrel Tasting,** held on the third full weekend in March. This event, which gives the public a glimpse of Sonoma Valley's finest future releases and raises money for the American Heart Association, is a 2-day fiesta of finger foods, pairings, demonstrations, and all the world-class wine you can drink—all for around $30 a ticket. Buy tickets well in advance. For details, call the St. Francis Winery, at © 800/543-7713.

Sonoma Valley's other major celebration is the **Vintage Festival,** held the last weekend in September at Sonoma's central plaza. This is a real blowout of a party, complete with live music, dancing, parades, arts-and-crafts shows, and of course, copious wine tasting. For more information, contact the **Sonoma Valley Visitors Bureau** (© 707/996-1090; www.sonomavalley.com).

For Napa Valley happenings, contact the **Napa Valley Conference and Visitors Bureau** (© 707/226-7459; www.napavalley.com).

Check out Healdsburg's festivities by contacting the **Healdsburg Chamber of Commerce & Visitors Bureau** (© 707/433-6935 or 800/648-9922, CA only, www.healdsburg.org).

But that's just the beginning. If you want to eat in any of the more renowned dining spots, you can pretty much count on shelling out at least $35 per person just for food—not including even one glass of wine. And don't even think of stepping foot in a high-end haunt such as Terra without dropping closer to $50 per person—and you can make that $175 per person for the French Laundry—and we're just talking lunch. (Don't worry: I'll get to some ways around that later.)

Is that cash register ringing in your head yet? Well, keep the tab open, 'cause there's more. Although some wineries offer free wine tastings, most now charge between $3 and $20. Stop by three or four in a day and—cha-ching!—they start to add up. Of course, you'll also want to buy a few bottles of your favorite *vino*. Cha-ching, cha-ching, cha-ching—it just keeps going. Don't let this deter you from a visit, but do expect to spend some money.

MONEY-SAVING TIPS   If you're starting to think that you just can't afford a Wine Country visit, don't despair yet: There are a few things you can do to keep your costs down and still enjoy the region to its fullest.

If you're on a budget, be sure to reserve your accommodations months in advance to secure the cheapest room; don't expect much more than a clean room and bed, and you won't be disappointed—but you're not planning to hang out in your room anyway, right? Here are some more money-saving tips:

- **Travel between November and March,** when accommodations rates are at their lowest. Stay at a place whose rates include breakfast and afternoon hors d'oeuvres, which will save you big bucks on dining out.
- If you want to dine at one of the Wine Country's more expensive restaurants, **have a late lunch** there and make it the day's biggest meal. The lunch menu is often served until mid-afternoon, and main courses usually cost several dollars less than the same dishes at dinner.
- There's no better place to **picnic** than the Wine Country. Stop at a grocery or gourmet shop—each valley has lots of wonderful ones, which are recommended in the chapters that follow—and pick up the picnic fixings for breakfast, lunch, or dinner. Head to one of the fabulous picnic spots I recommend in this book, pop the cork on a bottle you've picked up in your travels, and you've got the perfect alfresco feast—for a fraction of what it would cost you to eat in a restaurant.
- **Buy wines from local wine shops,** not from the wineries. Believe it or not, prices in the shops are often better than at wineries, and they're likely to have that extra-buttery chardonnay or that perfectly balanced cab that you fell in love with earlier in the day in stock. In Sonoma, your best bet is the **Wine Exchange,** on the plaza at 452 1st St. E. (© **707/938-1794**), which boasts more than 700 domestic wines and a remarkably

savvy staff. In Napa, head to St. Helena, where both **Dean & Deluca,** 607 St. Helena Hwy. (© **707/967-9980**), and **Safeway,** 1026 Hunt Ave. (© **707/963-3833**), have enormous wine selections; Safeway tends to offer some of the best deals around. In Healdsburg, my favorite is **Root's Cellar,** 113 Mill St. (© **707/433-4937**), just one block south of the square. They specialize in local bottlings plus international superstars. Resident expert Paul Root will point you toward little-known gems. Added bonus: They ship wine to virtually anywhere you like, so you don't have to tote your finds home with you.

PAYING YOUR WAY

Banks throughout Napa Valley and Sonoma Valley have **automated teller machines (ATMs),** which accept cards connected to networks such as Cirrus and PLUS. For specific ATM locations, call © **800/424-7787** for the Cirrus network, and call © **800/843-7587** for the PLUS system. You also can locate Cirrus ATMs on the Web at **www.mastercard.com** and PLUS ATMs at **www.visa.com**.

Traveler's checks are still the safest way to carry currency—Visa and American Express are the kinds most widely accepted. ***Remember:*** You'll need identification, such as a driver's license or passport, to change a traveler's check. And be sure to record the numbers of the checks and keep that information separate from your checks in the unlikely event that they get lost or stolen. Note that there are no American Express offices in either valley.

Rather than fuss with traveler's checks, it's easier just to use **credit cards**—most notably American Express, MasterCard, and Visa—which are almost as good as cash and are accepted in most Wine Country establishments. Also, ATMs make cash advances against MasterCard and Visa cards; make sure you have your PIN (personal identification number) with you.

4 Getting There

BY PLANE

If you're arriving by plane, Wine Country is easily accessed by the Bay Area's two major airports: San Francisco International and Oakland International.

SAN FRANCISCO INTERNATIONAL AIRPORT   Almost four dozen major scheduled carriers serve **San Francisco International Airport** (© **650/821-8211;** www.flysfo.com), which is 1½ to 2 hours southwest of Napa and Sonoma by car.

OAKLAND INTERNATIONAL AIRPORT   About 5 miles south of downtown Oakland and a little more than a 1-hour drive from downtown Napa, at the Hegenberger Road exit of California 17 (U.S. 880), **Oakland International Airport** (© **510/577-4000;** www.oaklandairport.com) is less crowded than SFO and is a very accessible airport, but it offers fewer carrier selections.

RENTING A CAR   Regardless of which airport you fly into, you should rent a car and drive to the Wine Country (see "By Car," below, for driving directions). Although for $20 you can hitch a ride to Napa Valley from SFO with **Evans Airport Service** (© **707/ 255-1559**), and the **Sonoma Airporter** (© **707/938-4246**) offers door-to-door service six times daily from SFO to hotels and inns in most areas of Sonoma ($35 for home pickup, $30 for standard downtown pickup locations), there's no useful public transportation in either valley, which makes it almost impossible to explore the region without wheels.

   All the major companies have desks at the airports. Currently, you can get a compact car for about $200 a week, including all taxes and other charges (but remember that rates are always subject to change). Some of the national car-rental companies operating in San Francisco include the following: **Alamo,** © 800/327-9633, www.go alamo.com; **Avis,** © 800/331-1212, www.avis.com; **Budget,** © 800/ 527-0700, www.budget.com; **Enterprise,** © 800/325-8007, www. enterprise.com; and **Hertz,** © 800/654-3131, www.hertz.com.

BY CAR
All these routes to the Wine Country are very well marked, with plenty of signs along the way.

TO NAPA
FROM SAN FRANCISCO   Cross the Golden Gate Bridge and go north on U.S. 101; turn east on Highway 37 (toward Vallejo), then north on Highway 29, the main road through Napa Valley. You can also take Highway 121/12 from Highway 37 and follow the signs.

FROM OAKLAND   Head eastbound on I-80 toward Sacramento; a few miles past the Carquinez Bridge ($2 toll) and the city of Vallejo, exit on Highway 12 west, which, after a few miles, intersects with Highway 29 and leads directly into Napa.

TO SONOMA VALLEY
FROM SAN FRANCISCO   From San Francisco, cross the Golden Gate Bridge and stay on U.S. 101 north. Exit at Highway

37; after 10 miles, turn north onto Highway 121. After another 10 miles, turn north onto Highway 12 (Broadway), which will take you directly into the town of Sonoma.

FROM OAKLAND Head eastbound on I-80 toward Sacramento. A few miles past the city of Vallejo (and after paying a $2 toll to cross the Carquinez Bridge), exit on Highway 12, which, after a few miles, intersects with Highway 29 at the southern foot of Napa Valley. Just before entering the city of Napa, you'll come to a major intersection, where Highway 29 meets Highway 12/121. Turn left onto Highway 12/121, which will take you directly to Sonoma Valley.

TO NORTHERN SONOMA

FROM SAN FRANCISCO From San Francisco, cross the Golden Gate Bridge and stay on U.S. 101 north. Exit anywhere from Santa Rosa to Healdsburg, depending on your final destination.

FROM OAKLAND Head eastbound on I-80 toward Sacramento. A few miles past the city of Vallejo (and after paying a $2 toll to cross the Carquinez Bridge), exit on Highway 12, which, after a few miles, intersects with Highway 29 at the southern foot of Napa Valley. Just before entering the city of Napa, you'll come to a major intersection, where Highway 29 meets Highway 12/121. Turn left onto Highway 12/121, turn right onto California 116/Arnold Drive. When the road forks, veer right onto Adobe road. Turn left on East Washington Street, merge onto Highway 101 North when you see the onramp, and exit at the town of your choice.

5 Getting Around

With hundreds of wineries scattered amidst Napa's 34,000 acres and Sonoma's 13,000 acres of vineyards, it's virtually impossible to explore the Wine Country without wheels. If you're arriving by air from another part of the country or abroad, see "Getting There," above, for details on renting a car.

CROSSING FROM COUNTY TO COUNTY

The easiest way to get from Napa to Sonoma Valley and vice versa is to head to the southern end of either valley (the Carneros District) and cross over along the Sonoma Highway (California 12/121). From Napa to Sonoma, the trip takes about 20 minutes, assuming that there's no traffic. Another option is to take the Oakville Grade (aka Trinity Rd.) over the Mayacamas Range, which links Oakville in Napa with Glen Ellen in Sonoma. It's an extremely steep and

---

Tips **Napa Valley Traffic Tip**

Travel the Silverado Trail as often as possible to avoid Highway 29's traffic. Avoid passing through Main Street in St. Helena during high season (May–Oct). Although a wintertime cruise from Napa to Calistoga can take 25 minutes, in summer you can expect the trek to take you closer to 50 minutes. Plan your time accordingly.

---

windy road, but it can be a real timesaver if you're headed to the northern end of either valley.

Getting to Northern Sonoma is a snap from Sonoma Valley. Just follow Highway 12, which runs north to south and connects Sonoma Valley's towns, north to get to Santa Rosa. From there, jump on Highway 101 north and exit at the town of your choice. From downtown Napa, take Sonoma Highway California 12/121 to Highway 16 to Adobe Road (veer right) to Highway 101 North. The trip is about 1 hour and 15 minutes. From northern Napa towns like Calistoga or St. Helena, it's easier to follow Highway 29 north past downtown Calistoga when it becomes Highway 128. Follow Highway 128 for a few blocks and turn left onto Petrified Forest Road. Turn right onto Porter Creek Road and follow it; it will become Mark West Springs Road, which will lead you to Highway 101 north.

DRIVING AROUND THE WINE COUNTRY You might be wondering: Does that mean visitors are drinking and driving up here? And how. The catch is, most of the year there's so much traffic that a major high-speed collision is virtually out of the question. Meanwhile, getting totally trashed while wine tasting is the exception, and the valley has somehow avoided having a major problem with drunk-driving accidents.

Of course, we're not condoning driving under the influence. But since there's no decent public transportation (other than taxis), my best recommendation is that you take it slow, monitor the amount of wine you drink, and bring along a designated driver or take a tour (see the following section, "Strategies for Touring the Wine Country").

TAXIS You can avoid the driving issue altogether by calling either of Napa's two main taxi services: **Napa Valley Cab** (© 707/257-6444) or **Yellow Cab** (© 707/226-3731). Sonoma is serviced by **Valley Cab** (© 707/996-6733). In Northern Sonoma **Healdsburg**

Taxi Cab (© 707/433-7099) is your best bet; they also offer a car and driver for $55 per hour (plus 20% tip) with a 3-hour minimum.

6 Strategies for Touring the Wine Country

Tour smarter, not harder, is the mantra you need to chant to yourself as you pore over this book in the process of planning your trip—because the less time you spend driving in circles, the more time you can spend sticking your schnozzle in wineglasses and saying silly things such as "full-bodied, yet corky."

NAPA VERSUS SONOMA: WHICH AREA IS RIGHT FOR YOU?

Determining whether to spend your wine country vacation in Napa Valley, Sonoma Valley, or Northern Sonoma—or some combination of two or three—depends on what kind of vacation you're looking for and how much time you have to spend. If you've got only a long weekend, it's better to choose one destination and make the most of it rather than spend a good portion of your vacation driving and checking in and out of hotels or B&Bs. Longer stays can inspire further exploration, although you could easily tour nothing but Napa, where the concentration of wineries and restaurants could keep you busy—and sated—for weeks. But when creating your ideal itinerary, most important for you to consider is the character and very different experiences of each area.

Napa Valley is the most condensed region with nearly 300 wineries packed into a 35-mile-long valley. It is also the more commercial of the options, boasting world-class wineries such as Robert Mondavi, which offer the most interesting and edifying wine tours in North America, more big-name wineries, many more spas (some at cheaper rates) to choose from, and a far superior selection of fine restaurants, hotels—including a few world-class options—and quintessential Wine Country activities such as hot-air ballooning. To misquote Gertrude Stein, *there's more there there.* If your intention is to immerse yourself in the culture of the Wine Country, then there's no better place to start than by cruising down Napa Valley's Highway 29, the Sunset Boulevard of the Wine Country. It's along this high-rent route that all the big players in the California wine industry—Beringer, Beaulieu, Charles Krug, Rubicon Estate—dazzle you with their multimillion-dollar estates and pricey art collections. This is where top-notch restaurants such as The French Laundry and Terra serve world-class cuisine to casually clad diners while Silicon Valley millionaires play croquet at the exclusive resorts just up the hill.

As you might expect, humility isn't one of Napa's strongest attributes. So don't be surprised if you encounter a bit of snobbishness at some Napa wineries (but by no means all), as well as a pricey tasting fee or two. More importantly, if you come during high season expect to be met by lots of traffic and crowds practically everywhere you go.

Sonoma Valley and Northern Sonoma, on the other hand, maintain backcountry ambience. Though Sonoma County is home to nearly 200 wineries, it seems far less commercial than Napa, primarily because the attractions are scattered over a far greater area so there's a lower density of wineries, restaurants, hotels, and manmade structures in general (vineyards aside). However, though both the "valley" and the environs to the north are technically in Sonoma, they offer dramatically different experiences.

Sonoma Valley may not be condensed, but the majority of its attractions are in relatively close proximity and easily accessed if you follow a few main roads. Its nearly 40 wineries, though mostly family owned, still seem pretty polished compared to the more mom 'n' pop stops in Northern Sonoma. Its centerpiece historic square includes one of California's famed missions along with mid-priced boutiques and restaurants, and accommodations range from one of Wine Country's most fancy spa resorts to an abundance of lacy B&Bs. To me, Sonoma Valley is an excellent weekend—or extended weekend—excursion for anyone who wants serious R&R and better deals on sleeping and eating and isn't too concerned with shopping outlets or visiting more than a handful of wineries each day.

Though I'm a Napa resident and big fan of Napa and Sonoma valleys, my current favorite destination is Northern Sonoma's Healdsburg area, especially because I've done the other two, and in the last few years, this area has seen the addition of truly exceptional dining and accommodations. But don't trust my opinion. Consider its offerings: You can cruise vast vine-trellised countryside and wind down tiny dirt roads to discover small gem wineries often manned by the winemakers, feast on excellent cuisine in chic new restaurants and longstanding casual local haunts, shop or people-watch at Healdsburg's historic square, and even float down a lazy river on an inner tube if you wish. To me, it's got the best of both Napa and Sonoma Valleys. It certainly feels the least commercial.

If you have the luxury of time, don't just visit one destination: Tour two so you can compare and contrast these very different—and very wonderful—worlds of winemaking.

THE GOLDEN RULE OF WINE TASTING: LESS IS MORE

Yes, they all sound great. Unfortunately, it's almost impossible to hit every winery. Actually, your best plan of action is to take it slow. **Pick three or four wineries** for a single day's outing, and really get to know not only the wines but also the story behind each winery: its history, the types of wines it makes and where the grapes are grown, and the colorful people who make the wines. You can *taste* California wines just about anywhere in the world, but only by visiting the Wine Country can you learn about the painstaking, delicate, and very personal processes and years of collective experience that go into each and every bottle. Like a fine glass of wine, the Wine Country should not be rushed, but savored.

When planning your trip to the Wine Country, consider the following: Is there a specific wine you want to taste? A specific tour you'd like to take? Maybe it's the adjoining restaurant, picnic setting, or art collection that piques your interest most. Whatever your intentions might be, the best advice I can give you about visiting your chosen wineries is to **arrive early:** Most tasting rooms open at 10am, and even on the busiest of weekends, most are empty that early in the morning. "What? Start drinking at 10am?" Absolutely. First of all, you're not drinking, you're tasting and learning. Second, the staff pouring the wines will have considerably more time to discuss their product. Come 1 or 2pm, the tasting room will probably be packed, and other visitors will be waiting in line simply to get a sample—while you're relaxing under an oak tree, finished with your wine-tasting rounds, enjoying a picnic lunch, and seriously contemplating an afternoon nap. Afterward, why not spend your time visiting Old Faithful in Calistoga or doing a little window-shopping while the late-birds duke it out over a sip of chardonnay?

Another consideration when wine tasting is money. It used to be that none of the wineries charged for sampling their wares, but when the popularity of the Wine Country began to soar (along with a growing intolerance for drinking and driving), wineries—particularly those in Napa—began requesting **tasting fees.** It wasn't to make additional profit, but to discourage what the winery staffs usually refer to as "recreational drinkers": visitors who, whether they're aware of it or not, prefer quantity to quality. Nowadays, the norm at Napa Valley wineries is to charge anywhere between $2 and $8 per tasting, which usually includes the tasting glass (etched with the winery's logo) and/or a refund toward a purchase.

The wineries in Sonoma Valley, however, are less likely than those in Napa Valley to charge for tasting wines. The exceptions are wineries that offer samples of their reserve wines (usually at a separate tasting area) and champagne houses.

DEALING WITH THE CROWDS

Anyone who's visited the Wine Country on a sunny August weekend knows how insane the traffic can be. Napa Valley's roads simply weren't designed to handle the influx of vehicles that can turn a 30-minute drive along Highway 29 from Napa to Calistoga into 2 hours of maddening gridlock. It's ironic, of course: People arrive for a vacation in the countryside, only to be stuck in traffic for hours.

 Some Wine-Buying Strategies

Just because you're buying wine directly from the people who made it doesn't mean that you'll save money by purchasing bottles in the tasting room. In fact, it's usually the other way around. You'll probably end up spending a bit more at a winery than you would at superstores that buy cases in bulk and pass the per-bottle savings on to the customer. (**Safeway** in St. Helena is one of the best places to buy wine in Napa Valley.)

If you want to save money, the smart approach is to make a list of your favorite wines as you taste at the wineries, and then make your purchases when you return from your vacation. You'll not only save money on the wine, you'll save a bundle on packaging and shipping fees—but be sure to ask the winery if the release you're interested in is available in your state and where you can purchase it.

In Healdsburg, you'll find an amazing selection, good prices, and vast knowledge of wines both local and international if you drop by **Root's Cellar**, 113 Mill St., Healdsburg, (② **707/433-4937**), located just one block south of the square.

Exceptions to this strategy are wineries that offer big discounts on cases of wine and wineries that only sell their wines directly (that is, they have no distribution). *Note:* If you're able to ship your wine directly from the winery, you'll avoid having to pay sales tax; for more information, see the section "The Ins & Outs of Shipping Wine Home."

If you want to avoid the masses altogether, the solution is simple: Either **visit during the off season** (Nov–May) **or visit midweek.** Though the optimum time to plan your trip is during the "crush"— the grape harvest season starting in late August and continuing through October, when the grapes are harvested, sorted, crushed, and fermented—this is also the Wine Country's peak tourist season. This is a good time to schedule a midweek visit, if possible.

Even if your only option is to arrive on a high-season weekend, there are still ways to avoid the Napa Valley cattle drive. The smartest option is to **avoid the big wineries** such as Mondavi and Beringer and opt for the smaller, family-run places tucked into the hillsides such as Prager and Heitz. Even the wineries along the Silverado Trail, which parallels the main highway through Napa Valley, receive significantly less traffic than those on Highway 29; locals use it as their main thoroughfare during high season.

Another high-season option is to avoid Napa Valley altogether and stick to **Sonoma Valley** or **Northern Sonoma.** Although they, too, suffer from traffic congestion, Sonoma usually gets far less saturated with visitors than Napa does.

A FEW MORE WORDS OF WINE-COUNTRY WISDOM

Here are a few final tips that should help make your visit a more pleasant experience:

- **Chart your winery tours** on a map before venturing into the countryside. It'll save you time and traffic frustration, as well as a lot of unnecessary backtracking.
- **Plan a picnic lunch** at the last winery you're going to visit for the day. (Let's face it—you'll probably be too pooped to drink more wine late in the day.) Many wineries offer free picnic facilities, and though few provide food, many wonderful gourmet shops in both Napa and Sonoma specialize in picnic items; see p. 117, 161, and 192 for recommendations.
- Most wineries are open from 10am to 4:30 or 5pm and are closed on major holidays such as Thanksgiving, Christmas, and New Year's Day. Many also have restricted hours during the off season, so **call ahead** if there's a winery you don't want to miss.
- Fine wine is a temperamental beast that hates to be mistreated. If you let that $60 bottle of merlot cook in the back seat of your car all day, you'll probably be surprised at the new taste it has acquired. Buy a cheap Styrofoam cooler and a couple of

blue ice packs, place them in the trunk of your car, and *voilà!*—you have a **portable wine cellar.**

- Anyone who's ever lived in a one-road town knows that you can't avoid the law for long. Don't speed, and for heaven's sake, don't drive while intoxicated.

7 The Ins & Outs of Shipping Wine Home

Perhaps the only things more complex than that $800 case of cabernet you just purchased are the rules and regulations about shipping it home. Because of absurd and forever fluctuating reciprocity laws—which supposedly protect the business of the country's wine distributors—wine shipping is limited by regulations that vary in each of the 50 states. Shipping rules also vary from winery to winery.

If you happen to live in a reciprocal state and the winery you're buying from offers shipping, you're in luck. You buy and pay the postage, and the winery sends your purchase for you. It's as simple as that. If that winery doesn't ship, it can most likely give you an easy solution.

If you live in a nonreciprocal state, the winery might still have shipping advice for you, so definitely ask. Some refuse to ship at all; others are more than accommodating. Be cautious of wineries that tell you they can ship to nonreciprocal states, and make sure you get a firm commitment. If they can't help you, ask them who can. Everyone knows how to get around these rules.

You may face the challenge of finding a shipping company yourself. If that's the case, keep in mind that it's technically illegal to box your own wine and send it to a nonreciprocal state; the shipper could lose its license, and you could lose your wine. If you do get stuck shipping illegally (not that we're recommending you do that), you might want to package your wine in an unassuming box and head to a post office, UPS, or other shipping company outside the Wine Country area. It's less obvious that you're shipping wine from Vallejo or San Francisco than from Napa Valley.

NAPA VALLEY SHIPPING COMPANIES

The UPS Store, at 3212 Jefferson St., in the Grape Yard Shopping Center, Napa (© **707/259-1398**), claims to pack and ship anything anywhere. Rates for a case of wine were quoted at approximately $25 for ground shipping to Los Angeles and $64 to New York.

St. Helena Mailing Center, 1241 Adams St., at Highway 29, St. Helena (© **707/963-2686**), says they will pack and ship to reciprocal states within the U.S. Rates for pre-wrapped shipments are around $30 per case for ground delivery to Los Angeles, $92 to New York.

SONOMA VALLEY SHIPPING COMPANIES

Mail Boxes, Etc., 19229 Sonoma Hwy., at Verano Street, Sonoma (*(C)* **707/935-3438**), has a lot of experience with shipping wine. It claims it will ship your wine to any state. Prices vary from $22 to Los Angeles to as much as $73 to the East Coast and $140 to Hawaii and Alaska.

The **Wine Exchange of Sonoma,** 452 First St. E., between East Napa and East Spain streets, Sonoma (*(C)* **707/938-1794**), will ship your wine, but there's a catch: You must buy an equal amount of any wine at the store (which they assured me would be in stock, and probably at a better rate). Shipping rates range from $20 to Los Angeles to $50 to the East Coast.

NORTHERN SONOMA SHIPPING COMPANIES

Fitch Mountain Packaging Company, 424A Center St., Healdsburg, (*(C)* **707/433-1247**) will pack and ship your wine. Shipping rates vary based on destination, packing materials, time frame, and more, but they are pretty much in sync with other shippers within the region. They're also conveniently located just off Healdsburg's main square.

FAST FACTS: The Wine Country

For valley-specific information, also see the "Fast Facts" sections in chapters 4 and 5.

Area Code The local area code is **707**.

Banks Most banks are open Monday through Friday from 9am to 3pm; several stay open until about 5pm at least 1 day a week and offer limited hours on Saturday. **Bank of America** has several branches throughout the area, including a location at 1001 Adams St. in St. Helena (*(C)* **707/963-6807**). You'll also find **Wells Fargo** throughout the region, including a branch in Napa at 217 Soscol Ave., inside Raley's supermarket (*(C)* **707/254-8690**). The Sonoma Wells Fargo is located at 480 W. Napa St. (*(C)* **707/996-2360**). For information on how to locate the nearest ATM, see "Money Matters," earlier in this chapter.

Car Rentals See "Getting Around," earlier in this chapter.

Emergencies Dial 🕾 **911** for police, ambulance, or the fire department. No coins are needed from a public phone.

Liquor Laws Liquor and grocery stores, as well as some drugstores, can sell packaged alcoholic beverages between 6am and 2am. Most restaurants, nightclubs, and bars are licensed to serve alcoholic beverages during the same hours. The legal age for purchase and consumption is 21; proof of age is required.

Safety The Wine Country still has a remarkably safe, sleepy-town atmosphere. The only safety consideration you will need to heed is your own basic common sense.

Taxes A 7.75% sales tax is added at the register for all goods and services purchased in Napa Valley and Sonoma County, except in the city of Santa Rosa where the tax is 8%. (Note that you won't have to pay sales tax if you have your purchases shipped directly from the store out of state.) Napa Valley hotel taxes range from 10% to 12%; in Sonoma Valley, the hotel tax is 10.5%; in Northern Sonoma it's 10% (with the threat of 12%).

Time The Wine Country is in the Pacific Standard Time zone, which is 8 hours behind Greenwich Mean Time (GMT) and 3 hours behind Eastern Standard Time (EST). For the local time, call 🕾 **707/767-8900.**

Weather A general weather phone recording does not exist, but the emergency number (in operation only during very wet weather) provides information on flood conditions: **Travel Advisory 🕾 888/854-NAPA.**

4

Napa Valley

Compared to its sister valleys, Sonoma and Northern Sonoma counties, Napa is a bit farther east from San Francisco, encompasses a far more condensed selection of wineries, and has more of an overall touristy, big-business feel to it. You'll still find plenty of rolling, mustard flower–covered hills and vast stretches of vineyards, but they come hand in hand with large, upscale restaurants; designer discount outlets; rows of hotels; and in the summer, plenty of traffic. Even with hordes of visitors year-round, Napa Valley is still pretty sleepy, with a focus on daytime attractions—wine tasting, outdoor activities, and spas—and fabulous food. Nightlife is very limited, but after indulging all day, most visitors are ready to turn in early anyway.

1 Orientation & Getting Around

Napa Valley is relatively compact. Just 35 miles long, it claims more than 34,000 acres of vineyards, making Napa the most densely planted wine-growing region in the U.S. Still, it's an easy jaunt from one end to the other: You can drive it in just over half an hour—closer to an hour during high season.

Conveniently, most of the large wineries—as well as most of the hotels, shops, and restaurants—are along a single road, **Highway 29,** which starts at the mouth of the Napa River, near the north end of San Francisco Bay, and continues north to Calistoga and the top of the growing region. All of the Napa Valley coverage in this chapter—every town, winery, hotel, and restaurant—is organized below from south to north, beginning in the city of Napa, and can be reached from Highway 29.

ALONG HIGHWAY 29: NAPA'S TOWNS IN BRIEF

Although, road signs aside, it's virtually impossible to tell when you cross from one town into the next in Napa Valley, each does have its own distinct personality. The **City of Napa** serves as the commercial center of the Wine Country and the gateway to Napa Valley—hence the high-speed freeway that whips you right past it and on to the tourist towns of St. Helena and Calistoga. However, if you do veer off the highway, you'll be surprised to discover a small but burgeoning community of more than 72,000 residents with the most cosmopolitan (relatively) atmosphere in the county and some of the most affordable accommodations in the valley. It is also in the process of gentrification, thanks to (relatively) affordable housing and new restaurants and attractions like Restaurant Budo and Copia: The American Center for Wine, Food & The Arts. Heading north on either Highway 29 or the Silverado Trail leads you to Napa's wineries and the more idyllic pastoral towns beyond.

Yountville, with an approximate population of 3,000, was founded by the first white American to settle in the valley, George Calvert Yount. Although it lacks the small-town charm of neighboring St. Helena and Calistoga—primarily because it has no rambunctious main street—it serves as a good base for exploring the valley, and it's home to a handful of excellent wineries, inns, and restaurants, including the world-renowned restaurant The French Laundry (p. 108).

Driving farther north on the St. Helena Highway (Hwy. 29) brings you to **Oakville,** most easily recognized by Oakville Cross Road and the Oakville Grocery Co. (p. 117), a great place to pick up gourmet picnic fare and one of the only indications that you've reached the small town. If you so much as blink after Oakville, you're likely to overlook **Rutherford,** the next small town, which borders on St. Helena. Each has spectacular wineries, but you won't see most of them while driving along Highway 29.

Next comes **St. Helena,** located 17 miles north of Napa on Highway 29. St. Helena is a former Seventh-Day Adventist village that manages to maintain an old-fashioned feel while simultaneously catering to upscale shoppers with deep pockets and its generally wealthy resident population of about 6,000 and growing. This quiet, attractive little town is home to a slew of beautiful old houses, as well as great restaurants, the region's best shopping street (alas, that's not saying much), and exceptional wineries.

Calistoga, the last tourist town in Napa Valley, was named by Sam Brannan, entrepreneur extraordinaire and California's first millionaire. After making a bundle supplying miners during the gold rush, he went on to take advantage of the natural geothermal springs at the north end of Napa Valley by building a hotel and spa in 1859. Flubbing up a speech in which he compared this natural California wonder to New York State's Saratoga Springs resort, he serendipitously coined the name "Calistoga" and it stuck. Today, this small, simple resort town with just over 5,200 residents and an old-time main street (no building along the 6-block stretch is more than two stories high) is popular with city folk who come here to unwind. Calistoga is a great place to relax and indulge in mineral waters, mud baths, Jacuzzis, massages, and, of course, wine. The vibe is more casual—and a little groovier—than you'll find in neighboring towns to the south.

VISITOR INFORMATION

Even if you plan to skip the town of Napa, you might want to stop at the **Napa Valley Conference and Visitors Bureau,** 1310 Napa Town Center (off 1st St.), Napa, CA 94559 (© **707/226-7459**), www.napavalley.org, to pick up a variety of local information and money-saving coupons.

WINE-TASTING TOURS

Driving gives you the most touring freedom, but if the whole point of this vacation is to drink too much, eat too much, and avoid all mental exertion, consider hiring one of the companies below to figure out the sightseeing and wine-tasting details.

RIDING THE NAPA VALLEY WINE TRAIN *Overrated* One of the most leisurely ways (not to mention boring, if you ask me) to view the Wine Country is aboard the **Napa Valley Wine Train,** a rolling restaurant that makes a 3-hour, 36-mile journey through the vineyards of Napa, Yountville, Oakville, Rutherford, and St. Helena. This is a lazy, slow cruise through the valley on vintage-style cars finished with polished Honduran mahogany paneling and etched-glass partitions and sadly dirt-stained windows. In other words, there's nothing to do but enjoy the company you keep, peek out the window, and eat (if you opted for a ticket that included a meal).

The staff, who serve optional "gourmet" meals complete with all the finery—damask linen, bone china, silver flatware, and etched crystal—is attentive, if not overly enthusiastic. Plainly put, if you're in it for the food, forget it. Go somewhere else where $75 per person will get you a memorable meal. The point here is the train ride, period. For that reason, definitely do it by day.

The train consists of nine cars including the dining cars, lounges, and the glass-topped Vista Dome. Passengers can visit all of them. Two bummers: The train doesn't stop except during one daytime ride, which includes an optional stop in Yountville and at the Grgich Winery in Rutherford for a tour followed by a tasting, and the pre-boarding wine tasting was flat-out patronizing and unpolished, which was emphasized when our instructor consistently mispronounced the grape varietal "pinot meunier" (say "*pee*-noh muh-*nyay*").

The train departs from the McKinstry Street Depot, 1275 McKinstry St. (near 1st St. and Soscol Ave.), Napa (© **800/427-4124** or 707/253-2111; www.winetrain.com). Train fare without meals is $48 for daytime rides; fare with meals is $80 for brunch, from $78 for lunch, and $95 for dinner. To sit in the ultraswank and modern 1950s Vista Dome Car with elevated seating and a glass top, you must opt for the pricier lunch or dinner served within it. Including train fare, lunch is between $110 and $140 for a four-course French affair; dinner is five courses and costs between $120 and $150. Boarding times are Monday through Friday at 11am and 6pm; Saturday, Sunday, and holidays at 9am, noon, and 6pm. (The dinner schedule is abbreviated in Jan and Feb.) *Tip:* Sit on the west side for the best views.

BICYCLING AROUND THE WINE COUNTRY   Cycling enthusiasts can embark on full-day group tours with **Getaway Adventures BHK** (© **800/499-BIKE** or 707/568-3040; www.getawayadventures.com). Prices are $115 per person, including lunch and a visit to four or five wineries, or $105 per person for private groups of 6 or more. Basic Bike rental without a tour costs $28 per day plus a $20 delivery fee. You can also inquire about the company's kayaking and hiking tours. Another shop offering bike rentals is St. Helena Cyclery, 1156 Main St., St. Helena (© **707/963-7736**), which offers bikes for $7 per hour or $30 a day, including rear rack, helmet, lock, and bag in which you can pack a picnic.

FAST FACTS: Napa Valley

Hospitals   **Queen of the Valley Hospital,** 100 Trancas St., Napa (© **707/257-4008**), offers minor emergency care from 10am to 10pm and also has emergency-room care 'round the clock. You can also head to **St. Helena Hospital,** about 5 minutes from the town of St. Helena, at 650 Sanitarium Rd., Deer Park (© **707/963-6425**).

Information   See "Visitor Information," above.

Newspapers/Magazines   The **Napa Valley Register** covers the entire Napa Valley; it's available at newspaper racks on the main streets in towns throughout the county. Other local town weeklies include the **Weekly Calistogan** and the **St. Helena**

Star, which are both free. Essential for all visitors is the *Napa Valley Guide,* an annual, glossy magazine packed with valuable tourist information; it's sold in most shops and hotels and is also available at the **Napa Valley Conference and Visitors Bureau,** 1310 Napa Town Center, off 1st Street (© **707/226-7459**).

Pharmacies **Smith's St. Helena Pharmacy,** 1390 Railroad Ave. (at Adams St.), St. Helena (© **707/963-2794**), is open Monday through Friday from 9am to 6pm and Saturday from 9am to 5pm. **Vasconi Drug Store,** 1381 Main St., St. Helena (© **707/963-1447**), is open Monday through Friday from 11am to 7pm, Saturday from 10am to 2pm. **Raley's Pharmacy,** 217 Soscol Ave., Napa (© **707/224-1269**), is open Monday through Friday from 9am to 7pm and Saturday from 9am to 5pm.

Police Call © **707/967-2850** or, in an emergency, © **911.**

Post Offices Each town has its own post office. **Franklin Post Office,** 1351 2nd St., at Randolf Street, Napa (© **707/255-0621**), is open Monday through Friday from 8:30am to 5pm. **Napa Downtown,** 1625 Trancas St., at Claremont Street (© **707/255-0190**), is open Monday through Friday from 8:30am to 5pm. You'll find local branches in **Yountville** at 6514 Washington St. at Mulberry (© **707/944-2123**), open Monday through Friday from 8am to 4pm, Saturday from 9:30am to noon; in **Oakville** at 7856 St. Helena Hwy., at Oakville Cross Road (© **707/944-2600**), open Monday through Friday from 8am to noon and 1 to 4pm, Saturday from 8 to 11:30am; and in **Rutherford** at 1190 Rutherford Rd., at Highway 29 (© **707/963-7488**), operating Monday through Friday from 8am to 1pm and 2 to 4pm, Saturday from 8am to noon. The **St. Helena Post Office,** 1461 Main St., between Adams and Pine streets (© **707/963-2668**), is open Monday through Friday from 8:30am to 5pm and Saturday from 10am to 1pm. In **Calistoga,** head to 1013 Washington St., at Lincoln (© **707/942-6661**), open Monday through Friday from 9am to 4pm.

Shipping Companies See "The Ins & Outs of Shipping Wine Home," in chapter 3.

Taxis Call **Napa Valley Cab,** at © **707/257-6444,** or **Yellow Cab,** at © **707/226-3731.**

2 Touring the Wineries

Touring Napa Valley takes a little planning. With more than 280 wineries, each offering distinct wines, atmosphere, and experience, the best thing you can do is decide what you're most interested in and chart your path from there. (For more on this, see "Strategies for Touring the Wine Country," in chapter 3.)

The towns and wineries listed below are organized geographically, from the city of Napa in the south to Calistoga in the north. Bear in mind that because some wineries are on Highway 29 and others are on the Silverado Trail (which parallels Hwy. 29), the order in which they're listed is not necessarily the best path to follow.

While you're exploring, keep in mind that some of the most memorable Wine Country experiences aren't all made on tours or in formal tasting halls, but at the mom-and-pop wineries that dot the region. These are the places where you'll discover bottles sold from the proprietor's front room and get to talk one-on-one with winemakers.

NAPA

Artesa Vineyards & Winery *(Finds)*   Views, modern architecture, seclusion, and region-specific pinot noir flights are the reasons this is one of my favorite stops. Arrive on a day when the wind is blowing less than 10 mph, and the fountains are captivating; they automatically shut off with higher winds. Step into the winery, and

---

Tips **Reservations at Wineries**

Plenty of wineries' doors are open to anyone who walks through the doors between 10am and 4:30pm. But some wineries require reservations just to visit. But don't think it's because they've got an attitude (although some definitely do). Most of them do so because of local permit laws. It's always best to call ahead if you have your heart set on visiting a certain winery. A few wineries limit the number of guests to create a more intimate experience. In many cases, however, they'll be just as happy to see you if you arrive unannounced. Another word of advice: If you're planning on taking a winery tour, be sure to call in advance and confirm they're still offered, the time at which they begin, and that there's space available. Wineries update their schedules more frequently than I can keep up with, so seriously, do call if you're bent on a tour; arriving to find you're out of luck would definitely be a buzz kill.

Napa Valley Wineries

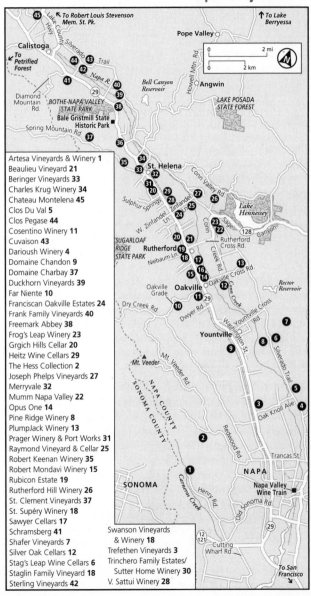

To Robert Louis Stevenson Mem. St. Pk.

To Lake Berryessa

Cal&istoga

To Petrified Forest

Pope Valley

Angwin

Lake County Hwy.

Silverado Trail

Napa R.

Diamond Mountain Rd.

BOTHE-NAPA VALLEY STATE PARK

Bale Gristmill State Historic Park

Spring Mountain Rd

LAKE POSADA STATE FOREST

Howell Mtn. Rd.

Bell Canyon Reservoir

St. Helena

Conn Valley Rd

Lake Hennessey

Sulphur Springs

W. Zinfandel Ln.

Zinfandel Ln.

SUGARLOAF RIDGE STATE PARK

Rutherford

Niebaum Ln.

Conn Creek Rd.

Sage

Rutherford Cross Rd.

Rutherford Cross Rd.

Oakville Grade

Oakville

Dry Creek Rd

Dwyer Rd.

Oakville Cross Rd.

Conn Creek Rd.

Rector Reservoir

Yountville

Mt. Veeder

Mt. Veeder Rd.

NAPA COUNTY

SONOMA COUNTY

Redwood Rd

Oak Knoll Ave.

Washington St.

Yountville Cross Rd.

Silverado Trail

Trancas St.

NAPA

SONOMA

Carneros Creek

Henry Rd

Old Sonoma Rd.

Napa Valley Wine Train

Cutting Wharf Rd.

To San Francisco

Artesa Vineyards & Winery **1**
Beaulieu Vineyard **21**
Beringer Vineyards **33**
Charles Krug Winery **34**
Chateau Montelena **45**
Clos Du Val **5**
Clos Pegase **44**
Cosentino Winery **11**
Cuvaison **43**
Darioush Winery **4**
Domaine Chandon **9**
Domaine Charbay **37**
Duckhorn Vineyards **39**
Far Niente **16**
Franciscan Oakville Estates **24**
Frank Family Vineyards **40**
Freemark Abbey **38**
Frog's Leap Winery **23**
Grgich Hills Cellar **20**
Heitz Wine Cellars **29**
The Hess Collection **2**
Joseph Phelps Vineyards **27**
Merryvale **32**
Mumm Napa Valley **22**
Opus One **14**
Pine Ridge Winery **8**
PlumpJack Winery **13**
Prager Winery & Port Works **31**
Raymond Vineyard & Cellar **25**
Robert Keenan Winery **35**
Robert Mondavi Winery **15**
Rubicon Estate **19**
Rutherford Hill Winery **26**
St. Clement Vineyards **37**
St. Supéry Winery **18**
Sawyer Cellars **17**
Schramsberg **41**
Shafer Vineyards **7**
Silver Oak Cellars **12**
Stag's Leap Wine Cellars **6**
Staglin Family Vineyard **18**
Sterling Vineyards **42**

Swanson Vineyards & Winery **18**
Trefethen Vineyards **3**
Trinchero Family Estates/ Sutter Home Winery **30**
V. Sattui Winery **28**

there's plenty to do. You can wander through the very tasteful gift shop, browse a room that outlines history and details of the Carneros region, or head to the long bar for $2 to $4 tastes or $10 to $15 flights of everything from chardonnays and pinot noirs to cabernet sauvignon and zinfandel. Sorry, but Artesa's permits don't allow for picnicking.

1345 Henry Rd., Napa. ✆ 707/224-1668. www.artesawinery.com. Daily 10am–5pm; tours daily at 11am and 2pm. From Hwy. 12/121, turn north on old Sonoma Rd., turn left on Dealy Lane which becomes Henry Rd.

The Hess Collection ✦✦ *(Finds)*   Tucked into the hillside of rural Mount Veeder, one of the region's sexiest wineries brings art and wine together like no other destination in the valley. Swiss art collector Donald Hess is behind the 1978 transformation of the Christian Brothers' 1903 property into a winery–art gallery exhibiting huge, colorful works by the likes of Frank Stella, Francis Bacon, and the latest addition, an Anselm Kiefer. A free self-guided tour leads through the collection and allows glimpses through tiny windows into the winemaking facilities. Equally alluring is the picturesque courtyard and exceptionally tasteful gift shop. *The only downside:* Staff can be cold and stuffy. For $5, you can sample the current cabernet and chardonnay and one other featured wine. For bottles, current-release prices start at $9.95 and top off at around $90.

4411 Redwood Rd., Napa. ✆ 707/255-1144. www.hesscollection.com. Daily 10am–4pm, except some holidays. From Hwy. 29 north, exit at Redwood Rd. west, and follow Redwood Rd. for 6½ miles.

Trefethen Vineyards   Listed on the National Register of Historic Places, the vineyard's main building was built in 1886 and is Napa's last example of a 19th-century, wooden, gravity-flow winery. Although Trefethen is one of the valley's oldest wineries, it didn't produce its first chardonnay until 1973—but thank goodness it did. The award-winning whites and reds are a pleasure to the palate. Tastings are $10 for four estate wines, but if you want to sample a reserve, it'll cost you $20.

1160 Oak Knoll Ave. (east of Hwy. 29), Napa. ✆ 707/255-7700. www.trefethen.com. Daily 10am–4:30pm. From Hwy. 29 north, take a right onto Oak Knoll Ave.

Darioush Winery   If you want to get in on the ground floor of a winery that's sure to be a contender, visit this newbie, which opened in 2000 and was already selling out of its most coveted varietals from a double-wide trailer. The new winery and visitor center, which were finished in 2004, accentuate the homeland of the owner, Persian-American Darioush Khaledi, who immigrated during the Islamic

Revolution and found his fortune in a grocery chain. With architecture based on Persepolis, the capital city of ancient Persia, this 22,000-square-foot winery is one for history buffs and wine lovers alike. It features dazzling architectural references such as the 16 monumental 18-foot-tall freestanding columns at its entrance as well as a state-of-the-art visitor center and lush landscaping. Tastings of their wines, including a red table wine, shiraz, merlot, cabernet sauvignon, viognier, and chardonnay, are $10 to $15 (including Persian pistachios), but opt for the appointment-only $35 private tasting with cheese pairing, and you'll get to taste local Sonoma artisan cheeses along with your wine and take a tour of the facilities.

4240 Silverado Trail (south of Oak Knoll Ave.), Napa. ℂ **707/257-2345.** www. darioush.com. Daily 10:30am–5pm. Private Tasting with Cheese Pairing daily at 11am and 3pm by appointment only. Tours available by appointment.

Clos Du Val Outside, French and American flags mark the entrance to the ivy-covered building and well-manicured rose garden. Inside, you'll experience a friendly, small-business atmosphere along with a matter-of-fact tasting room pouring California wines made in subtler French style.

Cabernet makes up 70% of the winery's production, but other varietals include chardonnay, pinot noir, and merlot. There's a $5 tasting charge (refunded with purchase) for about four wines, which may include a library selection or two.

Lovely picnic facilities and free access to the lawn game *pétanque* are available in grassy nooks along the grounds.

5330 Silverado Trail (north of Oak Knoll Ave.), Napa. ℂ **707/259-2200.** www. closduval.com. Daily 10am–5pm. Tours by appointment only.

Stag's Leap Wine Cellars Founded in 1972, Stag's Leap shocked the oenological world in 1976 when its 1973 cabernet won first place over French wines in a Parisian blind tasting. Visit the charmingly landscaped, unfussy winery and its very cramped "tasting room" where, for $10 per person, you can judge the four to six current releases; or you can fork over up to $30 for estate samples. A 1-hour tour and tasting runs through everything from the vineyard and production facilities to the ultraswank $5-million wine caves (used to store and age wine), which premiered in mid-2001.

5766 Silverado Trail, Napa. ℂ **707/944-2020.** www.cask23.com. Daily 10am–4:30pm. Tours by appointment only. From Hwy. 29, go east on Trancas St. or Oak Knoll Ave., then north to the cellars.

Pine Ridge Winery More for the serious wine taster than the casual winery hopper, Pine Ridge welcomes guests with a pretty hillside location, less tourist traffic than most, and good wines. Outside, vineyards surround the well-landscaped property, and picnic tables are perfectly perched on a knoll. (However, the winery prefers to extend lunch courtesies to refined revelers who taste first and don't just show up with coolers full of beer.) Across the parking lot is a demonstration vineyard, which is somewhat educational if you know something about grape growing and even more helpful if you take their $20 tour (by appointment), which also covers the cellar and barrel tastings. Otherwise, tastings, which are held inside a modest room, start at $10 for current releases. Their appointment-only Cab and Hillside barrel-to-bottle tastings are $20 and $30 respectively and are held at 11am, 1pm, and 3pm. If you're visiting in summer and want to know about food and wine pairing, call to learn whether they're holding their tasty weekend seminars.

5901 Silverado Trail, Napa. © **800/575-9777** or 707/253-7500. www.pineridge winery.com. Daily 10:30am–4:30pm. Tours by appointment at 10am, noon, and 2pm.

Shafer Vineyards *(Finds*   For an intimate, off-the-beaten-track wine experience, make an appointment to tour and taste at this Stags Leap destination. Unlike many Napa wineries, this one is family owned—by John Shafer, who after 23 years in publishing bought 209 Wine Country hillside acres and planted vines on 50 of them. Today, he and his son Doug, joined by winemaker Elias Fernandez, use sustainable farming and solar energy to make exceptional chardonnay, merlot, sangiovese-cab blend (their answer to a Super Tuscan and my personal favorite!), cabernet sauvignon, and syrah. Though they only produce 34,000 cases per year, their wines are well known and highly regarded. But more importantly, they share their wine and their winemaking philosophy with you during a really enjoyable and relaxed $25-per-person 1½-hour tour and tasting, which includes sipping at one long wooden table within a bright, homey room with a fireplace, pitched ceiling and windows overlooking vineyards from every angle, and perhaps patting their yellow Lab, Parker. Most wines go for $37 to $60, but their Hillside Select cabernet will cost you $150.

6154 Silverado Trail, Napa. © **707/944-2877.** www.shafervineyards.com. By appointment only Mon–Fri 10:30am–1:30pm.

YOUNTVILLE

Domaine Chandon *(★★* *(Finds*   Founded in 1973 by French champagne house Moët et Chandon, the valley's most renowned sparkling winemaker rises to the grand occasion with truly elegant grounds and atmosphere. Here quintessentially manicured gardens showcase locally made sculpture, and guests linger—their glasses fizzing with bubbly—under the patio's umbrella shade. In the restaurant, diners indulge in a somewhat formal French-inspired meal (there's a more casual menu at lunchtime). If you can pull yourself away from the Salon's bubbly (sold in tastings for $9–$14), the comprehensive tour of the facilities is interesting, very informative, and friendly. There's also a boutique. *Note:* The restaurant, which is closed on Tuesday and Wednesday and has even more restricted winter hours, usually requires reservations.

1 California Dr. (at Hwy. 29), Yountville. ✆ 707/944-2280. www.chandon.com. Daily 10am–6pm; hours vary by season, so call to confirm. Call for free tour schedules.

Cosentino   Known for its friendly, laid-back atmosphere and vast selection of wines, Cosentino's tasting room is a great stop for anyone interested in covering a lot of wine-tasting ground under one roof. Pay $5 to taste ($10 for reserve wines) and you'll get to keep the glass, plus sample an array of wines from their portfolio, which includes the brands Cosentino, CE2V, and Crystal Valley Cellars. With nearly 40 different wines on sale ($12–$100), there's lots of entertainment value at the long, copper-top bar. Join the wine club for free tastings and 25% off purchases.

7415 St. Helena Hwy. (Hwy. 29), Yountville. ✆ 707/944-1220. www.cosentino winery.com. Daily 10am–5pm (until 5:30pm during daylight saving time).

OAKVILLE
Far Niente   This storybook stone winery is a serious treat for wine, garden, and classic car lovers. Founded in 1885, it was abandoned for 60 years around prohibition, purchased in 1979 by Gil Nickel (also of nearby Nickel & Nickel winery), and opened to the public for the first time in spring 2004. The tour includes a walk of the beautiful historic stone property, caves, private car collection (truly stunning!), and azalea garden. It finishes with a sampling of five delicious wines (including a delicious chardonnay, cabernet sauvignon, and "Dolce"—their spectacular semillon and sauvignon blanc dessert blend sure to make converts of even sweet wine naysayers). Tours and tastings of five wines are $40 and by appointment only. Wines aren't cheap either—from around $52 for the chardonnay to $110 for their estate cabernet sauvignon.

1350 Acacia Dr., Oakville. ✆ 800/FN-DOLCE or 707/944-2861. www.farniente.com. Tours and tastings by appointment only Mon–Sat 10am–4pm; closed Sun.

Silver Oak Cellars   Colorado oil man Ray Duncan and former Christian Brothers monk Justin Meyer formed a partnership and a mission to create the finest cabernet sauvignon in the world. The answer was this winery, which produces one of the valley's cabernet kings.

A narrow, tree-lined road leads to the handsome Mediterranean-style winery, where roughly 25,000 cases of Napa Valley cabernet sauvignon are produced annually (an additional 50,000 cases are produced annually at their Alexander Valley winery in Geyserville). The elegant tasting room is refreshingly quiet and soothing, adorned with redwood panels stripped from old wine tanks and warmed by a wood fire. Tastings, which include a keepsake burgundy glass, are $10. No picnic facilities are available.

915 Oakville Cross Rd. (at Money Rd.), Oakville. ✆ **707/944-8808.** www.silver oak.com. Tasting room Mon–Sat 9am–4pm. Tours Mon–Fri at 1:30pm, by appointment only.

PlumpJack Winery If most wineries are like a Brooks Brothers suit, PlumpJack stands out as the Todd Oldham of wine tasting: chic, colorful, a little wild, and popular with a young, hip crowd as well as a growing number of aficionados. Like the franchise's PlumpJack San Francisco restaurants and wine shop, and Lake Tahoe resort, this playfully medieval winery is a welcome diversion from the same old same old. With Getty bucks behind what was once Villa Mt. Eden winery, the budget covers far more than just atmosphere: There's some serious winemaking going on here, too. For $5 you can sample the cabernet, merlot, and chardonnay. Alas, there are no tours or picnic spots.

620 Oakville Cross Rd. (just west of the Silverado Trail), Oakville. ✆ **707/ 945-1220.** www.plumpjack.com. Daily 10am–4pm.

Robert Mondavi Winery 🌟 *Finds* At mission-style Mondavi, computers control almost every variable in the winemaking process—it's fascinating to watch, especially since Mondavi gives the most comprehensive tours in the valley. Basic jaunts, which cost $20 and last about 1¼ hours, take you through the vineyards—complete with examples of varietals—and through their newest winemaking facilities. Ask the guides anything; they know a heck of a lot. After the tour, you taste the results of all this attention to detail in selected current wines. If you're really into learning more about wine, ask about their myriad in-depth tours, such as the $50 "essence tasting," which explores the flavor profiles of wine by sniff-comparing varietals alongside the scents of fresh fruits, spices, and nuts, or their $105 "Celebrating California Wine and Food" tour, which includes a presentation on the history of wine, a tour of the winery, and a three-course luncheon with wine pairing. In summer, the winery also schedules some great outdoor concerts; previous performers included Buena Vista Social Club and Chaka Kahn. Call about upcoming events.

7801 St. Helena Hwy. (Hwy. 29), Oakville. ℂ **800/MONDAVI** or 707/226-1395. www.robertmondaviwinery.com. Daily 10am–4pm, until 5pm in summer. Reservations recommended for guided tour; book 1 week ahead, especially for weekend tours.

Opus One   A visit to Opus One is a serious and stately affair developed in a partnership between Robert Mondavi and Baron Philippe de Rothschild, who, after years of discussion, embarked on this state-of-the-art collaboration. Architecture buffs in particular will appreciate the tour, which takes in both the impressive Greco-Roman-meets-20th-century building and the no-holds-barred ultra-high-tech production and aging facilities.

This entire facility caters to one ultrapremium wine, which is offered here for a whopping $25 per 4-ounce taste (and a painful $160 per bottle). But wine lovers should happily fork over the cash: It's a memorable red. Grab your glass and head to the redwood rooftop deck to enjoy the view.

7900 St. Helena Hwy. (Hwy. 29), Oakville. ℂ **707/944-9442**. www.opusonewinery. com. Daily 10am–4pm. Tours daily by appointment only; in high season, book a month in advance.

RUTHERFORD

Swanson Vineyards & Winery ⟨ *Finds*   The valley's most posh and unique wine tasting is yours with a reservation and a $25 to $55 fee at Swanson. Here the shtick is more like a private party, which they call a "*Sa*-lon." You and up to seven other guests sit at a centerpiece round table in a vibrant coral parlor adorned with huge paintings, seashells, and a fireplace, and take in the uncommonly refined yet whimsical atmosphere. The table's set more for a dinner party than for a tasting, with Reidel stemware, slivers of a fine cheese or two, crackers, and one Alexis ganache-filled bonbon, which you will be glad to know can be purchased on the premises. Over the course of the hour-or-more snack-and-sip event, a winery host will pour four to seven wines, perhaps a bright pinot grigio, merlot, and hearty Alexis, their signature cab-syrah blend, and you're bound to befriend those at the table with you. Definitely a must-do for those who don't mind spending the money.

1271 Manley Lane, Rutherford. ✆ **707/967-3500**. www.swansonvineyards.com. Appointments available Wed–Sun 11am, 1:30pm, and 4pm.

Sawyer Cellars *Finds*　The most attractive thing about Sawyer, aside from its clean and tasty wines, is its dedication to extremely high quality while maintaining a humble, accommodating attitude. Step into the simple, restored 1920s barn to see what I mean. Whatever you ask, the tasting-room host will answer. Whatever your request, they do their best to accommodate it. Want to picnic on the back patio overlooking the vineyards? Be their guest. Like to participate in a crush? Come on over and get your hands dirty. Reserve their charming wine library for a private luncheon? Pay a minimal fee and make yourself at home. Here you can tour the property on a little tram or learn more about winemaker Brad Warner, who spent 30 years at Mondavi before embarking on this exclusive endeavor. Plunk down $5 to taste delicious estate-made wines: sauvignon blanc, merlot, cabernet sauvignon, and Meritage ($16–$46 for current releases), which some argue are worth twice the price. With a total production of only 4,200 cases and a friendly attitude, this winery is a rare treat.

8350 St. Helena Hwy. (Hwy. 29), Rutherford. ✆ **707/963-1980**. www.sawyercellars. com. Daily 10am–5pm. Tasting by appointment. Tours by appointment.

St. Supéry Winery *Kids*　The outside looks like a modern corporate office building, but inside you'll find a functional, welcoming winery that encourages first-time tasters to learn more about oenology. On the self-guided tour, you can wander through the demonstration vineyard, where you'll learn about growing techniques. Inside, kids gravitate toward coloring books and SmellaVision, an interactive display that teaches you how to identify different wine ingredients. Adjoining the main building is the Atkinson House, which chronicles more than 100 years of winemaking history during public tours at 1 and 3pm. For $10, you'll get lifetime tasting privileges and a tour, which includes samples of four wines, which hopefully includes their excellent and very well-priced sauvignon blanc. Even the prices make visitors feel at home: Bottles start at $19, although the tag on their high-end Bordeaux red blend is $50.

8440 St. Helena Hwy. (Hwy. 29), Rutherford. ✆ **800/942-0809** or 707/963-4507. www.stsupery.com. Daily 10am–5pm, until 5:30pm in summer. $10 tour at 1 and 3pm daily.

Rubicon Estate　Hollywood meets Napa Valley at Francis Ford Coppola's historic Inglenook Vineyards, previously known as Niebaum-Coppola (*Nee*-bom *Coh*-pa-la) and now named after their most prestigious wine. You'll have to fork over $25 to visit the estate, but that includes a tasting of five wines, tour of various historic properties, and valet parking. Outside the spectacular 1880s ivy-draped stone winery and grounds are historic grandeur. Inside, downstairs is one giant wine bar and retail center. Upstairs displays his film memorabilia, from Academy Awards to trinkets from *The Godfather* and *Bram Stoker's Dracula*. Wine, food, and gift items dominate the cavernous tasting area, where wines such as an estate-grown blend, cabernet franc, merlot, and zinfandel made from organically grown grapes are sampled. Bottles range from around $19 to more than $100. Along with the basic tour, you can pay extra for more exclusive, specialized tours as well.

1991 St. Helena Hwy. (Hwy. 29), Rutherford. © **800/RUBICON** or 707/968-1100. www.rubiconestate.com. 10am–5pm daily. Tours daily.

Beaulieu Vineyard   Bordeaux native Georges de Latour founded the third-oldest continuously operating winery in Napa Valley in 1900. With the help of legendary oenologist André Tchelistcheff, he has produced world-class, award-winning wines that have been served by every president of the United States since Franklin D. Roosevelt. The brick-and-redwood tasting room isn't much to look at, but with Beaulieu's (*Bowl*-you) stellar reputation, it has no need to visually impress. Appellation tastings cost $5, and a variety of bottles sell for under $20. The recently remodeled Reserve Tasting Room offers a "flight" of five reserve wines to taste for $25, but if you want to take a bottle to go, it may cost upward of $100.

1960 St. Helena Hwy. (Hwy. 29), Rutherford. © **707/967-5230**. www.bvwines.com. Daily 10am–5pm.

Grgich Hills Cellar   Croatian émigré Miljenko (Mike) Grgich (*Grr*-gitch) made his presence known to the world when his 1973 Chateau Montelena chardonnay bested the top French white burgundies at the famous 1976 Paris tasting. Since then, the master vintner teamed up with Austin Hills (of the Hills Brothers coffee fortune) and started this extremely successful and respected winery featuring estate grown wines from organically and biodynamically farmed vineyards.

The ivy-covered stucco building isn't much to behold, and the tasting room is even less appealing, but people don't come here for the scenery: As you might expect, Grgich's chardonnays are legendary—and priced accordingly. The smart buys are the outstanding zinfandel and cabernet sauvignon, which cost around $28 and

$50, respectively. The winery also produces a fantastic fumé blanc for $21 a bottle. Before you leave, be sure to poke your head into the barrel-aging room and inhale the divine aroma. Tastings cost $5 (which includes the glass). No picnic facilities are available.

1829 St. Helena Hwy. (Hwy. 29), north of Rutherford Cross Rd., Rutherford. 𝄢 **707/963-2784.** www.grgich.com. Daily 9:30am–4:30pm. $10 tours by appointment only, Mon–Fri 11am and 2pm; Sat–Sun 11am and 1:30pm.

Mumm Napa Valley   At first glance, Mumm, housed in a big redwood barn, looks almost humble. Once you're through the front door, however, you'll know that they mean business—big business. Just beyond the extensive gift shop (filled with all sorts of namesake mementos) is the tasting room, where you can purchase sparkling wine by the glass ($5–$8), three-wine flights ($8–$25), or the bottle ($16–$70), and appreciate breathtaking vineyard and mountain views on the open patio. You can also take a 45-minute free educational tour and stroll the impressive photography gallery, which features a permanent Ansel Adams collection and ever-changing photography exhibits. Sorry, there's no food or picnicking here.

8445 Silverado Trail (just south of Rutherford Cross Rd.), Rutherford. 𝄢 **800/686-6272** or 707/942-3434. www.mummnapa.com. Daily 10am–5pm. Tours offered every hour daily 10am–3pm.

Staglin Family Vineyard   This, one of the area's prestige wineries, was never open to the public until winter 2001, when Staglin debuted its new wine caves and private tours. Now you can turn off Highway 29, through a quiet residential area, to beautifully trellised vineyards and the daily private wine tasting with no more than 10 guests. During the visit, they'll tell you about the winery history and the famed "Rutherford dust" and taste you through four wines—two chardonnays and two cabernet sauvignons under two labels, Staglin Family and their secondary brand Salus. Wines range from $35 to $100 and are served at a sit-down tasting in the caves. At $20 a pop and with little in the way of bells and whistles (other than the wine, of course), this excursion is best for those who want a more intimate understanding of Staglin rather than winemaking in general and for those who want to purchase some of Staglin's product.

P.O. Box 680, Rutherford. 𝄢 **707/944-0477.** www.staglinfamily.com. One tasting daily, by appointment.

Frog's Leap Winery   One of the valley's leaders in organic farming, Frog's Leap is known for its killer zinfandels (but its sauvignon blancs, merlots, cabernets, and chardonnays are nothing to sneeze at). The new Hospitality Center is slated to open in spring 2006, and that's where you'll start the 45-minute expedition which gives "a scintillating history" of how Frog's Leap began, a tour of the barn and gardens, and wine tasting—the wine may even be poured directly from the tanks. If there's action on the vines, you might get to pick and eat fresh grapes.

Considering that Frog's Leap is a favorite on restaurant wine lists and has a small annual production of 50,000 cases, the wine is well priced, ranging from $12 for a dry rosé to $65 for the Rutherford (a blend of cabernet sauvignon and cabernet franc).

8815 Conn Creek Rd. (west of Silverado Trail), Rutherford. ✆ **800/959-4704** or 707/963-4704. www.frogsleap.com. Mon–Sat 10am–4pm. Tastings and tours by appointment only. From Hwy. 29, take Rutherford Cross Rd. and turn left at the fork.

Rutherford Hill Winery   Rutherford Hill Winery isn't particularly well known for its wine, although it does produce a wide array—chardonnay, cabernet, zinfandel port, sangiovese, cabernet sauvignon, and merlot, which makes up around 80% of its entire wine production. But it does have lots of reasons to pay a visit. For example, thanks to massive drilling machinery imported from England, nearly a mile has been carved into the limestone slopes behind the winery, where more than 8,000 barrels of wine are stored in a naturally temperature-controlled environment. Half-hour tours include a trip through the caves and take you into the bowels of the immense wooden structure that houses the fermentation tanks and tasting room. A tour costs $10 and includes a wineglass for current-release tasting; for $15 you get the tour, a special reserve glass, and a reserve tasting.

Perched high above the valley, Rutherford Hill is also the Wine Country's premier picnicking site, offering the same superb views of the valley that guests of Auberge du Soleil (see "Where to Stay," later in this chapter) pay big bucks for. Prices for current wines range from $15 for the sauvignon blanc to $92 for their reserve merlot.

200 Rutherford Hill Rd. (off Silverado Trail), Rutherford. ✆ **800/MERLOT-1** or 707/963-7194. www.rutherfordhill.com. Daily 10am–5pm. Tours daily at 11:30am, 1:30pm, and 3:30pm.

Franciscan Oakville Estates   Franciscan's tasting room is Pottery Barn chic with its slick zinc centerpiece bar, dark wood shelving, high ceilings, and suave displays. But the point of a visit is less superficial. Here it's $5 for the entry-level tasting of current releases and reserve wines for $10. For an even more in-depth experience, book a space in one of the private educational tastings, which range from an "essence" tasting (how to identify sensory elements in wine) to wine and cheese pairing. Each class is around an hour long and is held in the posh, wood-paneled, library like, private section of the new building. The private tasting/educational classes cost $10 to $20 and should be reserved in advance.

1178 Galleron Rd. (east of Hwy. 29), Rutherford. © **800/529-WINE** or 707/963-7111. www.franciscan.com. Daily 10am–5pm; closed major holidays. Reservations suggested for classes.

ST. HELENA

Raymond Vineyard & Cellar As fourth-generation vintners from Napa Valley and relations of the Beringers, brothers Walter and Roy Raymond have had plenty of time to develop terrific wines—and an excellent wine-tasting experience. The short drive through vineyards to reach the friendly, unintimidating cellar is a case in point: Passing the heavy-hanging grapes (in summer) makes you feel like you're really in the thick of things before you even get in the door. The spacious, warm room, complete with dining table and chairs, is a perfect setting for sampling the four tiers of wines, and a Limited Edition tasting is $10 (fee is waived with a purchase). The Amber Hill label starts at $9 a bottle for chardonnay and $13 for cab; the reserves range from $12 to $35, and the Generations cab costs $70. Along with the overall experience, there's a great gift selection, which includes barbecue sauces, mustards, chocolate wine syrup, and gooey hazelnut merlot fudge sauce. Private reserve tastings cost $5. Sorry, there are no picnic facilities.

849 Zinfandel Lane (off Hwy. 29 or Silverado Trail), St. Helena. © **800/525-2659** or 707/963-3141. www.raymondwine.com. Daily 10am–4pm. Tours by appointment only.

V. Sattui Winery *Kids* *Finds* So what if it's touristy and crowded? This enormous winery is also a fun picnic-party stop thanks to a huge gourmet deli and grassy expanse. It's especially great for families since you can fill up on wine, pâté, and cheese samples without ever reaching for your pocketbook, while the kids romp around the grounds. The gourmet store stocks more than 200 cheeses, sandwich meats, pâtés, breads, exotic salads, and desserts such as white-chocolate cheesecake. (It would be an easy place to graze were it not for the continuous mob scene at the counter.) Meanwhile, the extensive wine offerings flow at the long wine bar in the back. Wines aren't distributed, so if you taste something you simply must have, buy it. (With a case purchase, you receive membership to their private cellar and access to the less crowded, private tasting room.) Wine prices start around $9, with many in the $16 neighborhood; reserves top out at around $75. *Note:* To use the picnic area, you must buy food and wine here.

1111 White Lane (at Hwy. 29), St. Helena. ⓒ 707/963-7774. www.vsattui.com. Winter daily 9am–5pm; summer daily 9am–6pm.

Heitz Wine Cellars   If you're looking for a big wine-tasting hullabaloo, don't come here. At Heitz's tiny, modest tasting room, the point is the wine and the wine alone. Joe Heitz, who passed away in December 2000, launched his winery in 1961, when there were fewer than 20 wineries in the valley. Today, his son David oversees the production of 40,000 cases per year, and although his reputation was built on cabernets (such as the Martha's Vineyard cab, which will set you back $105 to $150 depending on the vintage), he's also produced a Napa Valley chardonnay ($16–$30) as well as less costly cabs, zins, more unusual offerings such as the Grignolino rosé ($17), and two ports ($20–$25). Tastings are complimentary, but if you want to take home the fruits of Heitz's labors, count on spending upwards of $20 per bottle.

436 St. Helena Hwy. (Hwy. 29), St. Helena. ⓒ 707/963-3542. www.heitzcellar.com. Daily 11am–4:30pm. Tours of the winery are Mon–Fri by appointment only (the winery itself is located at 500 Taplin Road).

Merryvale   Merryvale may be approachable and low-key, but not because it's yet to be discovered. Wines here have received plenty of attention from the likes of *Wine Spectator* and *Wine & Spirits*—especially in recent years. Actually, the winery has a much longer history. It was originally built around the time of Prohibition. And allegedly, Peter and Robert Mondavi started their winemaking careers at this site. The property's current identity (Merryvale was founded in 1983 and was previously Sunny St. Helena) celebrates its history with a tasting room and the cask room, complete with century-old 2,000-gallon casks. As for the wine, a $5 tasting fee gets you access to current releases; it's $7 for reserve selections and $10 for the classic reserve prestige selection. Varietals include sauvignon blanc, chardonnays, semillon, merlot, pinot noir, cabernet sauvignon, and antigua (a muscat dessert wine). Current releases begin at $15 for semillon and top off at $90 for the delicious Profile (a proprietary Bordeaux varietal blend).

Every weekend morning at 10:30am there's a 2-hour $15 seminar (reserve in advance); three Saturdays of the month you can make a reservation for a wine component–tasting seminar and the fourth Saturday of the month you can sign up for the food and wine pairing seminar. Another fun reason to stop by is the barrel tastings, which happen every second weekend of every month from 1 to 5pm; for $7 you can sample wine aging in the barrel. Also worth noting: While most wineries close around 5pm, this one keeps on pouring until dinnertime!

1000 Main St. (Hwy. 29), St. Helena. © 707/963-7777. www.merryvale.com. Daily 10am–6:30pm.

Joseph Phelps Vineyards ℛ Visitors interested in intimate, comprehensive tours and a knockout tasting should schedule a tour at this winery. A quick turn off the Silverado Trail in Spring Valley (there's no sign—watch for Taplin Rd., or you'll blast right by), Joseph Phelps was founded in 1973 and is a major player in both the regional and the worldwide wine market. Phelps himself accomplished a long list of valley firsts, including launching the syrah varietal in the valley and extending the 1970s Berkeley food revolution (led by Alice Waters) to the Wine Country by founding the Oakville Grocery Co. (p. 117).

A favorite stop for serious wine lovers, this modern, state-of-the-art winery with a big-city vibe is proof that Phelps's annual 95,000 cases prove fruitful in more ways than one. When you pass the wisteria-covered trellis to the entrance of the redwood building, you'll encounter an air of seriousness that hangs heavier than harvest grapes. Fortunately, the mood lightens as the well-educated $20 "seminar" leader explains the details around samples of six wines, which may include viognier, chardonnay, syrah, merlot, cab, Rhone blends, and Bordeaux blends. Unfortunately, some wines are so popular that they sell out quickly; come late in the season, and you may not be able to taste or buy them. The three excellently located picnic tables, on the terrace overlooking the valley, are only available for Phelps wine club members (join and get wine shipped a certain number of times per year) by reservation.

200 Taplin Rd. (off the Silverado Trail; P.O. Box 1031), St. Helena. © 800/707-5789. www.jpvwines.com. Mon–Sat 9am–5pm; Sun 10am–4pm. $20 seminars and tastings by appointment only; $10 per person for 2-oz. pour of Insignia.

Prager Winery & Port Works (Finds If you want a real down-home, off-the-beaten-track experience, Prager's can't be beat. Turn the corner from Sutter Home winery and roll into the small gravel parking lot; you're on the right track, but when you pull open the creaky old wooden door to this shack of a wine-tasting room, you'll begin to wonder. Don't turn back! Pass the oak barrels, and you'll quickly come upon the clapboard tasting room, made homey with a big Oriental rug and a Prager family host. Fork over $10 (includes a complimentary glass), and they'll pour you samples of late-harvest Johannesburg Riesling and the tawny port (which costs $45–$65 per bottle). Also available is "Prager Chocolate Drizzle," a chocolate liqueur that tops ice creams and other desserts. If you're looking for a special gift, consider their bottles, which can be custom etched in the design of your choice for around $75, plus the cost of the wine.

1281 Lewelling Lane (just west of Hwy. 29, behind Sutter Home), St. Helena. ℂ **800/ 969-PORT** or 707/963-7678. www.pragerport.com. Daily 10:30am–4:30pm.

Trinchero Family Estates/Sutter Home Winery This winery's been around since 1874, but its widespread reputation stems from the early 1980s, when its introduction of white zinfandel to the mass market made pink the prominent color in America's wineglasses. Although wine-drinking trends have evolved, Sutter Home's department store–like tasting room is a fair indication that this winery is still pouring for the people. In the friendly, bustling room, visitors surround the enormous U-shaped bar to sample a slew of Sutter Home wines, with chardonnay, cabernet, zin, and other varietals topping out at $8 a bottle. (Alcohol-free wines are as low as $4; Trinchero reserve cab is $45.) Along the periphery of the room is an endless selection of food products, ranging from mustard and barbecue to pasta and chocolate sauces, as well as a Sutter Home wardrobe line, featuring everything from boxers to baseball-style jackets.

Tastings range from free to $7 for reserves (plus a souvenir glass). No tours are offered, but you're invited to take a self-guided walk through the surrounding Victorian gardens.

277 St. Helena Hwy. S. (at Thomann Lane), St. Helena. ℂ **707/963-3104**. www.sutter home.com. Daily 10am–5pm, except major holidays.

Robert Keenan Winery *(Finds)* It's a winding, uphill drive to reach secluded Robert Keenan, but this far off the tourist track you're guaranteed more elbowroom at the tasting bar and a quieter, less commercial experience. When you drive in, you'll pass a few modest homes and wonder whether one of the buildings is the family winery. It's not. Keep driving (slowly—kids and dogs at play) and you'll know when you get to the main building and its redwood tasting room.

The 10,000 cases produced here per year are the result of yet another fast-paced professional who left his business behind and headed for the hills. In this case, it's native San Franciscan Robert Keenan, who ran his own insurance agency for 20 years. When his company merged with another firm and was bought out in 1981, he had already purchased his "retirement property," the winery's 176 acres (48 of which are now planted with grapes), and he soon turned his fascination with winemaking into a second career. The renovated stone building has a much older history, dating back to the old Conradi Winery, which was founded in 1890.

Today, Robert Keenan Winery is known for its big, full-bodied reds, such as the Mountain cab and merlot. Chardonnay, cabernet franc, and zin sold exclusively at the winery range from $22 to $38 per bottle. Older vintages, which you won't find elsewhere, are for sale here as well. Take the tour to learn about the vineyards, production facilities, and winemaking in general. Those looking for a pastoral picnic spot should consider spreading your blanket out here. The three tables, situated right outside the winery and surrounded by vineyards, offer stunning views.

3660 Spring Mountain Rd. (off Hwy. 29), St. Helena. © 707/963-9177. www. keenanwinery.com. Weekends 11am–4pm. Call for an appointment on weekdays. Free tours and tastings weekends 11am–4pm.

Domaine Charbay Winery & Distillery   After you finally reach this mountaintop hideaway, affectionately called "the Still on the Hill," you immediately get the sense that something special is going on here. Miles Karakasevic, the owner of this family operation, considers himself more of a perfume maker than the 12th-generation master distiller he is, and it's easy to see why. The tiny distillery is crammed with bottles of his latest fragrant projects-in-the-making, such as brandy, whole-fruit-flavor-infused vodkas, grappa, and pastis. He's also become known in the valley for other elixirs: black walnut liqueur, apple brandy, a line of ports, several cabernet sauvignons, and the charter product—Charbay (pronounced *Sharbay*)—a brandy liqueur blended with chardonnay.

The tour—which costs $20 per person and is a private and exclusive visit—centers around a small, 25-gallon copper alembic still; you'll be lovingly guided through an explanation of the distilling process by either daughter Laura, gregarious sons Miles and Marko, or his wife Susan. Alas, there's no tasting other than wine and port due to legal limitations. It's all very low-key and laughter-filled at Domaine Charbay, one of the most unique and interesting places to visit in the Wine Country. Sadly, there are no picnic facilities. *Note:* Do not show up without an appointment; you'll be turned away.

4001 Spring Mountain Rd. (5 miles west of Hwy. 29), St. Helena. © 800/634-7845 or 707/963-9327. www.charbay.com. Mon–Sat (except holidays) by appointment only.

Beringer Vineyards ☆ (Finds)   You won't find a personal experience at this tourist-heavy stop. But you will find a regal 1876 estate founded by brothers Jacob and Frederick and hand-dug tunnels in the hillside. The oldest continuously operating winery in Napa Valley, Beringer managed to stay open even during Prohibition by making "sacramental" wines. White zinfandel is the winery's most popular seller, but plenty of other varietals are available to enjoy. Tastings of current vintages ($5–$16) are conducted in new facilities, where there's also a large selection of bottles for less than $20. Reserve wines are available for tasting in the remarkable Rhine House and tours range from the $5 standard or $18 historical to the $30 1½-hour vintage legacy tour. That said, check the website for current tour prices; rumor has it they're changing.

2000 Main St. (Hwy. 29), St. Helena. © **707/963-7115**. www.beringer.com. Off season daily 10am–5pm (last tour 3:30pm, last tasting 4:30pm); summer 10am–6pm (last tour 3:30pm, last tasting 5:30pm).

Charles Krug Winery   Founded in 1861, Krug was the first winery built in the valley. The family of Peter Mondavi (yes, Robert is his brother) owns it today. It's worth paying your respects here by dropping $5 to sip current releases, $8 to sample reserves. On the grounds are picnic facilities with umbrella-shaded tables overlooking vineyards or the wine cellar.

2800 Main St. (St. Helena Hwy.; just north of the tunnel of trees at the northern end of St. Helena), St. Helena. © **707/963-5057**. www.charleskrug.com. Daily 10:30am–5pm.

Duckhorn Vineyards   With quintessential pastoral surroundings, brand new digs, and a unique wine-tasting program, Duckhorn Vineyards has much to offer for visitors interested in spending a little money and time to relax and taste. The airy Victorian farmhouse is very welcoming; you can stand on the veranda and look out on the surrounding meadow, and the interior affords equally bucolic views. If you're going to taste wine in the surprisingly modern tasting room, complete with cafe tables and a centerpiece bar, it's $10 for a current release tasting. The fee may sound steep, but this not your run-of-the-mill drink-and-dash. You get plenty of attention and information on their sauvignon blanc, merlot, and cabernet sauvignon. Wanna really ante up? Make a reservation and drop $25 for the hour-long estate wine tasting—which includes five reserve wines and some yummy snacks such as cheese and pâté.

1000 Lodi Lane (at Silverado Trail), St. Helena. © **707/963-7108**. www.duckhorn. com. Daily 10am–4pm. Reservations required for parties of 5 or more for the Estate Wine Tasting (11am, 1pm, and 3pm) and for the single daily tour at noon.

Freemark Abbey   Set in a low-key shopping mall, Freemark Abbey's friendly tasting room has a hunting-lodge feel. The huge space features open-beamed ceilings, a roaring fire (in winter), and comfy couches. There's a $5 charge for a keepsake wineglass in which you might sample chardonnay, cabernet, and merlot (ranging from $19–$65 per bottle). They also offer a Napa Valley Reserve Flight for $10 that includes some of their limited production and library wines such as cabernet franc, petite sirah, viognier, and sangiovese. During summer, you can take your taste out onto the lovely outdoor terrace. No picnic facilities are available.

3022 St. Helena Hwy. N. (Hwy. 29, at Lodi Lane), St. Helena. © 800/963-9698. www.freemarkabbey.com. Daily 10am–5pm, until 6pm in summer. Tour by appointment only.

CALISTOGA

Frank Family Vineyards *★ (Finds*   "Wine dudes" Dennis, Tim, Jeff, Grant, and Pat will do practically anything to maintain their rightfully self-proclaimed reputation as the "friendliest winery in the valley." In recent years the name may have changed from Kornell Champagne Cellars to Frank-Rombauer to Frank Family, but the vibe's remained constant; it's all about down-home, friendly fun. No muss, no fuss, no intimidation factor. At Frank Family, you're part of their family—no joke. They'll greet you like a long-lost relative and serve you all the bubbly you want (three to four varieties: blanc de blancs, blanc de noir, reserve, rouge, at $20–$70 a bottle). Still-wine lovers can slip into the equally casual back room to sample truly tasty chardonnay, cabernet sauvignon, and zinfandel. Behind the tasting room is a choice picnic area, situated under the oaks and overlooking the vineyards.

1091 Larkmead Lane (just off the Silverado Trail), Calistoga. © 707/942-0859. www.frankfamilyvineyards.com. Daily 10am–5pm. Tours by appointment.

Schramsberg *★★ (Finds*   This 217-acre champagne estate, a landmark once frequented by Robert Louis Stevenson, has a wonderful old-world feel and is one of the valley's all-time best places to explore. Schramsberg is the label that presidents serve when toasting dignitaries from around the globe, and there's plenty of historic memorabilia in the front room to prove it. But the real mystique begins when you enter the champagne caves, which wind for 2 miles (reputedly the longest in North America) and were partly hand-carved by Chinese laborers in the 1800s. The caves have an authentic Tom Sawyer ambience, complete with dangling cobwebs and seemingly endless passageways; you can't help but feel you're on an adventure. The comprehensive, unintimidating tour ends in a charming tasting room, where you'll sit around a big table and sample four surprisingly varied selections of bubbly. Tastings are a bit dear ($20 per person), but it's money well spent. Note that tastings are offered only to those who take the free tour, and you must reserve in advance.

1400 Schramsberg Rd. (off Hwy. 29), Calistoga. *(C)* **707/942-2414.** www.schramsberg.com. Daily 10am–4pm. Tours and tastings by appointment only.

Clos Pegase *(R)* *(Finds)*   Renowned architect Michael Graves designed this incredible oasis, which integrates art, 20,000 square feet of aging caves, and a luxurious hilltop private home. Viewing the art is as much the point as tasting the wines—which, by the way, don't come cheap: Prices range from $13 for the 2000 Vin Gris merlot to as much as $75 for the 1998 Hommage Artist Series Reserve, an extremely limited blend of the winery's finest lots of cabernet sauvignon and merlot. Tasting current releases costs $5 for three whites and $10 for five reds. The grounds at Clos Pegase (Clo Pey-*goss*) feature an impressive sculpture garden as well as scenic picnic spots.

1060 Dunaweal Lane (off Hwy. 29 or the Silverado Trail), Calistoga. *(C)* **707/942-4981.** www.clospegase.com. Daily 10:30am–5pm. Tours daily at 11am and 2pm.

Sterling Vineyards *(R)* *(Kids)* *(Finds)*   No, you don't need climbing shoes to reach this dazzling white Mediterranean-style winery, perched 300 feet up on a rocky knoll. Just fork over $15 ($10 for kids—including a goodie bag) and take the aerial tram, which offers stunning bucolic views along the way. Once you're back on land, follow the self-guided tour (one of the most comprehensive in the Wine Country) of the winemaking process. Wine tastings of four varietals in the panoramic tasting room are included in the tram fare, but more sophisticated sips—a la limited releases or reserve flights—will set you back anywhere from $3 and $25 respectively. Expect to pay anywhere from $14 to $75 for a souvenir bottle ($20 is the average).

1111 Dunaweal Lane (off Hwy. 29, just south of downtown Calistoga), Calistoga. *(C)* **707/942-3344.** www.sterlingvineyards.com. Daily 10:30am–4:30pm.

Cuvaison   In 1969, Silicon Valley engineers Thomas Cottrell and Thomas Parkhill began Cuvaison (pronounced Koo-vay-*sawn*, a French term for the fermentation of wine on the skins) with a 27-acre vineyard of cabernet. Today, that same vineyard has expanded to 400 acres, producing 63,000 cases of premium wines every year. Known mainly for chardonnays, winemaker Steven Rogstad also produces a limited amount of merlot, pinot noir, cabernet sauvignon, and zinfandel within the handsome Spanish mission–style structure.

Tastings are $8 and $10, which includes a glass. Wine prices range from $22 for a chardonnay to as much as $40 for a cabernet sauvignon. Beautiful picnic grounds are situated amidst 350-year-old moss-covered oak trees.

4550 Silverado Trail (just south of Dunaweal Lane), Calistoga. ℂ 707/942-6266. www.cuvaison.com. Daily 10am–5pm. Tours at 10:30am daily.

Chateau Montelena   Perhaps you've heard of the California chardonnay that revolutionized the world of wine when it won the legendary Paris tasting test of 1976, beating out France's top white burgundies? That wine was a Chateau Montelena 1973 chardonnay, the product of Mike Grgich's (who now owns his own winery, Grgich Hills) second vintage as winemaker for Chateau Montelena. Though the tasting room is rather plain, the winery itself—housed in a replica of the great châteaux of Bordeaux—is a feast for the eyes, as are the Chinese-inspired lake and gardens behind the chateau. Basic tastings are $10, or splurge for the $25 estate cabernet tasting, held in the Estate Room. Bottle prices are on the steep side, ranging from $18 for a Riesling to $125 for the Montelena estate cabernet sauvignon. After sampling the winery's superb chardonnay, cabernet, and Napa Valley cabernet sauvignon (a blend of cabernet sauvignon and merlot), wander around back to marvel at this classic French castle and picturesque grounds, replete with wild fowl, lush foliage, and romantic walkways. Unfortunately, picnicking is not an option here. Reservation-only tours are a hefty $25, but include a 2-hour tour and sit-down tasting.

1429 Tubbs Lane (off Hwy. 29, just past the Old Faithful Geyser), Calistoga. ℂ 707/942-5105. www.montelena.com. Daily 9:30am–4pm. Estate Tastings from 9:30am–1:30pm. Guided tours by appointment only, at 9:30am and 2pm, $25 per person.

3 More to See & Do

I'm not going to lie to you: If days filled with wine tasting, dining on fancy food, and just lounging around in the country excite you about as much as a trip to the DMV, buy a *TV Guide* and make yourself real cozy—it's going to be one helluva long stay in the Wine Country.

However, there are a few daytime attractions—such as golf, spectacular spas, a few wonderful shops, and museums—that will perk up anyone who simply can't take one more glass of wine.

NAPA

If you have plenty of time and a penchant for Victorian architecture, check out the **Napa Valley Conference and Visitors Bureau,** 1310 Napa Town Center, off 1st Street (℃ **707/226-7459;** www.napa valley.com), which offers self-guided walking tours of the town's historic buildings.

Anyone with an appreciation for art absolutely must visit the **di Rosa Preserve.** Rene and Veronica di Rosa collected contemporary American art for more than 40 years and then converted their 215 acres of prime property into a monument to Northern California's regional art and nature. Veronica has passed on, but Rene still carries the torch through his world-renowned collection featuring 2,000 works in all media, by more than 900 Greater Bay Area artists. The di Rosas' treasures are on display practically everywhere—along the shores of the property's 35-acre lake and in each nook and cranny of their 125-year-old winery-turned-residence, adjoining building, two newer galleries, and gardens. With hundreds of surrounding acres of rolling hills (protected under the Napa County Land Trust), this place is a must-see for both art and nature lovers. It's at 5200 Carneros Hwy. (Hwy. 121/12); look for the gate. Each tour lasts 2 to 2½ hours, has a maximum of 25 guests, and costs $12 per person on weekdays, $15 on Saturday (10am tour is free every Wed). Reservations recommended. Call ℃ **707/226-5991** to make reservations. Open Tuesday through Friday from 9:30am to 3pm and Saturday by appointment. Visit www.dirosa preserve.org for more information.

Napa's biggest attraction, a museum, **Copia: American Center for Wine, Food & the Arts** ✻, 500 1st St. (℃ **888/51-COPIA** or 707/259-1600; www.copia.org), attempts to explore how wine and food influence U.S. culture. This $50 million multifaceted facility, which was spearheaded and is chaired by Robert Mondavi, tackles the topic in myriad ways, including visual arts a la rotating exhibits, vast vegetable and herb gardens, culinary demonstrations, basic wine classes, concerts, and opportunities to dine and drink on the premises. Programs are geared toward all types of visitors. Kids get a kick out of identifying candy bars through pictures, and connoisseurs might slip into a lecture or cooking class by Rocco DiSpirito, Ming Tsai, or other famous chefs. Day passes include entrance into the building and gardens, exhibitions, tours, and free 30-minute introductory classes. More advanced food, wine, garden, and art classes cost extra. All the food exploration might get you hankering for a snack, so a cafe offers gourmet picnic items, and the adjoining restaurant, Julia's Kitchen, which is named after Chef Child, is a French-California affair.

If you're around in summer or fall definitely check out the Monday night outdoor concert series (usually around $20 per ticket). I

Moments **Up, Up & Away . . .**

Admit it: Floating across lush green pastures in a hot-air balloon is something you've always dreamed of but never gotten around to actually doing. Well, here's your best chance, because believe it or not, Napa Valley is the busiest hot-air balloon "flight corridor" in the *world*. Northern California's temperate weather allows for ballooning year-round, and on clear summer weekends in the valley, it's a rare day when you don't see at least one of the colorful airships floating above the vineyards.

Trips usually depart early in the morning, when the air is cooler and the balloons have better lift. Flight paths vary with the direction and speed of the changing breezes, so chase crews on the ground must follow the balloons to their undetermined destinations. Most excursions last between 1 and 3 hours and end with a traditional champagne celebration and breakfast. Reservations are required and should be made as far in advance as possible. Prices, which often include shuttle service from your local hotel, run close to $200 per person; wedding, wine-tasting, picnic, and lodging packages are also available. *Warning:* When the valley is fogged in, companies drive passengers outside the valley to nearby areas to balloon. Though they cannot guarantee the flight path until hours before liftoff, they should refund your money if you decide not to partake. For more information or reservations, call Napa's **Bonaventura Balloon Company** (✆ **800/FLY-NAPA**; www. bonaventuraballoons.com), a highly reputable organization owned and operated by master pilot Joyce Bowen. Another good choice is **Napa Valley Aloft** (✆ **800/944-4408** or 707/944-4408; www.nvaloft.com), Napa Valley's oldest hot-air-balloon company.

often grab a lawn chair and head to the amphitheater for spectacular vocal and dance performances under Napa's soothing night sky. It's Napa at its best.

Prices of admission are as follows: adult $13; seniors 65 and over $10; students of any age $7.50; young adults (13 to 20) $7.50; children under 13 free. The center is open Wednesday through Monday from 10am to 5pm. The restaurant stays open until 9:30pm Thursday through Sunday. Wednesday admissions are half-price for Napa and Sonoma residents.

HITTING THE LINKS   South of downtown Napa, 1⅓ miles east of Highway 29 on California 12, is the **Chardonnay Club** (© **707/257-8950**), a challenging 27-hole land-links golf complex with first-class service. You pay just one fee, which makes you a member for the day. Privileges include the use of a golf cart, the practice range (including a bucket of balls), and services usually found only at a private club (such as roving snack carts and complimentary clubs cleaning). The course ambles through and around 375 acres of vineyards, hills, creeks, canyons, and rock ridges. There are three nines of similar challenge, all starting at the clubhouse. Four sets of tees provide you with a course measuring from 5,300 to a healthy 7,100 yards. Starting times can be reserved up to 7 days in advance (8–21 days at a premium). Greens fees (including cart) from April 1 through November are $45 to $75 on weekdays and $55 to $95 on weekends. Rates are discounted in winter. Other spots to swing your clubs include the city's public course, **Napa Municipal Golf Course,** at Kennedy Park (2295 Streblow Dr., off Silverado Trail; © **707/255-4333**). At $31 for nonresidents on weekdays, and $41 on weekends, it's a bargain for travelers who would prefer to save their extracurricular funds for food and wine splurges. The optional cart is an additional $13.

HORSEBACK RIDING   If you like horses and venturing through cool, misty forests, then $90 will seem like a bargain for a 2-hour ride with a friendly tour guide and owner, Midori, from the **Napa Valley Trail Rides and Sonoma Cattle Company,** P.O. Box 6883, Napa, CA 94581 (© **707/255-2900;** www.napavalleytrail rides.com). After a lesson in the basics of horse handling at the stable, you'll be led on a leisurely stroll. The price includes photos and refreshments. The ride goes through beautiful Skyline Park in Napa.

NIGHTLIFE   If a swank but more low-key scene is what you're seeking and you're in downtown Napa, check out **The Bounty Hunter** 𝒢𝒢 , a wine bar, at 975 1st St. (© **707/255-0622;**

www.bountyhunterwine.com). Surrounded by dark woods, wine bottles, fun wines by the glass, and excellent sculpted gourmet appetizers such as seared salmon perched atop a cube of sticky rice with wasabi cream, it's downtown's sexiest place to sip and snack—and it stays open late-night on Thursday through Saturday.

YOUNTVILLE

It's worth peeking into **Mosswood Collection,** 6550 Washington St. (© **707/944-8151**), for Elizabeth Lampe's selection of pretty, perky, hand-painted martini glasses, wall tapestries, and fabulous customizable food-and-wine etchings. You'll also find antique corkscrews, garden art, tabletop items, children's toys, and a great selection of ribbons. Open daily 10am to 5pm.

RUTHERFORD

Want to bring home an unusual and beautiful handcrafted decoration for your home or yard? Seek out **Napa Valley Grapevine Wreath Company,** on Highway 128/Rutherford Crossroad, P.O. Box 67, Rutherford, CA 94573 (© **707/963-8893**), which weaves big and small indoor or outdoor sculptures made out of little more than cabernet grapevines. Call for directions, as this tiny shack of a shop is hidden on a side road among Rutherford's vineyards. Hours vary during winter, but are generally Thursday through Monday from 10am to 5:30pm.

ST. HELENA

Literature buffs and other romantics will want to visit the **Silverado Museum,** 1490 Library Lane (© **707/963-3757**), which is devoted to the life and works of Robert Louis Stevenson, who honeymooned here in 1880 in an abandoned Silverado Mine bunkhouse. The collection of more than 8,000 items includes original manuscripts, letters, photographs, and portraits, plus the desk he used in Samoa. Hours are Tuesday through Sunday from noon to 4pm; admission is free.

SPAS   If the Wine Country's slow pace and tranquil vistas aren't soothing enough for you, St. Helena's diverse selection of spas can massage, bathe, wrap, and steam you into an overly pampered pulp.

If you're a fitness freak, **Health Spa Napa Valley** ℱ, 1030 Main St. (Hwy. 29; © **707/967-8800**), is a mandatory stop after a few days of inevitable overindulgence. Here you can treadmill or StairMaster yourself silly and then reward yourself with spa treatments: Immerse yourself in Wine Country ways with a grape-seed mud wrap ($95), or go all-out with a Abhyanga treatment ($180), in which two massage therapists get out the knots with synchronized motion. Memberships are $25 per day Monday through Thursday, $40 per day Friday through Sunday, and free for guests of The Inn at Southbridge (see "Where to Stay," below). Open Monday through Friday from 5:45am to 8:30pm and Saturday and Sunday from 7am to 8:30pm.

SHOPPING   St. Helena's Main Street is the best place to go if you're suffering serious retail withdrawal. Though you'll find only a few blocks of stores that are credit-card worthy, a lot of damage can still be done. Take, for example, **Vanderbilt and Company** ⊛, 1429 Main St., between Adams and Pine streets (☏ **707/963-1010**), which offers the crème de la crème of cookware, hand-painted Italian dishware, linens, and everything else you could possibly convince yourself you need for your gourmet kitchen and dining room. Open daily from 9:30am to 5:30pm.

Another great gift shop is **Olivier,** 1375 Main St. (☏ **707/ 967-8777**). This shop claims to be the number-one supplier for Williams-Sonoma, and it's named for everything related to delicious Napa Valley olives. Taste and pour your own oil from huge copper tanks or grab a beautifully prepackaged bottle along with other food products galore. Open Monday through Saturday from 10am to 6pm and Sunday from 10am to 5pm.

I also have no bones to pick with **Fideaux,** 1312 Main St. (☏ **707/967-9935**), a wonderfully charming boutique that's like an Eddie Bauer for dogs and cats. Hand-painted feeders, beautiful ceramic water bowls, custom-designed scratching posts, silk-screened dog and cat pillows, rhinestone collars, unique toys, and gourmet dog treats are just a few pet must-haves you'll find here. The ultimate way to bring the Wine Country home to Spot? Try a wine-barrel doghouse. Hours are 9:30am to 5:30pm daily.

Napa's best deals on wine are found not in the wineries, but in a couple of St. Helena stores. **Dean & Deluca,** 607 S. St. Helena Hwy. (Hwy. 29; ☏ **707/967-9980**), and—believe it or not—**Safeway,** 1026 Hunt Ave. (☏ **707/968-3620**), have enormous wine selections.

One last favorite stop: **Napa Valley Olive Oil Manufacturing Company,** 835 Charter Oak Ave., at the end of the road behind Tra Vigne restaurant (☏ **707/963-4173**), a tiny market that presses and bottles its own oils and sells them at a fraction of the price you'd pay elsewhere. It also has an extensive selection of Italian cooking ingredients, imported snacks, and the best deals on dried mushrooms. You'll love the age-old method for totaling the bill, which you simply must find out for yourself. It's open daily from 8am to 5pm.

BICYCLING   The quieter northern end of the valley is an ideal place to rent a bicycle and ride the Silverado Trail. **St. Helena Cyclery,** 1156 Main St. (© **707/963-7736;** www.sthelenacyclery. com), rents bikes for $7 per hour or $30 a day, including rear rack, lock, helmet, and picnic bag.

NIGHTLIFE   The whole valley has little in the way of after-dinner entertainment, which leaves revelers with little choice but to turn to **1351 Lounge,** 1351 Main St. (© **707/963-1969**), a gussied-up, stone-walled former bank, complete with a shiny vault. Here locals and visitors settle around cocktail tables or at the old mahogany bar for cocktails and music, ranging from open-mike night to a DJ or live rock, blues, or funk.

CALISTOGA

Calistoga Depot, 1458 Lincoln Ave. (on the site of Calistoga's original 1868 railroad station) has a variety of shops, some of which are housed in six restored passenger cars dating from 1916.

NATURAL WONDERS   Old Faithful Geyser of California, 1299 Tubbs Lane (© **707/942-6463;** www.oldfaithfulgeyser.com), is one of only three "old faithful" geysers in the world. It's been blowing off steam at regular intervals for as long as anyone can remember. The 350°F (177°C) water spews at a height of about 40 to 60 feet every 40 minutes, day and night. The performance lasts about 3 minutes, and you can bring a picnic lunch to munch on between spews. An exhibit hall, gift shop, and snack bar are open every day. Admission is $8 for adults, $7 for seniors, $3 for children 6 to 12, and free for children under 6. The geyser is open daily from 9am to 6pm (to 5pm in winter). To get there, follow the signs from downtown Calistoga; it's between Highway 29 and California 128.

You won't see thousands of trees turned into stone, but you'll still find many interesting petrified specimens at the **Petrified Forest,** 4100 Petrified Forest Rd. (© **707/942-6667;** www.petrifiedforest. org). Volcanic ash blanketed this area after an eruption near Mount St. Helena 3 million years ago. You'll find redwoods that have turned to rock through the slow infiltration of silicates and other minerals, A .25-mile walking trail, museum, discovery shop, and picnic grounds. Admission is $6 for adults, $5 for seniors and juniors 11 to 17, $3 for children 6 to 11, and free for children under 6. The forest is open daily from 9am to 7pm (to 5pm in winter). Heading north from Calistoga on California 128, turn left onto Petrified Forest Road, just past Lincoln Street.

BICYCLING See "Bicycling around the Wine Country," p. 52.

MUD BATHS One thing you should do while you're in Calistoga is what people have been doing here for the past 150 years: Take a **mud bath** ✿. The natural baths are composed of local volcanic ash, imported peat, and naturally boiling mineral hot-springs water, all mulled together to produce a thick mud that simmers at a temperature of about 104°F (40°C). It's a Creature-from-the-Black-Lagoon experience for sure—some people love it and some can't get far enough away from it—but one thing's for sure: You've got to try it out.

After you've overcome the hurdle of deciding how best to maneuver your naked body into the tub filled with steamy-hot and clumpy mud, the rest is pure relaxation, as you soak with surprising buoyancy for about 10 to 12 minutes. A warm mineral-water shower, a mineral-water whirlpool bath, and a mineral-water steam-room visit follow. Afterward, a blanket wrap slowly cools down your body, and then—for a little extra cash—you get a half-hour muscle-melting massage. The outcome is a rejuvenated, revitalized, squeaky-clean you. *Note:* Mud baths aren't recommended for those who are pregnant or have high blood pressure.

The spas also offer a variety of other treatments, such as hand and foot massages, herbal wraps, acupressure face-lifts, skin rubs, and herbal facials. Prices for treatments range from $35 to $150, and appointments are necessary for all services; call at least a week in advance, and as far in advance as possible during the busy summer season.

Indulge yourself at any of these Calistoga spas: **Dr. Wilkinson's Hot Springs,** 1507 Lincoln Ave. (✆ 707/942-4102); **Golden Haven Hot Springs Spa,** 1713 Lake St. (✆ 707/942-6793); **Calistoga Spa Hot Springs,** 1006 Washington St. (✆ 707/942-6269); **Calistoga Village Inn & Spa,** 1880 Lincoln Ave. (✆ 707/942-0991); **Indian Springs Resort,** 1712 Lincoln Ave. (✆ 707/942-4913); or **Roman Spa Motel,** 1300 Washington St. (✆ 707/942-4441).

4 Where to Stay

With more than 2,200 hotel rooms available throughout Napa County, you'd think it'd be a snap to secure a room. Unfortunately, choosing and reserving accommodations—especially from April through November—can be a challenge. Adding to the frustration is that ever-burdening 2-night minimum.

Because Napa Valley is so small, it really doesn't much matter which town you base yourself in; everything's within a 30- or 45-minute drive from everything else (traffic permitting). There are, however, a number of other things you should think about when deciding where to stay. Consider whether you want to be in a modern hotel with all the expected conveniences or a quaint, Victorian B&B; surrounded by acres of vineyards or closer to the highway; in the company of the more conservative wealthy or those leading alternative lifestyles. Accommodations here run the gamut—from motels and B&Bs to world-class luxury retreats—and all are easily accessible from the main highway. Although I recommend shacking up in the more romantically pastoral areas such as Yountville, Rutherford, St. Helena, or the outskirt of Calistoga there's no question you're going to find better deals in the towns of Napa or Calistoga's laid-back downtown.

The accommodations listed below are arranged first by area and then by price, using the following categories: **Very Expensive,** more than $250 per night; **Expensive,** $200 to $250 per night; **Moderate,** $150 to $200 per night; and **Inexpensive,** less than $150 per night. (Sorry—the reality is that anything less than $150 a night qualifies as inexpensive 'round these parts.)

When planning your trip, keep in mind that during the high season—between June and November—most hotels charge peak rates and sell out completely on weekends; many have a 2-night minimum. Always ask about discounts. During the off season, you have far better bargaining power and may be able to get a room at almost half the summer rate.

RESERVATIONS SERVICES   Bed & Breakfast Inns of Napa Valley (© 707/944-4444), an association of B&Bs, provides descriptions and makes reservations. **Napa Valley Reservations Unlimited** (© 800/251-NAPA or 707/252-1985; www.napavalley reservations.com) is also a source for booking everything from hot-air-balloon rides to wine-tasting tours by limousine.

NAPA

Embassy Suites, 1075 California Blvd., Napa, CA 94559 (© **800/ 362-2779** or 707/253-9540; www.embassynapa.com), offers 205 of its usual two-room suites. Each includes a galley kitchen complete with coffeemaker, fridge, microwave, and wet bar; they've also got two TVs and access to indoor and outdoor pools and a restaurant. Rates range from $169 to $289 and include cooked-to-order breakfast, 2-hour beverage reception from 5:30 to 7:30pm, complimentary

Napa Valley Accommodations

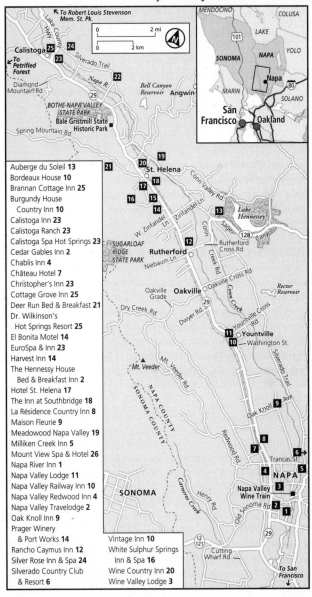

To Robert Louis Stevenson Mem. St. Pk.

Lake County Hwy.

Calistoga 25 24
To Petrified Forest 23
Silverado Trail
Diamond Mountain Rd.
Napa R. 22
Bell Canyon Reservoir
Angwin
BOTHE-NAPA VALLEY STATE PARK 29
Bale Gristmill State Historic Park
Spring Mountain Rd.

MENDOCINO   COLUSA
LAKE
101
SONOMA   NAPA   YOLO
Napa
MARIN   80
San Francisco   Oakland   SOLANO

19
21   20   St. Helena
18
17
16   15
14   13
W. Zinfandel Ln.   Un. Zinfandel Ln.   Lake Hennessey
Conn
12   Sage Canyon   128
SUGARLOAF RIDGE STATE PARK   Rutherford   Rutherford Cross Rd.
Niebaum Ln.   Creek Rd.   Rector Reservoir
Oakville Grade   Oakville   Oakville Cross Rd.
Dry Creek Rd.   29   Dwyer Rd.   Conn Creek   Yountville Cross Rd.
Mt. Veeder   Silverado Trail
Mt. Veeder Rd.   11   Yountville
10   Washington St.
NAPA COUNTY
SONOMA COUNTY   Oak Knoll Ave.   9
8
Redwood Rd.   7   6   Trancas St.
4   NAPA   5
SONOMA   Carneros Creek   Henry Rd.   Napa Valley Wine Train   3
Sonoma Rd.   2
Old Sonoma Rd.   1
12 121   29
Cutting Wharf Rd.
To San Francisco

Auberge du Soleil **13**
Bordeaux House **10**
Brannan Cottage Inn **25**
Burgundy House
   Country Inn **10**
Calistoga Inn **23**
Calistoga Ranch **23**
Calistoga Spa Hot Springs **23**
Cedar Gables Inn **2**
Chablis Inn **4**
Château Hotel **7**
Christopher's Inn **23**
Cottage Grove Inn **25**
Deer Run Bed & Breakfast **21**
Dr. Wilkinson's
   Hot Springs Resort **25**
El Bonita Motel **14**
EuroSpa & Inn **23**
Harvest Inn **14**
The Hennessey House
   Bed & Breakfast Inn **2**
Hotel St. Helena **17**
The Inn at Southbridge **18**
La Résidence Country Inn **8**
Maison Fleurie **9**
Meadowood Napa Valley **19**
Milliken Creek Inn **5**
Mount View Spa & Hotel **26**
Napa River Inn **1**
Napa Valley Lodge **11**
Napa Valley Railway Inn **10**
Napa Valley Redwood Inn **4**
Napa Valley Travelodge **2**
Oak Knoll Inn **9**
Prager Winery
   & Port Works **14**
Rancho Caymus Inn **12**
Silver Rose Inn & Spa **24**
Silverado Country Club
   & Resort **6**

Vintage Inn **10**
White Sulphur Springs
   Inn & Spa **16**
Wine Country Inn **20**
Wine Valley Lodge **3**

passes to a nearby health club, and free parking. The 272-room **Napa Valley Marriott,** 3425 Solano Ave., Napa, CA 94558 (© **800/ 228-9290** or 707/253-8600; www.napavalleymarriott.com), has an exercise room, a heated outdoor pool and spa, and two restaurants; rates range from $129 to $329 for rooms, $350 to $500 for suites. **Best Western Inn Napa Valley,** 100 Soscol Ave., Napa, CA 94559 (© **877/846-3729** or 707/257-1930), is a last-resort option, promising little more than 68 basic air-conditioned units in industrial surroundings. But at $99 to $259 per night, it's hard to complain.

VERY EXPENSIVE

Milliken Creek Inn 🎯🎯   This riverfront retreat, just north of downtown Napa, combines upscale boutique hotel accommodations with country living. Right off the Silverado Trail and surrounded by tranquil gardens, oaks, and redwoods, the 12 spacious and luxuriously appointed rooms are located in three neighboring buildings (including the restored 1857 Coach House). Soothing shades of brown and beige, greens, and yellows become even warmer and more welcoming when the fireplace is in action. King-size beds are firm and draped in Frette linens, tubs are the whirlpool variety, and fluffy robes await you. Delicious perks include a picnic breakfast delivered to your door, a wine-and-cheese tasting nightly in the equally sophisticated parlor, and the new spa rooms for facials and massages. Often live jazz piano accompanies the affair. No doubt this hotel is one of Napa's finest choices.

1815 Silverado Trail, Napa, CA 94558. © **888/622-5775** or 707/255-1197. Fax 707/255-3112. www.millikencreekinn.com. 12 units. $295–$695 double. AE, DC, DISC, MC, V. **Amenities:** Yoga gazebo; spa rooms. *In room:* A/C, TV/DVD plasma screen TV, dataport, minibar, hair dryer, iron on request, CD player, wireless Internet access throughout entire property.

Oak Knoll Inn 🎯🎯🎯   If you've got the bucks and want an extremely intimate luxury escape you can't do much better than this four-room French country–style B&B surrounded by 600 acres of vineyards. Each of the enormous stone-walled rooms are tastefully decorated in florals and have vaulted ceilings, working fireplaces, king-size feather beds, private entrances, and plenty of elbowroom. But no doubt you'll want to spend most of your time in the common areas, such as the vineyard-front back deck where arguably the best private tastings are held nightly and are hosted by the winemaker or a winery representative, and accompanied by an amazing appetizer spread that could easily substitute for dinner. The pool and whirlpool spa also beckon, as does the small sitting area complete with crackling fire in the fireplace during winter and the charming dining room where a fantastic full gourmet breakfast is served. Take my word for it: If you plan to hang around your hotel, this spot is definitely worth a splurge.

2200 E. Oak Knoll Ave. (between the Silverado Trail and Hwy. 29), Napa, CA 94558. © 707/255-2200. www.oakknollinn.com. 4 units. $250–$650. Rates include breakfast, wine and appetizers. MC, V. **Amenities:** Unheated pool; Jacuzzi. *In room:* AC, TV on request, hair dryer, iron, phone on request.

Silverado Country Club & Resort *&*

If you long for the opulence of an East Coast country club, bring your racquet and golf clubs to this 1,200-acre resort in the Napa foothills, where the focus is on the sporting life. Two cleverly designed golf courses by Robert Trent Jones, Jr., are the focal point; the 6,500-yard south course has a dozen water crossings, and the 6,700-yard north course is somewhat longer but a bit more forgiving. A staff of pros is on hand, and greens fees are $155 for 18 holes on either course (off-season is discounted), including a cart. The spacious, individually owned accommodations range from very large studios with king-size bed, kitchenette, and a roomy, well-appointed bathroom to one-, two-, or three-bedroom cottage suites. Each has a wood-burning fireplace. Cottage suites are in private, low-rise groupings tucked away in shared courtyards along peaceful walkways. All rooms are individually decorated, and manage to offer a sense of privacy despite the resort's size.

Though they've got restaurants on property, I'd recommend dining elsewhere. But when it comes to spa facilities, they've definitely got the goods.

1600 Atlas Peak Rd., Napa, CA 94558. © 800/532-0500 or 707/257-0200. Fax 707/257-2867. www.silveradoresort.com. 280 units. $290 junior suite; $360 1-bedroom suite; $460–$560 2- or 3-bedroom suite. Golf and spa promotional packages available. AE, DC, DISC, MC, V. Drive north on Hwy. 29 to Trancas St.; turn east to Atlas Peak Rd. **Amenities:** 2 restaurants (steak/seafood, Asian/Wine Country); bar; 2 heated outdoor pools; 8 unheated pools; 2 18-hole golf courses; 17 tennis courts; exercise room; full-service spa; concierge; business center; limited room service; in-room massage. *In room:* A/C, TV, dataport, kitchenette, minibar, coffeemaker, hair dryer, iron.

EXPENSIVE

Cedar Gables Inn *&& (Finds)* This grand, romantic B&B in Old Town Napa is in a stunning Victorian built in 1892. Rooms reflect that era, with rich tapestries and stunning gilded antiques. Four have fireplaces, five have whirlpool tubs, and all feature queen-size brass, wood, or iron beds. Guests meet each evening in front of the roaring fireplace in the lower—"tavern"—parlor for wine and cheese. At other times, the family room is a perfect place to cuddle up and watch the large-screen TV. Bonuses include a gourmet breakfast each morning, port in every room, and VIP treatment at many local wineries.

486 Coombs St. (at Oak St.), Napa, CA 94559. ℂ **800/309-7969** or 707/224-7969. Fax 707/224-4838. www.cedargablesinn.com. 9 units. $189–$319 double. Rates include full breakfast, evening wine and cheese, and port. AE, DISC, MC, V. From Hwy. 29 north, exit onto 1st St. and follow signs to downtown; turn right onto Jefferson, and left on Oak; house is on the corner. **Amenities:** Dataport (in the shared living room). *In room:* A/C, hair dryer, iron, ironing board, deluxe robes, free wireless Internet.

La Résidence Country Inn ℛ

If you consider a B&B too homespun and a luxury hotel too impersonal, La Résidence is a good alternative. Set on 2 acres on Highway 29, the inn's rooms are in either the late-18th-century revival-style main house or the newer French barn–style building. Rooms are individually decorated with wall-to-wall carpeting, period antiques, armoires, designer fabrics, fireplaces (in most), CD players, and patios or verandas. The pool area and large spa are secluded and well manicured. A full breakfast is served in the attractive dining room, which is often warmed by a roaring fire on chilly mornings; in the evening, wine and hors d'oeuvres are offered. If a recent four-star rating isn't enough encouragement to book a room, neighboring delicious Bistro Don Giovanni should be.

4066 Howard Lane, Napa, CA 94558. ℂ **707/253-0337**. Fax 707/253-0382. www.laresidence.com. 23 units. $240–$400; lower rates Dec–Mar. AE, DC, MC, V. **Amenities:** Heated outdoor pool; Jacuzzi; concierge. *In room:* A/C, TV in some units, CD player, fridge in some units, hair dryer, iron available.

Napa River Inn ℛℛ

Downtown Napa's most luxurious hotel manages an old-world boutique feel throughout most of its three buildings. The main building, part of the renovated Historic Napa Mill and Hatt Market Building, is an 1884 historic landmark. Each of its fantastically appointed rooms is exceedingly romantic, with burgundy-colored walls, original brick, wood furnishings, plush fabrics, seats in front of the gas fireplace, and a claw-foot tub in the bathroom. A newer and more modern themed addition overlooking the river and a patio boasts bright and airy accommodations. Yet another building houses the less luxurious, but equally well appointed, mustard-and-brown rooms that also overlook the riverfront, but have a nautical theme and less daylight. Perks abound and include instant access to downtown dining, complimentary vouchers to breakfast at adorable Sweetie Pie's bakery, and wine at nearby very swank wine bar The Bounty Hunter. A small but excellent spa is located in the hotel's parking lot.

500 Main St., Napa, CA 94559. ℭ **877/251-8500** or 707/251-8500. Fax 707/251-8504. www.napariverinn.com. 66 units. $179–$499 double. Rates include vouchers to a full breakfast and evening cocktails at one of the adjoining restaurants. Pets $25 per night. AE, DC, DISC, MC, V. **Amenities:** 2 restaurants; concierge; business services; same-day laundry service/dry cleaning. *In room:* A/C, TV, dataport, fridge, coffeemaker, hair dryer, iron, CD clock radio, wireless Internet access $9.99 per day.

INEXPENSIVE

Chablis Inn ⍟   There's no way around it: If you want to sleep cheaply in a town where the *average* room rate tops $200 per night in high season, you're destined for a motel. Look on the bright side: Because your room is likely to be little more than a crash pad after a day of eating and drinking, a clean bed and a remote control are all you'll really need anyway. And Chablis offers much more than that. All of the motel-style rooms are superclean, and some even boast kitchenettes or whirlpool tubs. Guests have access to an outdoor heated pool and hot tub.

3360 Solano Ave., Napa, CA 94558. ℭ **707/257-1944.** Fax 707/226-6862. www.chablisinn.com. 34 units. May to mid-Nov $99–$165 double; mid-Nov to Apr $79–$150 double. AE, DC, DISC, MC, V. **Amenities:** Heated outdoor pool; Jacuzzi. *In room:* A/C, satellite TV, dataport in some rooms, kitchenette in some rooms, fridge, coffeemaker, hair dryer.

Château Hotel   This contemporary two-story motel complex tries to evoke the aura of a French country inn, but it isn't fooling anybody—a basic motel's a basic motel. However, the plain-Jane rooms are C-H-E-A-P and bathrooms are spacious, and have separate vanity/dressing areas. Some units have refrigerators and ten rooms are specially designed for guests with disabilities. If you're used to a daily swim, you'll be glad to know that the Château also has a heated pool and spa. Bargain travelers, be sure to ask about discounts; some special rates will knock the price down by $20.

4195 Solano Ave., Napa, CA 94558. ℭ **800/253-6272** in CA or 707/253-9300. Fax 707/253-0906. 115 units. Apr–Oct $119–$169 double; Nov–Mar $99 double. Continental breakfast included. AAA, government, corporate, senior, and other discounts available. AE, DISC, DC, MC, V. From Hwy. 29 north, turn left just past Trower Ave., at the entrance to the Napa Valley wine region. **Amenities:** Restaurant; heated outdoor pool; hot tub. *In room:* A/C, TV.

The Hennessy House Bed & Breakfast Inn   This Eastlake-style Queen Anne Victorian may be old enough to be on the National Register of Historic Places, but its antiquity is contrasted by the fresh hospitality of owners Lorri and Kevin Walsh who escaped Silicon Valley in 2004 to purchase the inn. Rooms in the main house are quaint, with a combination of antique furnishings, queen-size bed, fireplace, and/or a claw-foot bathtub. Carriage-house accommodations, located just off the main house, are larger but less ornate and feature whirlpool tubs (a bummer to climb into if you're not agile); all have fireplaces. Because walls are thin throughout both structures, TVs are out of the question (except in a few rooms, where additional insulation was recently added), and if your neighbor's a snorer, you'll know it firsthand. But it'll make for fun conversation over breakfast, when guests meet in the dining room for an impressive full meal. The adjoining living room allows TV junkies to stay tuned. The small garden is a nice spot for a bit of morning sun.

1727 Main St. (between Lincoln and 1st sts.), Napa, CA 94559. ☎ **707/226-3774.** Fax 707/226-2975. www.hennessyhouse.com. 10 units. Mid-Mar to mid-Nov $145–$285 double; mid-Nov to mid-Mar $135–$265 double. Rates include full breakfast, afternoon tea and cookies, and nightly wine-and-cheese hour. AE, DC, DISC, MC, V. **Amenities:** Sauna; off-street parking. *In room:* A/C.

Napa Valley Redwood Inn   This no-frills lodging (read: seriously basic) has an excellent location and simple, clean, comfortable rooms. Local calls are free, and guests can enjoy the complimentary coffee in the lobby and the small pool on the premises (heated in summer only).

3380 Solano Ave., Napa, CA 94558. ☎ **707/257-6111.** Fax 707/252-2702. www. napavalleyredwoodinn.com. 58 units, all with bathroom (shower only). May–Oct from $83 queen weekday and from $150 on weekends; Nov–Apr from $67 queen weekday and $90 on weekends. Rates include continental breakfast. AE, DC, DISC, MC, V. **Amenities:** Small seasonally heated pool. *In room:* A/C, TV, high-speed Internet dataport.

Napa Valley Travelodge *Value*   In these parts, rarely does so much come so cheaply. This Travelodge has been around for a while, but in early 1998, the owners gutted the entire place with the intent of turning it into a "New Orleans–style" motel (including a cobblestone center courtyard/parking area). Although there are no wild partiers hanging over the balconies throwing beads, there's still plenty to celebrate. Every room has a VCR, a 36-inch TV, and a coffeemaker; some feature a Jacuzzi tub; and they are all in a great part of downtown Napa—within walking distance of the city's best dining. If you're lucky enough to secure a room, you will have gotten one of the best deals around. Ask about discounts for AAA and other clubs.

853 Coombs St., Napa, CA 94559. ✆ **800/578-7878** or 707/226-1871. Fax 707/226-1707. 45 units. $109–$189 double. DC, DISC, MC, V. **Amenities:** Heated outdoor pool; access to nearby fitness center (fee); video library; coin-operated laundry. *In room:* A/C, TV/VCR, hair dryer, iron.

Wine Valley Lodge ⟨ℛ⟩ *Value*   Dollar for dollar, the Wine Valley Lodge offers a great deal. At the south end of town in a quiet residential neighborhood, the mission-style motel is extremely well kept and accessible, just a short drive from Highway 29 and the wineries to the north. The reasonably priced two-bedroom deluxe units are great for families.

200 S. Coombs St. (between 1st and Imola sts.), Napa, CA 94559. ✆ **800/696-7911** or 707/224-7911. www.winevalleylodge.com. 54 units. $89–$124 double; $150–$165 deluxe. AE, DC, DISC, MC, V. **Amenities:** Heated outdoor pool (closed during the winter). *In room:* A/C, TV.

YOUNTVILLE
EXPENSIVE

Napa Valley Lodge ⟨ℛ⟩ *Finds*   Just off Highway 29, beyond a wall that does a good job of disguising the road from the lodge's guest rooms, which were upgraded in 2001, this hotel boasts rooms that are large, ultraclean, and better appointed than many in the area. Many have vaulted ceilings, and 39 have fireplaces. Each comes with a king- or 2 queen-size beds, wicker furnishings, robes, and a private balcony or a patio. Ground-level units are smaller and get less sunlight than those on the second floor. Suites boast king-size beds and Jacuzzi tubs. Extras are a concierge, afternoon tea and cookies in the lobby, Friday-evening wine tasting in the library, and a full champagne breakfast—with all this, it's no wonder AAA gave the Napa Valley Lodge the four-diamond award for excellence. Ask about winery tour packages and winter discounts, the latter of which can be as high as 30%.

2230 Madison St., Yountville, CA 94599. ✆ **800/368-2468** or 707/944-2468. Fax 707/944-9362. www.napavalleylodge.com. 55 units. $252–$475 double. Rates include champagne breakfast buffet, afternoon tea and cookies, and Fri-evening wine tasting. AE, DC, DISC, MC, V. **Amenities:** Heated outdoor pool; small exercise room; Jacuzzi spa; redwood sauna; concierge; free wireless Internet in lobby and conference rooms. *In room:* A/C, TV w/pay movies, minibar, coffeemaker, hair dryer, iron, high-speed Internet access, ceiling fan.

Vintage Inn ⟨ℛℛ⟩   This contemporary, French-country complex situated on an old 23-acre winery estate in the heart of Yountville feels far more corporate than "inn" would suggest. But big business does have its perks, like a very professional staff and bright cozy rooms, each of which comes equipped with a fireplace and private veranda, oversize bed, Jacuzzi tub, plush bathrobes, and welcoming bottle of wine. If you're looking for a workout, you may rent a bike, reserve one of the two tennis courts, or take a dip in the 60-foot swimming pool or outdoor whirlpool, both heated year-round. A champagne breakfast buffet and afternoon tea are served daily in the lobby. If they're booked, ask about their sister property, the spa-centric Villagio Inn & Spa, a Tuscan-style hotel complex just down the road.

6541 Washington St. (between Humboldt St. and Webber Ave.), Yountville, CA 94599. © **800/351-1133** or 707/944-1112. Fax 707/944-1617. www.vintage inn.com. 80 units. $230–$545 double; $345–$585 minisuites and villas. Rates include champagne breakfast buffet, complimentary wine upon arrival, and afternoon tea. AE, DC, MC, V. Free parking. From Hwy. 29 north, take the Yountville exit and turn left onto Washington St. Pets $30. **Amenities:** Concierge; business center; secretarial services; room service; in-room massage; laundry service; dry cleaning. *In room:* A/C, TV/VCR w/movie library, fridge, coffeemaker, hair dryer, iron, complimentary wireless high-speed Internet access.

MODERATE

Maison Fleurie 𝓖𝓖   It's impossible not to enjoy your stay at Maison Fleurie. One of the prettiest garden-set B&Bs in the Wine Country, it's comprised of a trio of beautiful 1873 brick-and-fieldstone buildings overlaid with ivy. The main house—a charming Provençal replica with thick brick walls, terra-cotta tile, and paned windows—holds seven rooms; the rest are in the old bakery building and the carriage house. Some feature private balconies, patios, sitting areas, Jacuzzi tubs, and fireplaces. An above-par breakfast is served in the quaint little dining room; afterward, you're welcome to wander the landscaped grounds or hit the wine-tasting trail, returning in time for afternoon hors d'oeuvres and wine.

6529 Yount St. (between Washington St. and Yountville Cross Rd.), Yountville, CA 94599. © **800/788-0369** or 707/944-2056. Fax 707/944-9342. www.maisonfleurie napa.com. 13 units. $120–$285 double. Rates include full breakfast and afternoon hors d'oeuvres. AE, DC, DISC, MC, V. **Amenities:** Heated outdoor pool; Jacuzzi; free use of bikes. *In room:* A/C, TV, dataport, hair dryer, iron.

INEXPENSIVE

Bordeaux House   Considering the name, I was expecting this centrally located hotel on a quiet Yountville street to be some kind of romantic, antique French–style structure. I was way off. How far? Try 1980 two-story brick. Nonetheless, there are eight ultratidy and simple rooms here, each renting for what in this neck of the woods is a very reasonable price. Each has a private entrance; six have fireplaces and private patios, and while interiors border on motel-bland (especially the small bathrooms), the few furnishings do have a homier, more stylish quality than most motels. Added bonuses include complimentary port, brandy, sherry, and homemade treats served in the common area and proximity to The French Laundry, just down the block.

6600 Washington St., Yountville, CA 94599. ℂ **800/677-6370** or 707/944-2855. Fax 707/945-0471. www.bordeauxhouse.com. 8 units. Sun–Thurs $135–$230 double, Fri–Sat $195–$230 double. Additional person $35 extra. 2-night minimum during high season. Rates include full breakfast and complimentary port and sherry. MC, V. *In room:* Central A/C, TV, dataport, hair dryer, iron.

Burgundy House Inn   This distinctly French country inn, built of local fieldstone and river rock in the early 1890s as a brandy distillery, is tiny but atmospheric. The interior features thick stone walls and hand-hewn post and lintel beams, enhanced today by antique country furnishings. The five cozy guest rooms (all untraditionally French in their nonsmoking status) have colorful quilted spreads and comfortable queen-size beds, along with very small bathrooms. Sweet touches include fresh flowers in each of the units, a continental breakfast, and complimentary port and sherry in the common area. Breakfast can be eaten inside or out in the pretty garden.

6711 Washington St. (P.O. Box 3246), Yountville, CA 94599. ℂ **707/944-0889.** www.burgundyhouseinn.com. 5 units, all with bathroom (shower only). $135–$175 double. MC, V. From Hwy. 29 north, take the Yountville exit and turn left onto Washington St. *In room:* Central A/C, no phone.

Napa Valley Railway Inn 🐾   This is a favorite place to stay in the Wine Country. Why? Because it's inexpensive and it's cute as all get-out. Looking hokey as heck from the outside, the Railway Inn consists of two rows of sun-bleached cabooses and rail cars sitting on a stretch of Yountville's original track and connected by a covered wooden walkway. Things get considerably better when you enter your private caboose or car, especially since they're redecorating each one as this book goes to press. Each is sumptuously appointed, with comfy love seat, king- or queen-size brass bed, and tiled bathroom. The coups de grâce are the bay windows and skylights, which let in plenty of California sunshine.

6503 Washington St., Yountville, CA 94599. ℂ **707/944-2000.** 9 units. $90–$170 double. AE, MC, V. *In room:* A/C, heater, TV, coffeemaker, hair dryer upon request.

OAKVILLE & RUTHERFORD
VERY EXPENSIVE

Auberge du Soleil 🐾🐾🐾 *(Moments*   This spectacular Relais & Châteaux member is the kind of place you'd imagine movie stars frequenting for clandestine affairs or weekend retreats. Set high above Napa Valley in a 33-acre olive grove, it's quiet, indulgent, and luxuriously romantic. The "Contemporary California bungalow" –like rooms, which were completely renovated in 2005, are large enough to get lost in, and you might want to once you discover all the amenities. The bathtub alone—an enormous hot tub with a skylight overhead—will entice you to grab a glass of California red and settle in for awhile. Oversized, cushy furniture surrounds a wood-burning fireplace—the ideal place to relax and listen to CDs. (The stereo comes with a few selections) or watch one of the room's two flatscreen TVs. Fresh flowers, original art, wood floors, cozy new burnt orange couches and a wet bar complete with complimentary sodas and snacks are the best of luxury home-away-from-home. Each sun-washed private deck has views of the valley that are nothing less than spectacular. Those with money to burn should opt for the $2,500–$3,500-per-night cottage; the 1,800-square-foot hideaway has two fireplaces, two full baths, a den, and a patio Jacuzzi. Now that's living.

Guests have access to a celestial swimming pool, exercise room, and the most fabulous spa in the Wine Country, which opened in 2001. Only guests can use the spa, but if you want to get all the romantic grandeur of Auberge without staying here, have lunch on the patio at the restaurant overlooking the valley (see "Where to Dine," later in this chapter, for more information). Overall, this is one of my favorite Wine Country places. *Parents take note:* This is not the kind of place you take the kids.

180 Rutherford Hill Rd., Rutherford, CA 94573. © 800/348-5406 or 707/ 963-1211. Fax 707/963-8764. www.aubergedusoleil.com. 50 units. $400–$750 double, $675–$1275 suites. AE, DC, DISC, MC, V. From Hwy. 29 in Rutherford, turn right on California 128 and go 3 miles to the Silverado Trail; turn left and head north about 200 yd. to Rutherford Hill Rd.; turn right. **Amenities:** Restaurant; 3 outdoor pools ranging from hot to cold; 3 tennis courts; health club and full-service spa; sauna; steam room; bikes; concierge; secretarial services; salon; 24-hr. room service; massage; same-day laundry service and dry cleaning. *In room:* A/C, TV/DVD w/pay movies, dataport, kitchenette, minibar, fridge, coffeemaker, hair dryer, iron.

MODERATE

Rancho Caymus Inn ⟨R⟩   This cozy Spanish-style hacienda, with two floors opening onto wisteria-covered balconies, was the creation of sculptor Mary Tilden Morton (of Morton Salt). Morton wanted each room in the hacienda to be a work of art, so she employed the most skilled craftspeople she could find. As a result you'll find Morton-designed adobe fireplaces in 22 of 26 rooms, and artifacts she gathered in Mexico and South America.

Decent-size guest rooms surround a whimsical garden courtyard with an enormous outdoor fireplace. The mix-and-match decor is on the funky side, with overly varnished imported carved wood furnishings and braided rugs. But it's hard to balk when they include wet bars, sitting areas with sofa beds, hardwood floors, small private patios, and new beds and wall paint added in 2005. Most of the suites have fireplaces, one has a kitchenette, and five have whirlpool tubs. Breakfast, which includes fresh fruit, granola, orange juice, and pastries, is served in the inn's dining room. Next door is fancy, formal, and French-influenced La Toque restaurant (see p. 112 for complete details).

1140 Rutherford Rd. (P.O. Box 78), Rutherford, CA 94573. ② **800/845-1777** or 707/963-1777. Fax 707/963-5387. www.ranchocaymus.com. 26 units. $145–$300 double; $185–$400 master suite; $265–$440 2-bedroom suite. Rates include continental breakfast. AE, MC, V. From Hwy. 29 N., turn right onto Rutherford Rd./California 128 E.; the hotel is on your left. **Amenities:** Restaurant. *In room:* A/C, TV, dataport, kitchenette in one room, minibar, fridge, coffeemaker, microwaves in master suites, hair dryer, iron in some rooms.

ST. HELENA
VERY EXPENSIVE
The Inn at Southbridge ★★   It's absurdly expensive for what it is, but if you want to be in St. Helena and prefer upscale Pottery Barn decor to lace and latticework, this is a good place to shack up. Along with modern digs you'll find terry robes, fireplaces, bathroom skylights, down comforters, private balconies, and a host of other luxuries. One notable bummer: The inn is along the highway, so it lacks that reclusive feel offered by many other upscale hotels. Additionally, this isn't the ideal stop for families, but the adjoining casual and cheap Italian restaurant Pizzeria Tra Vigne does lure the little ones with games, TV, and pizzas.

1020 Main St., St. Helena, CA 94574. ② **800/520-6800** or 707/967-9400. Fax 707/967-9486. 21 units. $255–$625 double. AE, DC, MC, V. **Amenities:** Restaurant; large heated outdoor pool; excellent health club and full-service spa; Jacuzzi; concierge; limited room service; massage; same-day dry cleaning. *In room:* A/C, TV, dataport, minibar, coffeemaker, hair dryer, iron, high-speed Internet.

Meadowood Napa Valley ★★★ *(Finds)*   Originally a private country club for Napa's well-to-do families, Cape Cod–like Meadowood is one of California's top-ranked privately owned resorts. On 250 secluded acres of pristine mountainside dotted with madrones and oaks, it's a favorite retreat for celebrities and CEOs. Units, which vary in size tremendously depending on the price, are furnished with

American country classics and have beamed ceilings, private patios, stone fireplaces, and views of the forest. Many are individual suite-lodges so far removed from the common areas that you must drive to get to them. Lazier folks can opt for more centrally located rooms.

The resort offers a wealth of activities: golf on a challenging 9-hole course, tennis on seven championship courts, and croquet (yes, croquet) on two international regulation lawns. There are private hiking trails, a health spa, two heated pools, and two whirlpools.

900 Meadowood Lane, St. Helena, CA 94574. ⓒ **800/458-8080** or 707/963-3646. Fax 707/963-3532. www.meadowood.com. 85 units. $475–$825 double; 1-bedroom suite from $775–$1,250; 2-bedroom from $1,275–$2,075; 3-bedroom from $1,775–$2,900; 4-bedroom from $2,275–$3,725. Ask about promotional offers and off-season rates. 2-night minimum stay on weekends. AE, DC, DISC, MC, V. **Amenities:** 2 restaurants; 2 large heated outdoor pools; golf course; 7 tennis courts; health club and full-service spa; Jacuzzi; sauna; concierge; secretarial services; business center; 24-hr. room service; same-day laundry service/dry cleaning weekdays only; 2 croquet lawns. *In room:* A/C, TV, dataport, kitchenette in some rooms, minibar, coffeemaker, hair dryer, iron, free high-speed Internet access.

EXPENSIVE

Harvest Inn 👫 *Kids*   Ornate brick walkways lead through beautifully landscaped grounds to pools and freestanding accommodations at this sprawling Tudor-style resort. Each of the immaculate rooms is furnished with dark-oak beds and dressers, brown leather chairs, and antique furnishings; most have brick fireplaces, wet bars, refrigerators, CD players, feather beds, down comforters, and a 25-inch TV with VCR. (Videos are for rent on the property.) With four-diamond ratings from AAA and all the big-hotel bells and whistles, it's not surprising that this spot is on the wedding and conference circuit.

1 Main St., St. Helena, CA 94575. ⓒ **800/950-8466** or 707/963-9463. Fax 707/963-4402. www.harvestinn.com. 54 units. $255–$535 double; $645–$675 suite. AE, DC, DISC, MC, V. **Amenities:** Wine and beer bar; 2 outdoor heated pools; 2 outdoor Jacuzzis; concierge; business center. *In room:* A/C, TV/VCR, CD player, dataport, minibar, fridge, coffeemaker, hair dryer, iron.

MODERATE

Deer Run Inn 👫   If romantic solitude is a big part of your vacation plan, Deer Run should be on your itinerary. Situated 4½ miles (10 min. by car) from downtown St. Helena along a winding mountain road, this four-room B&B is a heavenly hideaway. All of the wood-paneled rooms look onto owners Tom and Carol Wilson's 4 acres of forest, and each features gorgeous antiques, a feather bed, a private entrance, a deck, a decanter of brandy, a fridge, coffee and tea, robes, fireplaces, and access to hiking trails. One unit adjoins the cedar-shingled main house and boasts a king-size bed, Ralph Lauren textiles, a wood-burning fireplace, and an open-beam ceiling. The Carriage House Suite coddles guests with an antique queen-size bed, Spanish tile floors, a gas stove, and a huge bathroom. The Studio Bungalow is fashioned after Ralph Lauren, with Spanish tile, a cathedral ceiling, and whitewashed cedar walls. Outside, you'll find a very small pool and perhaps the owner's chocolate Labrador, Cocoa.

3995 Spring Mountain Rd., P.O. Box 311, St. Helena, CA 94574. ℂ **877/333-7786** or 707/963-3794. Fax 707/963-9026. 4 units, all with bathroom (shower only). $160–$195 double. Rates include full breakfast. AE, MC, V. **Amenities:** Outdoor unheated pool. *In room:* A/C, TV, fireplaces, robes, coffeemaker, fridge, hair dryer.

Hotel St. Helena   This downtown hotel occupies a historic 1881 building, the oldest wooden structure in St. Helena. The hotel keepers celebrated the building's 100th birthday with a much-needed renovation; now it's more comfortable than ever. The hallways are cluttered with stuffed animals, wicker strollers, and other memorabilia. Most of the rooms have been decorated with brass beds, wall-to-wall burgundy carpeting, and oak or maple furnishings. There's a garden patio and a wine and coffee bar. Perhaps most enjoyable is the hotel's downtown location, front-and-center to the area's best shopping and restaurants. Smoking is discouraged.

1309 Main St., St. Helena, CA 94574. ℂ **888/478-4355** or 707/963-4388. www. hotelsthelena.com. 18 units, 14 with private bathroom. $95–$155 double without bathroom; $125–$185 double with bathroom; $250–$325 1-bedroom suite. Rates discounted up to 30% in winter. Rates include continental breakfast. AE, DC, DISC, MC, V. *In room:* A/C, TV.

Prager Winery & Port Works   The two suites at Prager Winery are one of the best-kept secrets in the valley. Their incognito location—on a residential side street behind Trinchero Family Estates/Sutter Home Winery—gives no indication of the affordable accommodations within. The smaller "Winery" suite, which is still huge, is perched above the winery (see "Touring the Wineries," earlier in this chapter), up a flight of stairs. It boasts a bedroom with a queen-size bed, living room with fireplace, fridge, coffeemaker, and a lovely private sundeck. The garden cottage, or "Vineyard Suite," is also enormous and immaculate, and has a bedroom, living room with piano, TV/VCR, fireplace, and private garden. Both are homey, sleep up to four, and come with a full, delivered breakfast and unlimited wine tastings; the Pragers don't rent for about 3 days around Christmas so they can accommodate their large and festive family.

1281 Lewelling Lane, St. Helena, CA 94574. © **707/963-3720.** Fax 707/963-7679. www.pragerport.com. 2 units. $225–$325 double. Rates include a full breakfast en suite and unlimited tastings in the tasting room. MC, V. *In room:* A/C.

Wine Country Inn ☞☞   Just off the highway behind Freemark Abbey vineyard is one of Wine Country's most personable choices. The attractive wood-and-stone inn, complete with a French-style mansard roof and turret, overlooks a pastoral landscape of vineyards. The individually decorated rooms contain antique furnishings, and handmade quilts; most have fireplaces and private terraces overlooking the valley, and others have private hot tubs. The five luxury cottages include king-size beds, a single bed (perfect for the tot in tow), sitting areas, fireplaces, private patios, and two-person Jacuzzi tubs. One of the inn's best features is the heated outdoor pool, which is attractively landscaped into the hillside. Another favorite feature is the selection of suites, which come with stereos, plenty of space, and lots of privacy. The family that runs this place makes guests feel extra welcome and serves wine and plenty of appetizers nightly, along with a hotel-staff hospitality in the inviting living room. A full buffet breakfast is served there, too. *Note:* TV junkies book elsewhere. You won't be able to tune in in rooms here.

1152 Lodi Lane, St. Helena, CA 94574. © **888/465-4608** or 707/963-7077. Fax 707/963-9018. www.winecountryinn.com. 29 units, 12 with shower only. $195–$525 double, $495–$555 for cottages. Rates include breakfast and appetizers. MC, V. **Amenities:** Heated outdoor pool; Jacuzzi; concierge; free Internet access at a computer station; big-screen TV in common room. *In room:* A/C, hair dryer, iron.

INEXPENSIVE

El Bonita Motel ☞ *Kids* *Value*   This 1930s Art Deco motel is a bit too close to Highway 29 for comfort, but the 2½ acres of beautifully landscaped gardens behind the building (away from the road) help even the score. The rooms, while small and nothing fancy (think motel basic), are spotlessly clean and decorated with newer furnishings and kitchenettes; some have a whirlpool bathtub. It ain't heaven, but it is cheap for St. Helena.

195 Main St. (at El Bonita Ave.), St. Helena, CA 94574. © **800/541-3284** or 707/963-3216. Fax 707/963-8838. www.elbonita.com. 41 units. $89–$259 double. Rates include continental breakfast. AE, DC, DISC, MC, V. **Amenities:** Heated outdoor pool; spa; Jacuzzi; free high-speed Internet access in lobby. *In room:* A/C, TV, fridge, coffeemaker, hair dryer, iron, microwave, free wireless Internet.

White Sulphur Springs Inn & Spa ☞   If your idea of the ultimate vacation is a cozy cabin on 45 acres, paradise is a short, winding drive away from downtown St. Helena. Established in 1852, Sulphur Springs claims to be the oldest resort in California. The property holds a creek, a waterfall, a naturally heated sulfur hot spring, and redwood, madrone, and fir trees. Guests stay in different-size creek-side cabins (which were renovated in 1998 and 1999), the inn, or the carriage house. The cabins are decorated with simple but homey furnishings; cabin no. 9 has two queen-size beds and a kitchenette. From here you can take a dip in the natural hot sulfur spring; lounge by the large outdoor unheated pool; sit under a tree and watch for deer, fox, raccoon, spotted owl, or woodpecker; or schedule a day of massage (fantastic massage!), aromatherapy, and other spa treatments in their spa, which was completed in early 2001. *Note:* No RVs are allowed. All rooms are nonsmoking. Call well in advance; the resort is often rented by large groups.

3100 White Sulphur Springs Rd., St. Helena, CA 94574. ℂ 800/593-8873 in California, or 707/963-8588. Fax 707/963-2890. www.whitesulphursprings.com. 37 units, 14 with shared bathroom; 9 cottages. Carriage House (shared bathroom) $95–$120; small creek-side cottages $170–$190; large cottages $185–$200; cottage number 9 $190–$210. Rates include continental breakfast. 2-night minimum stay on weekends Apr–Oct and all holidays. AE, DC, DISC, MC, V. **Amenities:** Heated outdoor pool; soaking pool; full-service spa; Jacuzzi; free Internet hook-up in hospitality room. *In room:* A/C in some rooms, refrigerator, hair dryer, iron in large cottage.

CALISTOGA
VERY EXPENSIVE
Calistoga Ranch ✿✿✿   Napa Valley's hottest new luxury resort is my absolute favorite. Tucked into the eastern mountainside on 157 pristine hidden-canyon acres, each of the 46 rural-chic freestanding luxury cottages may cost more than $525 per night. But it combines the best of sister property Auberge du Soleil and rival Meadowood, is beautifully decorated, and is packed with every conceivable amenity (including fireplaces, outdoor patios along a wooded area, and cushy outdoor furnishings). Reasons not to leave include a giant swimming pool, reasonably large gym, incredibly designed indoor-outdoor spa with a natural thermal pool and individual pavilions with private-garden soaking tubs, and a breathtakingly beautiful restaurant with stunning views of the property's Lake Lommel. Add the fact that the food here is startlingly good and can only be experienced by guests and the resort architecture that intentionally tries to blend with the natural surroundings and you've got a romantically rustic slice of Wine Country heaven.

580 Lommel Rd., Calistoga, CA 94515. ℂ 707/254-2800. Fax 707/942-4706. www.calistogaranch.com. 46 cottages. $450–$1025 double. AE, DC, DISC, MC, V.

Amenities: Restaurant; spa; gym; large heated outdoor pool; Jacuzzi; steam room; concierge; 24-hr. room service; massage; laundry service; dry cleaning (next-day). *In room:* A/C, TV/VCR w/DVDs, fax upon request, dataport, 1 room with full kitchen, minibar, fridge, coffeemaker, hair dryer, iron, safe.

EXPENSIVE

Cottage Grove Inn 🦋🦋   Standing in two parallel rows at the end of the main strip in Calistoga is my top pick for a romantic splurge in downtown Calistoga—adorable cottages that, though on a residential street (with a paved road running between two rows of accommodations), seem removed from the action once you've stepped across the threshold. Each one-room guesthouse has a wood-burning fireplace, homey furnishings, king-size bed with down comforter, and an enormous bathroom with a skylight and a deep, two-person Jacuzzi tub. Guests enjoy such niceties as gourmet coffee, a stereo with CD player, a DVD player (the inn has a complimentary DVD library), and a wet bar. Smoking is allowed only in the gazebos, bicycles are provided for cruises around town, and guests can recoup a few bucks spent by using the complimentary tasting passes to more than a dozen nearby wineries. *Take note:* If you're the type that likes accommodations with good common areas, stay elsewhere.

1711 Lincoln Ave., Calistoga, CA 94515. 🕿 **800/799-2284** or 707/942-8400. Fax 707/942-2653. www.cottagegrove.com. 16 cottages. $250–$325 double. Rates include continental breakfast and evening wine and cheese. AE, DC, DISC, MC, V. *In room:* A/C, TV/DVD, dataport, fridge, coffeemaker, hair dryer, wet bar, iron, robes, safe, 40 digital music channels.

MODERATE

Christopher's Inn 🦋 *(Kids)*   A cluster of seven buildings makes up one of Calistoga's more attractive B&B-like options. Ten years of renovations and expansions by architect-owner Christopher Layton turned sweet old homes at the entrance to downtown into hotel rooms with a little pizzazz. Options range from somewhat simple but tasteful rooms with colorful and impressive antiques and small bathrooms to huge lavish abodes with four-poster beds, rich fabrics and brocades, and sunken Jacuzzi tubs facing gas fireplaces. Most rooms have gas fireplaces, and some have flatscreen TVs and DVDs (with cable). Those who prefer homey accommodations will feel comfortable here, since the property doesn't have corporate polish or big-business blandness. The two rather plain but very functional two-bedroom units are ideal for families, provided you're not expecting the Ritz. An extended continental breakfast is delivered to your room daily.

1010 Foothill Blvd., Calistoga, CA 94515. (*C*) **866/876-5755** or 707/942-5755. Fax 707/942-6895. www.chrisinn.com. 24 units. $150–$475 double; $330–$350 house sleeping 5 or 6. Rates include continental breakfast. AE, MC, V. *In room:* TV, dataport, wi-fi wireless, free computer hookups, massage studio.

Euro Spa & Inn 🍷🍷   In a quiet residential section of Calistoga, this small European-style inn and spa provides a level of solitude and privacy that few other spas can match. The horseshoe-shaped inn consists of 13 stucco bungalows, a spa center, and an outdoor patio, where a light breakfast and snacks are served. The rooms, although small, are pleasantly decorated in Pottery Barn decor that was implemented in 2000, whirlpool tubs, decks, gas wood stoves, and kitchenettes. Spa treatments range from clay baths and foot reflexology to minifacials.

1202 Pine St. (at Myrtle), Calistoga, CA 94515. (*C*) **707/942-6829.** Fax 707/ 942-1138. 13 units. $119–$229 double. Rates include deluxe continental breakfast. Off-season and midweek package discounts available. AE, DC, DISC, MC, V. **Amenities:** Outdoor heated pool; Jacuzzi. *In room:* A/C, TV, kitchenette, hair dryer, iron, robes, free high-speed wireless Internet in most rooms.

Mount View Hotel & Spa 🍷   Located on the main road in the middle of downtown Calistoga, this National Historical Landmark is the best hotel in town. Rooms within the main building and cottages are cheerily decorated in either Victorian or Art Deco–style and trimmed with beautiful hand-painted accents. Some units are small, but they are well appointed, considering most of the area's funkier options. The three self-contained cottages are fab for romantics; each cozy nest has a queen-size bed (including featherbed and down duvet), a wet bar, a private deck, and a secluded fenced-in outdoor hot tub. Almost everything in town is within walking distance, although once you settle in, you might not want to leave the quiet, sunny swimming-pool area or spa.

1457 Lincoln Ave. (on California 29, near Fairway St.), Calistoga, CA 94515. (*C*) **800/ 816-6877** or 707/942-6877. Fax 707/942-6904. www.mountviewhotel.com. 32 units, including 3 cottages. $139–$179 double; $209–$289 suite; $269–$329 cottage. Rates include continental breakfast. Packages available. 2-night minimum on weekends. AE, DISC, MC, V. **Amenities:** Large heated outdoor pool; full-service spa; hot tub; wi-fi hotspot. *In room:* A/C, TV, DVD and fridge in some units, coffeemaker, hair dryer, iron, robes.

Silver Rose Inn & Spa 🍷   If you'd like a big, ranch-style spread complete with a large wine bottle–shaped heated pool, a smaller unheated pool, two hot tubs, dual tennis courts, and even a chipping and putting green, then you'll love the Silver Rose Inn & Spa. Situated on a small oak-covered knoll overlooking the upper Napa

Valley, the inn, which is known for its polished hospitality, offers so many amenities that you'll have a tough time searching for reasons to leave (other than to eat dinner). Each of the spacious guest rooms, which surround a centerpiece two-story atrium living room, is individually—and whimsically—decorated in sometimes over-the-top themes ranging from the peach-colored Peach Delight to the Oriental room, complete with shoji screens and Oriental rugs, to the Mardi Gras room adorned with colorful masks. Several rooms come with fireplaces, whirlpool baths, and private balconies or terraces. Guests can partake of the exclusive full-service spa as well as an afternoon "hospitality hour" of wine, cheese, and crackers. Also, the winery is open and offers free samples ($5 for outside guests) as well as daily 11am barrel tastings ($10 for outsiders).

351 Rosedale Rd. (off the Silverado Trail), Calistoga, CA 94515. ℂ 800/995-9381 or 707/942-9581. www.silverrose.com. 20 units. $165–$255 double weekdays; $195–$300 double weekends. Rates include continental breakfast. AE, DISC, MC, V. **Amenities:** 2 pools; spa; 2 Jacuzzis. *In room:* A/C, dataport, hair dryer, iron upon request.

INEXPENSIVE

Brannan Cottage Inn   This cute little 1860 cottage, complete with the requisite white picket fence, sits on a quiet side street. One of Sam Brannan's original resort cottages, the inn was restored through a community effort to salvage an important piece of Calistoga's heritage; it's now on the National Register of Historic Places. The six spacious rooms are decorated with down comforters and white lace curtains; each room also has a ceiling fan, private bathroom, and its own entrance; three rooms have four-poster beds. There's a comfortable parlor and a pleasant brick terrace furnished with umbrella tables.

109 Wapoo Ave. (at Lincoln Ave.; P.O. Box 81), Calistoga, CA 94515. ℂ 707/942-4200. www.brannancottageinn.com. 6 units. $135–$200 double. Extra person $25. Rates include full buffet breakfast. Off-season discounts available. MC, V, AE. *In room:* A/C, TV in some units, fridge.

Calistoga Inn   Would the fact that the Calistoga Inn has its own brewery influence my decision to recommend it? You betcha. Here's the deal: You're probably in town for the spa treatments, but unfortunately, the guest rooms at almost every spa are lacking in the personality and warmth department. A better bet for the budget traveler is to book a room at this homey inn, then walk a few blocks up the street for a mud bath and massage. You'll have to share the bathrooms, and the rooms above the inn's restaurant can be noisy, but otherwise, you get a cozy little room with a queen-size bed, washbasin, and continental breakfast, for a weekend rate that's half the average in these parts. What's more, there's no minimum stay, and the best beer in town is served downstairs. *Tip:* Request a room as far from the bar/restaurant as possible.

1250 Lincoln Ave. (at Cedar St.), Calistoga, CA 94515. ℂ **707/942-4101.** Fax 707/942-4914. www.calistogainn.com. 18 units, none with bathroom. $65–$90 double. Rates include continental breakfast. AE, MC, V.

Calistoga Spa Hot Springs ℛ *Kids* *Value*   Very few hotels in the Wine Country cater specifically to families with children, which is why I recommend Calistoga Spa Hot Springs if you're bringing the little ones: They classify themselves as a family resort and are very accommodating to visitors of all ages. In any case, it's a great bargain, offering unpretentious yet comfortable rooms, as well as a plethora of spa facilities. All of Calistoga's best shops and restaurants are within easy walking distance, and you can even whip up your own grub at the barbecue grills near the large pool and patio area.

1006 Washington St. (at Gerrard St.), Calistoga, CA 94515. ℂ **866/822-5772** or 707/942-6269. www.calistogaspa.com. 57 units. Winter $104–$185 double, summer $127–$185 double. MC, V. **Amenities:** 3 heated outdoor pools; kids' wading pool; exercise room; spa. *In room:* A/C, TV, kitchenette, fridge, coffeemaker, hair dryer, iron.

Dr. Wilkinson's Hot Springs Resort ℛ   This retro spa/"resort," located in the heart of Calistoga, is one of the best deals in Napa Valley. The rooms range from attractive Victorian-style accommodations to modern, cozy, recently renovated guest rooms in the main 1950s-style motel. All rooms are spiffier than most in the area's other hotels, with surprisingly tasteful textiles and basic motel-style accouterments. Larger rooms have refrigerators and/or kitchens. Facilities, which are the highlight of a Calistoga visit, include three mineral-water pools (two outdoor and one indoor), a Jacuzzi, a steam room, and mud baths. All kinds of body treatments are available in the spa, including famed mud baths, steams, and massage—all of which I highly recommend. Be sure to inquire about their excellent midweek packages and their new, fantastic facial held in your very own facial cottage

1507 Lincoln Ave. (California 29, between Fairway and Stevenson aves.), Calistoga, CA 94515. ℂ **707/942-4102.** www.drwilkinson.com. 42 units. $109–$199 double. Weekly discounts and packages available. AE, MC, V. *In room:* A/C, TV, dataport, coffeemaker, hair dryer.

5 Where to Dine

Napa Valley's restaurants draw as much attention to the valley as its award-winning wineries. Nowhere else in the state are kitchens as deft at mixing fresh, seasonal, local, organic produce into edible magic, which means that menus change constantly to reflect the best available ingredients. Add that to a great bottle of wine and stunning views, and you have one heck of an eating experience.

To best enjoy the valley's restaurant scene, keep one thing in mind: Reserve—especially if you want a seat in a famous room. Beyond that, expect to spend some money! Aside from taco stands and great little Mexican joints tucked throughout the valley, quality doesn't come cheaply in these parts.

The restaurants listed below are classified first by town, then by price, using the following categories: **Expensive,** dinner from $50 per person; **Moderate,** dinner from $35 to $50 per person; and **Inexpensive,** dinner less than $35 per person. These categories reflect prices for an appetizer, a main course, and a dessert.

NAPA
MODERATE

Angèle 🦆🦆 COUNTRY FRENCH   I love this riverside spot for two reasons: The food is great and the surroundings are some of the best in the valley. Its cozy combo of raw wood beams, taupe-tinted concrete-block walls, concrete slab floors, bright yellow leather bar stools, candlelight, and a heated, shaded patio (weather permitting) has always been great for intimate dining. But chef Tripp Mauldin, previously at Michael Mina and the Ritz-Carlton in San Francisco, who arrived in mid-2005, has upped the culinary ante in a big way, offering fabulous crispy roast chicken with summer corn, chanterelles, lardoons, baby potatoes, and jus, outstanding burgers, and tasty seafood such as King salmon with arugula salad, heirloom tomatoes, olives, basil, and parmesan. During winter eves, opt for the rustic-chic indoors; for summer, settle into one of the outdoor seats. And whatever you do, if they're offering it, get the chocolate soup for dessert. It sounds weird, but trust me, it's shamelessly delicious.

540 Main St. (in the Hatt Building), Napa. ©️ **707/252-8115.** Reservations recommended. Main courses $16–$26. AE, MC, V. Daily 11:30am–10pm.

Bistro Don Giovanni 🦆🦆🦆 (Value) REGIONAL ITALIAN Donna and Giovanni Scala—who launched Scala's Bistro in San Francisco—own this bright, bustling, and cheery Italian restaurant, which also happens to be one of my favorite restaurants in Napa

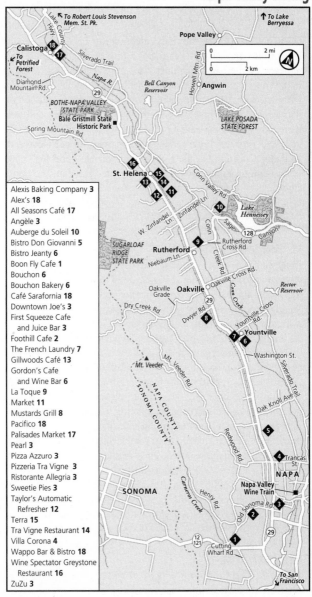

Napa Valley Dining

Calistoga

To Robert Louis Stevenson Mem. St. Pk.

To Lake Berryessa

Pope Valley

To Petrified Forest

Silverado Trail

Diamond Mountain Rd.

Napa R.

Bell Canyon Reservoir

Angwin

Lake County Hwy.

Howell Mtn. Rd.

0   2 mi
0   2 km

BOTHE-NAPA VALLEY STATE PARK

Bale Gristmill State Historic Park

Spring Mountain Rd.

LAKE POSADA STATE FOREST

St. Helena

Conn Valley Rd.

Lake Hennessey

W. Zinfandel Ln.

Zinfandel Ln.

Conn Creek Rd.

Sage Canyon

128

SUGARLOAF RIDGE STATE PARK

Rutherford

Niebaum Ln.

Rutherford Cross Rd.

Oakville Grade

Oakville

Oakville Cross Rd.

Conn Creek

Rector Reservoir

Dry Creek Rd.

29

Dwyer Rd.

Yountville Cross Rd.

Yountville

Washington St.

Mt. Veeder

Mt. Veeder Rd.

NAPA COUNTY

SONOMA COUNTY

Oak Knoll Ave.

Silverado Trail

Redwood Rd.

Carneros Creek

SONOMA

Trancas St.

NAPA

Napa Valley Wine Train

Henry Rd.

Old Sonoma Rd.

12 121

Cutting Wharf Rd.

29

To San Francisco

Valley. Fare prepared by chef/partner Scott Warner highlights quality ingredients and California flair and never disappoints, especially when it comes to the thin-crusted pizzas and house-made pastas. Every time I grab a menu, I can't get past the salad of beets and *haricots verts* or the pasta with duck Bolognese. On the rare occasion that I do, I am equally smitten with outstanding classic pizza Margherita fresh from the wood-burning oven, seared wild salmon filet perched atop a tower of buttermilk mashed potatoes, and steak frites. My only complaint: Over the past few years the appetizers have been getting skimpier and more expensive. But don't let it deter you. Alfresco dining in the vineyards is available—and highly recommended on a warm, sunny day. Midwinter, I'm a fan of ordering a bottle of wine (always expensive here) and dining at the bar.

4110 Howard Lane (at St. Helena Hwy.), Napa. ℂ **707/224-3300.** Reservations recommended. Main courses $12–$24. AE, DC, DISC, MC, V. Sun–Thurs 11:30am–10pm; Fri–Sat 11:30am–11pm.

Ristorante Allegria ⟲ NORTHERN ITALIAN   When all I really want is a quality dinner at everyday prices, I go directly to this downtown locals spot housed in a beautiful historic bank. High ceilings, faux-finished walls, mood lighting, an accordion player on Wednesdays (!), and a sectioned-off full bar create excellent atmosphere, the staff is very friendly, and you won't find a more perfectly prepared grilled salmon over Yukon gold potatoes, and baby spinach hash topped with lemon-caper aioli—especially at 17 bucks! They also make a generous and tasty Caesar salad, offer plenty of antipasti and pastas (the latter of which are not nearly as good as those at Don Giovanni), and offer the likes of filet mignon with garlic mashed potatoes and gorgonzola compound butter to satisfy red-meat lovers. Plus you can order their fixed-price menu of three courses plus dessert for a measly $39. You won't get the vineyard view "wine country" dining experience—or its corresponding high prices—here, but sometimes, that's exactly what the diner ordered. Oh! And one last perk: You can pay $10 to bring and drink your own bottle of wine *and* they waive the fee if you order a bottle from the list as well.

1026 1st St. (at Main St.), Napa. ℂ **707/254-8006.** www.ristoranteallegria.com. Most main courses $9–$16 lunch, $11–$18 dinner. AE, MC, V. Mon–Thurs lunch 11am–2:30pm, dinner 5–10pm, Fri–Sun 10am–11pm.

INEXPENSIVE

Alexis Baking Company ⟲ BAKERY/CAFE   Alexis (aka ABC) is a quaint, casual stop for residents and in-the-know tourists. On weekend mornings—especially Sunday, which is when you'll find me devouring their out-of-this-world Sunday-only huevos rancheros—the line stretches out the door. Once you order (from the counter during the week and at the table on weekends) and find a seat, you can relax and enjoy the coffeehouse atmosphere. Start your day with spectacular pastries, coffee drinks, and breakfast goodies like pumpkin pancakes with sautéed pears. Lunch also bustles with locals who come for simple, fresh fare like grilled hamburgers with Gorgonzola, grilled-chicken Caesar salad, roast lamb sandwich with minted mayo and roasted shallots on rosemary bread, and lentil bulgur orzo salad. (Sorry fries lovers; you won't find any here.) Desserts run the gamut; during the holidays, they include a moist and magical steamed persimmon pudding. Oh, and the pastry counter's cookies and cakes beg you to take something for the road.

1517 3rd St. (between Main and Jefferson sts.), Napa. ℂ 707/258-1827. www. alexisbakingcompany.com. Main courses $5–$10 breakfast, $7–$10 lunch. MC, V. Mon–Fri 6:30am–4pm; Sat 7:30am–3pm; Sun 8am–2pm.

The Boon Fly Café ℛ AMERICAN   Along the rural Carneros highway is a great bargain dining option: the gourmet roadhouse fronting the Carneros Inn. The slick and inviting interior is modern barn style complete with a corrugated metal water-shed-like pizza oven and light, airy, surroundings with dark wood tables and floors. The food similarly balances rustic and chic with fancy renditions of comfort classics like killer beer-battered onion rings, thin-crust pizza, great cobb salad, omelets, pancakes, and roasted half chicken with bacon, roasted potatoes, sautéed mushrooms and chicken stock and white wine reduction. With prices topping out in the mid teens, it's almost cheaper to eat here than dine at home. An added bonus: If you're passing by and in a hurry they offer tasty to-go items like donut holes and breakfast sandwiches. They've just changed chefs so keep your fingers crossed that the quality continues.

4048 Sonoma Hwy./121 (near Old Sonoma Road), Napa. ℂ 707/299-4900. Main courses $4–$9 breakfast, $15–$25 lunch and dinner. AE, DC, DISC, MC, V. Daily 7am–10pm.

Downtown Joe's AMERICAN BISTRO   Foodies will want to steer clear, but those looking for a good hangover breakfast, a down-home atmosphere, lots of beer on tap, and grooving tunes during the evenings will appreciate this well-priced restaurant. The menu is all over the place, offering everything from New York strip steaks to omelets, pasta, and seafood specials. The beers, such as the tart Golden Ribbon American beer, are made in-house, as are the breads and desserts. If the sun's out, request a table on the outside patio, adjacent to the park. Thursday through Sunday nights, rock, jazz, and blues bands draw in the locals.

Another reason to visit Joe's are their happy hours, which are Monday through Friday and feature changing daily specials such as $2 pints and half-price appetizers (on certain days) plus a drawing every hour to win free stuff.

902 Main St. (at 2nd St.), Napa. (✆ **707/258-2337.** Main courses $6–$10 breakfast, $9–$18 lunch and dinner. AE, DC, DISC, MC, V. Mon–Thurs 10:30am–10:30pm (lunch and dinner); Fri 10:30am–midnight; Sat 8:30am–2pm (brunch) and 2pm–midnight (dinner); Sun 8:30am–10:30pm.

First Squeeze Cafe and Juice Bar DELI/JUICE   Stay in town long enough, and you're bound to crave simple, wholesome, healthy fare, and First Squeeze is just the place to find it. I drop by for fresh smoothies such as a protein-powder shake with wheat grass, spirulina, ginseng, bee pollen, and brewer's yeast. But you can also order at the counter, settle amidst spartan furnishings (and decor to match), and dig into a full breakfast or a big, bulky sandwich.

1126 1st St. (in Clocktower Plaza), Napa. (✆ **707/224-6762.** Deli items $3–$7. AE, DC, MC, V. Mon–Fri 7am–3pm; Sat–Sun 8am–3pm.

Foothill Café ✿✿ AMERICAN   Unpretentious, not fancy, astounding value, and creative good-quality food are the name of the game at this hidden local favorite in a tiny mall. With a mere 42 seats and a serious following, the east-Napa neighborhood joint is always crowded, but the feeling is still intimate and casual. Chef/owner Jerry Shaffer's menu trots the backyard and the globe with items such as Thai salad, crab cakes, his famed oak-roasted baby back ribs, and duck breast with huckleberry sauce, garlic mashed potatoes, and sautéed vegetables. Sometimes dishes are complete winners; other times they're very good. In both cases they're served by a friendly staff and accompanied by affordable wines, making this stop a great choice for anyone interested in a fine Napa Valley meal without the fanfare or price tag of fine dining rooms.

2766 Old Sonoma Rd. (at Foothill Blvd.), Napa. (✆ **707/252-6178.** Reservations recommended. Main courses $14–$18. AE, MC, V. Wed–Sun 4:30–9:30pm.

Pizza Azzurro ✿ ITALIAN   This casual, cheery, family-friendly restaurant serves the best fancy thin-crust pies in downtown Napa. Unlike many Valley dining rooms, the place has an authentic neighborhood feel thanks to a very low-key atmosphere, and the continual presence of chef/owner Michael Gyetvan who spent 10 years in the kitchens of Tra Vigne, One Market, and Lark Creek Inn. While killer thin-crust pizzas—such as the incredible *Salsiccia* (tangy tomato sauce, rustic Sonoma-made fennel pork sausage, crunchy red onion, and mozzarella) star here, they've got great salads, too. Try the respectable Caesar or the marinated chickpea salad, a giant serving of chopped romaine, garbanzos, and canned albacore, cucumber, red pear tomatoes, and olives tossed in a lightly acidic citrus dressing that can easily serve four. Pastas, such as rigatoni in red sauce with hot Italian sausage and mushrooms, play it safe, while *manciatas*—soft, lightly cooked pizza dough meant to be folded and eaten like a soft taco—are very satisfying. (Try the B.B.L.T. version.) Although Bistro Don Giovanni is king of fancy pasta and pizza fixes, Azzurro is cheaper and far better if you've got the kids in tow or want to have a low-key or fast dinner. *Note:* There's no dessert here, but Ben & Jerry's is a quick stroll away.

1400 2nd St. (at Franklin St.). (C) 707/255-5552. No reservations. Main courses $9.95–$12. AE, MC, V. Mon–Fri 11:30am–9pm; Sat 5pm–9pm; closed Sun.

Sweetie Pies *☆ (Finds* CAFE/BAKERY   Simple breakfasts of granola, egg-and-cheese croissant sandwiches, quiche, and coffee are a perfect and light way to kick off each decadent day at this very adorable and aptly named country bakery. But yummy pastries, decadent individual cakes, huge cookies, and lunchtime edibles like ham and fontina panini and pizzettas with mixed green salads are equal reason to stop by and linger at one of the few tables. Got a sweet tooth? You can't go wrong with the dark chocolate and caramel ganache fudge cake or mud-pie cheesecake.

520 Main St., (at the south end), Napa. (C) 707/257-7280. Breakfast snacks $2.75–$4.50; pastries $2.25–$2.75; cake $6.75; sandwiches $5.50. MC, V. Mon–Wed 6:30am–6pm; Thurs 6:30am–7pm; Fri–Sat 6:30am–8pm; Sun 7am–5pm.

Villa Corona *☆* MEXICAN   The best Mexican food in town is served in this bright, funky, and colorful restaurant hidden in the southwest corner of a strip mall behind an unmemorable sports bar and restaurant. The winning plan here is simple: Order and pay at the counter, sit at either a plastic-covered table or at one of the few sidewalk seats, and wait for the huge burritos, enchiladas, and chimichangas to be delivered to your table. Those with pork preferences shouldn't miss the carnitas, which are abundantly flavorful and juicy. My personal favorites are hard-shell tacos or chicken enchiladas with light savory red sauce, a generous side of beans, and rice. Don't expect to wash down your menudo, or anything else for that matter, with a margarita. The place serves only beer and wine.

Don't hesitate to come for a hearty breakfast, too. Excellent *chilaquiles* (eggs scrambled with salsa and tortilla) and huevos rancheros are part of the package.

3614 Bel Aire Plaza, on Trancas St., Napa. ⓒ **707/257-8685**. Breakfast, lunch, and dinner $6–$10. MC, V. Mon–Fri 9am–9pm; Sat 8am–9pm; Sun 8am–8pm.

ZuZu 🌟🌟 TAPAS   A local place to the core, ZuZu lures neighborhood regulars with a no-reservation policy, a friendly cramped wine and beer bar, and very affordable Mediterranean small plates, which are meant to be shared. The comfortable, warm, and not remotely corporate atmosphere extends from the environment to the food, which includes sizzling mini skillets of tangy and fantastic paella, addictive prawns with requisite Pimento bread-dipping sauce, light and delicate sea scallop ceviche salad, and Moroccan barbecued lamb chops with a sweet-and-spicy sauce. Desserts aren't as fab, but with a bottle of wine and more tasty plates than you can possibly devour, who cares?

829 Main St., Napa. ⓒ **707/224-8555**. Reservations not accepted. Tapas $3–$13. MC, V. Mon–Thurs 11:30am–10pm; Fri 11:30am–midnight; Sat 4pm–midnight; Sun 4–9pm.

YOUNTVILLE
EXPENSIVE

The French Laundry 🌟🌟🌟 CLASSIC AMERICAN/FRENCH   It's almost futile to include this restaurant, because you're about as likely to secure a reservation—or get through on the reservation line, for that matter—as you are to drive Highway 29 without passing a winery. Several years after renowned chef-owner Thomas Keller bought the place and caught the attention of epicureans worldwide (including the judges of the James Beard Awards, who named him "Chef of the Nation" in 1997), this discreet restaurant is one of the hottest dinner tickets *in the world.*

Plainly put, The French Laundry is unlike any other dining experience, period. Part of it has to do with the intricate preparations, often finished tableside and always presented with uncommon artistry and detail, from the food itself to the surface it's delivered on. Other factors are the service (superfluous, formal, and attentive) and the sheer length of time it takes to ride chef Keller's culinary magic carpet. The atmosphere is as serious as the diners who quietly swoon over the ongoing parade of bite-size delights. Seating ranges from downstairs to upstairs to seasonal garden tables. Technically,

> ⌐Fun Fact **Trying a Tasting Menu**
>
> Never heard of a tasting menu? Basically, if you opt for one, it means you're committing to a set menu of smaller portions and more courses, which you choose from numerous selections. It's great for people who prefer to taste lots of things without overstuffing themselves—although that can still happen.

the prix-fixe menu offers a choice of seven or nine courses (including a vegetarian menu), but after a slew of cameo appearances from the kitchen, everyone starts to lose count. Signature dishes include Keller's "tongue in cheek" (a marinated and braised round of sliced lamb tongue and tender beef cheeks) and "macaroni and cheese" (sweet butter-poached Maine lobster with creamy lobster broth and orzo with mascarpone cheese). The truth is, the experience defies description, so if you absolutely love food, you'll simply have to try it for yourself. Portions are small, but only because Keller wants his guests to taste as many things as possible. Trust me, nobody leaves hungry.

The staff is well acquainted with the wide selection of regional wines; there's a $50 corkage fee if you bring your own bottle. *Hint:* If you can't get a reservation, try walking in—on occasion folks don't keep their reservation and tables open up, especially during lunch on rainy days. Also, insiders tell me that fewer people call on weekends, so you have a better chance at getting beyond the busy signal.

6640 Washington St. (at Creek St.), Yountville. ⌐ **707/944-2380.** Reservations required. Vegetarian menu $80; 5-course menu $105; chef's tasting menu $175. AE, MC, V. Fri–Sun 11am–1pm; daily 5:30–9pm. Dress code required: no jeans, shorts or tennis shoes; men should wear jackets.

MODERATE

Bistro Jeanty ⌐ FRENCH BISTRO This casual, warm bistro, with muted buttercup walls, two dining rooms divided by the bar, and patio seats, is where chef Phillipe Jeanty's staff serves seriously rich French comfort food for legions of fans. The all-day menu includes legendary tomato soup in puff pastry; foie gras pâté; steak tartare; and house-smoked trout with potato slices. No meal should start without a paper cone filled with fried smelt, and none should end without the crème brûlée, made with a thin layer of chocolate cream between classic vanilla custard and a caramelized sugar top. In between, it's a rib-gripping free-for-all including coq au vin, cassoulet, and juicy, thick-cut pork chop with jus, spinach, and mashed potatoes. Alas, quality has suffered since Jeanty has branched out to three restaurants, but when the kitchen is on it's still a fine place to sup.

6510 Washington St., Yountville. ✆ **707/944-0103.** www.bistrojeanty.com. Reservations recommended. Appetizers $8.50–$13; most main courses $15–$29. AE, MC, V. Daily 11:30am–10:30pm.

Bouchon ✍✍ FRENCH BISTRO   If you're looking for a delicious, moderately priced meal in city-chic, lovely environs, this is your best bet. Perhaps to appease the crowds who never get a reservation at French Laundry, Thomas Keller opened this far more casual, but still delicious, and very sexy French brasserie. Along with a raw bar, expect superb renditions of steak frites, mussels meunière, grilled-cheese sandwiches, and other heavenly French classics (try the expensive and rich foie gras pâté, which is made at Bouchon). My all-time favorite must-orders: the bibb lettuce salad (seriously, trust me on this), french fries (perhaps the best in the valley), and roasted chicken bathed in wild mushroom ragout. A bonus, especially for restless residents and off-duty restaurant staff, is the late hours, although they offer a more limited menu when the crowds dwindle.

6534 Washington St. (at Humboldt St.), Yountville. ✆ **707/944-8037.** Reservations recommended. Main courses $15–$27. AE, MC, V. Daily 11:30am–12:30am.

Gordon's Cafe and Wine Bar ✍ WINE COUNTRY CUISINE If you want to escape the town's highfalutin restaurants for an intimate brush with the locals, this is the place to do it. Sally Gordon opened this adorable Yountville favorite in May 1996. Part country store, part deli, and part restaurant, one wall is lined with an intriguing collection of jams, mustards, olive oils, wines, and other gourmet goods for sale; another posts the chalkboard breakfast and lunch menu above a glass display case housing a cornucopia of deli items. The floor is scuffed hardwood, and fewer than a dozen tables are spaciously dispersed throughout the airy room. Breakfast (oatmeal, omelets, and homemade pastries), lunch (soup, salads, and sandwiches), and real homemade flavor come from an open kitchen. Friday nights feature a Wine Bar Menu highlighting local hard-to-find wines by the glass, small plate meals, and special desserts.

6770 Washington St., Yountville. ✆ **707/944-8246.** Breakfast $5–$7; lunch $5–$12; wine bar plates $5–$15. MC, V. Breakfast daily 7:30–11am, until noon on weekends; lunch daily 11am–3pm. Coffee and wine bar until 4pm Sun–Thurs, 9pm Fri. Nov–Apr 1, closed Tues–Wed.

Mustards Grill ☆☆ CALIFORNIA   Mustards is one of those standby restaurants that everyone seems to love because it's dependable and its menu has something that suits any food craving. Housed in a convivial, barn-style space, it offers an 11-page wine list and an ambitious chalkboard list of specials. Options go from exotic offerings like tea-smoked Peking duck with almond onion sauce or Mongolian style pork chop with hot mustard sauce, to sautéed lemon-garlic chicken breast with mashed potatoes and fresh herbs. The menu includes something for everyone, from vegetarians to good old burger lovers, and the wine list features nothing but "New World" wines.

7399 St. Helena Hwy. (Hwy. 29), Napa. ℂ 707/944-2424. Reservations recommended. Main courses $11–$27. AE, DC, DISC, MC, V. Mon–Thurs 11:30am–9pm; Fri 11:30am–10pm; Sat 11am–10pm; Sun 11am–9pm.

INEXPENSIVE

Bouchon Bakery ☆ FRENCH BAKERY   In the summer of 2003, famed French Laundry chef Thomas Keller opened this adorable authentic French bakery next door to his restaurant Bouchon (see above). It ain't cheap, but that doesn't stop locals and visitors from lining up amid the pretty green-mosaic-tiled storefront for the outstanding bread baked twice daily, paper-wrapped panini, killer treats (think éclairs, cookies, tarts, and more), coffee drinks, classic sandwiches, and near-perfect pastry. Grab it to go or snack at one of the garden tables, which overlook Yountville's main drag.

6528 Washington St. (between Jefferson and Yount sts.). ℂ 707/944-2253. Pastries and sandwiches $2.25–$7. MC, V. Daily 7am–7pm.

OAKVILLE & RUTHERFORD
EXPENSIVE

Auberge du Soleil ☆ *Finds* WINE COUNTRY CUISINE   There is no better restaurant view than the one at Auberge du Soleil, perched on a hillside overlooking the valley. I recommend coming during the day (request terrace seating) to join the wealthy patrons, many of whom have emerged from their uberluxury guest rooms for a casual burger or salad lunch—especially since dinner is expensive, and while chef Robert Curry, previously at Domaine Chandon and the nearby Culinary Institute, does a fine job, there are better blow-the-bank dinners in these parts. No doubt he'll stick with seasonal local specialties. If you go for it, dress the part: The warm interior is somewhat formal.

180 Rutherford Hill Rd., Rutherford. ℂ 707/967-3111. Reservations recommended. Main courses $19–$25 lunch, $28–$34 dinner; 4-course fixed-price dinner $79. AE, DISC, MC, V. Daily 7–11am and 11:30am–2:30pm; Sun–Thurs 6–9:30pm; Fri–Sat 5:30–9:30pm.

La Toque ✸✸ FRENCH   Renowned chef Ken Frank attracts diners to one of Wine Country's most formal dining rooms with beautifully presented five-course extravaganzas. Well-spaced tables create plenty of room to showcase the chef-owner's memorable and innovative French-inspired cuisine, which might include an incredible Indian spice–rubbed foie gras with Madras carrot purée; Alaskan King salmon with lentils and house-cured bacon; or Niman Ranch rib roast with roasted root vegetables and red wine. But don't count on it. The menu changes weekly, so you might discover a completely different, but equally delicious, selection. Should you find room and the extra few bucks for the cheese course, try a few, served with walnut bread. For an additional $62 per person you can also drink well-paired wines with each course.

1140 Rutherford Rd., Rutherford. ✆ **707/963-9770.** www.latoque.com. Reservations recommended. Fixed-price menu $98. Wed–Sun 5:30–9:30pm. Closed Mon–Tues.

ST. HELENA
EXPENSIVE

Terra ✸✸✸ CONTEMPORARY AMERICAN   Terra is one of my favorite restaurants, because it manages to be humble even though it serves some of the most extraordinary food in Northern California. The creation of Lissa Doumani and her husband, Hiro Sone, a master chef who hails from Japan, it's a culmination of talents brought together more than 15 years ago, after the duo worked at L.A.'s Spago. Today, the menu reflects Sone's full use of the region's bounty and his formal training in classic European and Japanese cuisine. Dishes—all of which are incredible and are served in the rustic-romantic dining room—range from understated and refined (two must-tries: rock shrimp salad, broiled sake-marinated cod with shrimp dumplings and shiso broth) to rock-your-world flavorful (petit ragout of sweetbreads, prosciutto, mushroom, and white truffle oil; or grilled squab with leek and bacon bread pudding and roasted garlic foie gras sauce). I cannot express the importance of saving room for dessert (or forcing it even if you didn't). Doumani's recipes, which includes to-die-for tiramisu, are heavenly.

1345 Railroad Ave. (between Adams and Hunt sts.), St. Helena. ✆ **707/963-8931.** www.terrarestaurant.com. Reservations recommended. Main courses $19–$29. AE, DC, MC, V. Wed–Mon 6–10pm. Closed for 2 weeks in early Jan.

MODERATE

Tra Vigne Restaurant ✸ ITALIAN   As much as I want to love everything about this famous, absurdly scenic restaurant, I can't—

anymore. With lots of chef changes over the years and meals that range from barely so-so to totally rockin,' it's just not the sure thing it used to be. However, there is one thing you can count on. If the sun is shining or the stars are out on a warm eve and you sit in the Tuscany-evoking courtyard, you will have an incredible time regardless of whether the kitchen is on the money or missing the mark. Inside, the bustling, cavernous dining room and happening bar is fine for chilly days and eves, but it's not nearly as magical. You can also count on wonderful bread (served with house-cured olives) a menu of robust California dishes, cooked Italian-style, a daily oven-roasted pizza special, lots of pastas, and tried-and-true standbys like short ribs, fritto misto, and whole roasted fish.

1050 Charter Oak Ave., St. Helena. ⓒ **707/963-4444.** Reservations recommended. Main courses $13–$22. DC, DISC, MC, V. Daily 11:30am–10pm.

Wine Spectator Greystone Restaurant ⓕ CALIFORNIA

This place offers a visual and culinary feast that's unparalleled in the area, if not the state. The room is an enormous stone-walled former Christian Bros. winery, warmed by the festive decor and heavenly aromas. Cooking islands—complete with scurrying chefs, steaming pots, and rotating chickens—provide entertainment. The menu features creative dishes such as Liberty duck breast with cocoa nibs (toasted cocoa beans), wild mushrooms, and burnt orange coffee sauce or pan roasted halibut with French green lentils and whole grain mustard sauce. But since the chef just left when this book went to press, you'll have to wait for the next edition or taste for yourself to see if the change is for the better. In any case, I recommend that you opt for a barrage of appetizers for your table to share. You might also consider the "Flights of Fancy"—$14 to $25, which allows you to sample three 3-ounce pours of local wines such as white Rhone, pinot, or zinfandel. While the food is serious, the atmosphere is playful—casual enough that you'll feel comfortable in jeans or shorts. If you want to ensure a meal here, reserve far in advance. Personally, I prefer to stop by, have a snack at the bar, and eat big meals elsewhere.

At the Culinary Institute of America at Greystone, 2555 Main St., St. Helena. ⓒ **707/967-1010.** Reservations recommended. Temptations $9; main courses $17–$29. AE, DC, MC, V. Daily 11:15am–10pm.

INEXPENSIVE

Gillwoods Café AMERICAN

In a town like this—where if you order mushrooms on your burger, the waiter's likely to ask, "What kind?"—a plain old American restaurant can be a godsend. In St.

Helena, the land of snobs and broccoli rabes, Gillwoods is that place. At this homey haunt, with its wooden benches and original artwork, it's all about the basics. You'll find a breakfast of bakery goods, fruit, pancakes, omelets (with pronounceable ingredients), and a decent eggs Benedict; and a lunch menu of burgers, sandwiches, lots of salads, and chicken-fried steak. Lunch is available starting at 10:30am, but late risers can order breakfast until 3pm. A second location is in downtown Napa at 1320 Napa Town Center, ℂ **707/253-0409.**

1313 Main St. (Hwy. 29, at Spring St.), St. Helena. ℂ **707/963-1788.** Breakfast $9–$11; lunch $9–$12. AE, MC, V. Daily 7am–3pm. Napa location daily 8am–3pm.

Market AMERICAN In past editions I've highly recommended this upscale but cheap ode to American comfort food. But ever since the chef departed to open a high-end sister restaurant in Sonoma County's town Healdsburg (called Cyrus and it's incredible!), the food's gone downhill. Still, if you're in expensive St. Helena and want some casual glamour with your burger, you'll find it here with fancy stone-wall and Brunswick bar surroundings paired with clunky steak knives and simple white-plate presentations. Skip the lame chopped salad and perhaps go instead for barbecue sauce–glazed meatloaf over gravy, mashed potatoes, and carrots; or toast-it-yourself s'mores with crisp homemade graham crackers. At lunch, you can also opt for a three-course meal—a steal at a measly $15.

1347 Main St., St. Helena. ℂ **707/963-3799.** Most main courses $7–$17. AE, MC, V. Daily lunch 11:30am–10pm, bar menu.

Pizzeria Tra Vigne ℛ *Kids* *Value* ITALIAN After spending a week in Wine Country, I usually can't stand the thought of another decadent wine and foie gras meal. That's when I race here for a $5.95 chopped salad, a welcome respite from gluttonous excess. Families and locals come here for another reason: Although the menu is limited, it's a total winner for anyone in search of freshly prepared, wholesome food at atypically cheap Wine Country prices. A Caesar salad, for example, costs a mere $5.95. "Piadine"—pizzas folded like a soft taco—are the house specialty and come filled with such delights as fresh rock shrimp, Crescenza cheese sauce, scallions, and deep fried lemons. Pizzas are of the build-your-own variety, with gourmet toppings like sautéed mushrooms, fennel sausage, baby spinach, sun-dried tomatoes, and homemade pepperoni. The 14 respectable local wines come by the glass starting at a toast-worthy $5, or $18 per bottle. Dessert, at less than $4 a pop for gelato or biscotti, or $6 for tiramisu, is an overall sweet deal. Kids especially like the pool table and big-screen TV.

At the Inn at Southbridge, 1016 Main St., St. Helena. ℂ 707/967-9999. Pastas $8–$11; pizzas $9–$17. DC, DISC, MC, V. Daily 11:30am–9pm (Fri–Sat until 9:30pm).

Taylor's Automatic Refresher DINER   Yet another winner to slip from sublime status to buyer beware, this gourmet roadside burger shack built in 1949 still draws huge lines of tourists who love the notion of ordering at the counter and feasting alfresco. But the last few meals I had there left me knowing the $80 I coughed up for lunch for five would have been better spent as Oakville Grocery's deli. The burger, onion rings, and fries were mediocre at best, the iceberg salad was unwieldy, and only the shake left me satisfied. (How hard is it to make a great shake, after all?) Perhaps it's that the owners now have a closer eye on their San Francisco outpost, which is great, by the way. No matter. It's still the only casual burger joint in St. Helena (especially considering it offers ahi tuna burger and various tacos and salads) and its ever-bustling status proves everyone knows it.

933 Main St., St Helena. ℂ 707/963-3486. www.taylorsrefresher.com. Main courses $4–$13. AE, MC, V. Daily 11am–8pm, 9pm in summer.

CALISTOGA
MODERATE

All Seasons Café ⟳⟳ CALIFORNIA   All Seasons successfully balances old-fashioned down-home dining charm with today's penchant for sophisticated, seasonally inspired dishes. It also happens to have perhaps the best food in downtown Calistoga. Here vibrant bouquets, large framed watercolors, and windows overlooking busy Lincoln Avenue soften the look of the black and white checkered flooring, brick red ceiling, and long, black wine bar. Laid-back service belies what arrives on the plate—and the fact that they have 400-plus wines available from their adjoining wine shop (with a $15 corkage fee, buy next door and you're drinking for far cheaper than most restaurants). But it also makes the quality of crispy skin chicken with black truffle chicken jus and herb-roasted monkfish with fennel nage that much more of a delicious surprise. Alas, the kitchen was a wee slow on my last visit, but all was forgiven when the food far surpassed my expectations.

1400 Lincoln Ave. (at Washington St.), Calistoga. ℂ 707/942-9111. Reservations recommended on weekends. Main courses $9–$11 lunch, $19–$28 dinner. DISC, MC, V. Lunch Fri–Sun noon–2:30pm; dinner nightly 6–9pm.

INEXPENSIVE

Café Sarafornia AMERICAN   When Calistoga locals want a quick, inexpensive fix for breakfast or lunch, this is where they come. Café Sarafornia is pleasantly homey, a clean, bright, cheery bastion for late risers who prefer to eat their huevos rancheros or salmon and eggs at noon. (Breakfast is served all day.) The cafe consists of little more than a U-shaped counter, a few booths, wood and tile floors, and a series of bucolic wall murals. The menu is a lesson in simplicity—burgers, hot dogs, pastas, sandwiches, salads, and requisite small-town specials such as chicken-fried steak with red-eye gravy. And if you like to sweat and holler, be sure to sample the five-alarm chili. The cafe also offers kids' meals for a mere $4.75.

1413 Lincoln Ave. (at Washington St.), Calistoga. (*C*) **707/942-0555.** Main courses breakfast $6–$10, lunch $6–$12. DISC, MC, V. Daily 7am–3pm.

Pacifico MEXICAN   If you're in the mood for Mexican food, Pacifico is the place. The rather mundane-looking facade opens up into a surprisingly festive interior, complete with brilliantly colorful Mexican artwork and pottery, huge potted palm trees, and a south-of-the-border bar, complete with faux tile roof and waterfall. The menu is *muy grande,* covering just about every conceivable region in Mexico, from Tacos de Oaxaqueños (grilled, marinated chicken tacos topped with guajillo chile salsa) to Enchiladas del Ray (filled with Chihuahua cheese and covered with chile verde sauce).

1237 Lincoln Ave. (between Myrtle and Cedar sts.), Calistoga. (*C*) **707/942-4400.** Lunch and dinner main courses $6.75–$15. MC, V. Mon–Thurs 11:30am–10pm, Fri 11am–10pm, Sat–Sun 10am–10pm.

Palisades Market ✦✦ DELI/MARKET   Trust me, sandwiches as delicious as those served at this adorable, old-fashioned gourmet market are an absolute rarity and a sure-fire addiction. Drop in for wine, juice, soda, cheese, tamales, green salads, lasagna, crab cakes, soup, picnic items, and every kind of treat you can think of, but under no circumstances should you skip the sandwiches, which range from pesto, turkey, provolone, lettuce, and tomatoes on sun-dried tomato focaccia to ham, Gruyère cheese, onions, lettuce, mayo, and Dijon mustard on a baguette. Call 2 days in advance and Palisades will box a lunch for you; $16 will get you a sandwich, salad, fruit, cookie, and utensils.

1506 Lincoln Ave., Calistoga. (*C*) **707/942-9549.** Sandwiches $4.95–$7.95. AE, MC, V. Sun–Wed 7:30am–6pm; Thurs–Sat 7:30am–7pm.

Wappo Bar & Bistro GLOBAL   One of the best alfresco dining venues in the Wine Country is under Wappo's jasmine-and-grapevine–covered arbor. Unfortunately, food and service are a very distant second. But much can be forgiven when the wine's flowing and you're surrounded by pastoral splendor. The menu offers a global selection, from tandoori chicken to roast rabbit with gnocchi and mustard cream sauce. Desserts of choice are black-bottom coconut cream pie and strawberry rhubarb pie.

1226B Washington St. (off Lincoln Ave.), Calistoga. ℰ **707/942-4712.** www.wappo bar.com. Main courses $14–$25. AE, MC, V. Wed–Mon 11:30am–2:30pm and 6–9:30pm.

6 Where to Stock Up for a Picnic & Where to Enjoy It

You can easily plan your whole trip around restaurant reservations, but gather one of the world's best gourmet picnics, and the valley's your oyster.

One of the finest gourmet-food stores in the Wine Country, if not all of California, is the **Oakville Grocery Co.,** 7856 St. Helena Hwy., at Oakville Cross Road, Oakville (ℰ **707/944-8802**). You can put together the provisions for a memorable picnic or, with at least 24 hours' notice, the staff can prepare a picnic basket for you. The store, with its small-town vibe and claustrophobia-inducing crowds, can be quite an experience. You'll find shelves crammed with the best breads and choicest cheeses in the northern Bay Area, as well as pâtés, cold cuts, crackers, top-quality olive oils, fresh foie gras (domestic and French, seasonal), smoked Norwegian salmon, fresh caviar (beluga, sevruga, osetra) and, of course, an exceptional selection of California wines. The store is open daily from 9am to 6pm. There's also an espresso bar tucked in the corner (open Mon–Fri 7am–6pm, Sat–Sun 8am-6pm), offering lunch items, a complete deli, and house-baked pastries, and a few picnic tables behind the store.

Another of my favorite places to fill a picnic basket is New York's version of a swank European marketplace, **Dean & Deluca,** 607 S. St. Helena Hwy (Hwy. 29), north of Zinfandel Lane and south of Sulphur Springs Road, St. Helena (ℰ **707/967-9980;** www.dean anddeluca.com). The ultimate in gourmet grocery stores is more like a world's fair of foods, where everything is beautifully displayed and often painfully pricey. As you pace the barn-wood plank floors, you'll stumble upon more high-end edibles than you've probably ever seen under one roof. They include local organic produce (delivered daily); 200 domestic and imported cheeses (with an on-site aging room to ensure proper ripeness); shelves and shelves of tapenades, pastas, oils, hand-packed dried herbs and spices, chocolates, sauces, cookware, and housewares; an espresso bar; one hell of a bakery section; and more. Along the back wall, you can watch the professional chefs prepare gourmet takeout, including salads, rotisserie meats, and sautéed vegetables. You can also snag a pricy bottle from the wine section's 1,200-label collection. The store is open daily from 9am to 7pm (the espresso bar is open Mon–Sat at 7:30am and Sun at 9am). If you're itching to eat, you can indulge at patio tables outside. But there are far more picturesque places to nosh. (See below.)

If you're in the northern part of the valley, go directly to downhome and downright delicious Palisades Market, 1506 Lincoln Ave., Calistoga (© **707/942-9549**), which is open daily from 7:30am to 7pm.

Also see p. 66 for details on **V. Sattui Winery,** 1111 White Lane (at Hwy. 29), St. Helena (© **707/963-7774**). Besides an enormous selection of wines and gourmet deli items—including 200 kinds of cheeses and desserts such as white-chocolate cheesecake—you'll also find extensive picnic facilities, making this winery one of the most popular stops along Highway 29.

If you crave a quiet, more pastoral picnic spot, head for one of the four picnic tables at **Robert Keenan Winery** in St. Helena (p. 69), located right outside the winery and surrounded by vineyards, offering stunning views. Or try the beautiful picnic grounds situated amidst 350-year-old moss-covered oak trees at **Cuvaison** in Calistoga (p. 73); the spectacular grounds at **Rubicon Estate** in Rutherford (p. 62); or the Wine Country's premier picnicking site, **Rutherford Hill Winery** (p. 65), which boasts superb views of the valley.

Sonoma Valley

Sonoma Valley is often thought of as the "other" Wine Country, forever in the shadow of Napa Valley. It's true that Sonoma Valley doesn't have as much going on as Napa Valley. You won't find as many wineries, shopping outlets, or world-class restaurants here. But its less developed, more backcountry character is exactly its charm. Besides, there is more than enough to do here to fill your vacation time.

Sonoma Valley is far more rural and less traveled than its neighbor to the east, offering a more genuine away-from-it-all experience than its more commercial cousin. The roads are less crowded, the pace is slower, and the whole valley is still relatively free of slick tourist attractions and big-name hotels. Commercialization has, for the most part, not yet taken hold. Small, family-owned wineries are still Sonoma Valley's mainstay, just as in the old days of winemaking, when everyone started with the intention of going broke and loved every minute of it. (As the saying goes in these parts, "It takes a large fortune to make a small fortune.")

Unlike in Napa Valley, in Sonoma Valley you won't find palatial wineries with million-dollar art collections, aerial trams, and Hollywood ego trips (read: Rubicon Estate). Rather, Sonoma Valley offers a refreshing dose of reality, where modestly sized wineries are integrated into the community rather than perched on hilltops like corporate citadels. If Napa Valley feels like a fantasyland, where everything exists to service the almighty grape and the visitors it attracts, then Sonoma Valley is its antithesis, an unpretentious gaggle of ordinary towns and ranches. The result, as you wind your way through the valley, is a chance to experience what Napa Valley must have been like long before the Seagrams and Moët et Chandons of the world turned the Wine Country into a major tourist destination.

1 Orientation & Getting Around

Sonoma Valley is some 17 miles long and 7 miles wide, and it is bordered by two mountain ranges: the Mayacamas Mountains to the east and the Sonoma Mountains to the west. One major road, Highway 12 (also known as the Sonoma Hwy.), passes through the valley, starting at the northern edge of the Carneros District, leading though the communities of Sonoma, Glen Ellen, and Kenwood, and ending at the southern boundary, Santa Rosa. Conveniently, most of the wineries—as well as most of the hotels, shops, and restaurants—are either in the town of Sonoma, along Highway 12, or a short distance from it. Of the numerous side roads that branch off Highway 12, only Bennett Valley Road to the west and Trinity Road (aka Oakville Grade) to the east lead over the mountain ranges and out of the valley, and neither is easy to navigate. If you're coming from Napa, I strongly suggest that you take the leisurely southern route along Highway 12/121 rather than tackle Trinity Road, which is a real brake-smoker.

ALONG HIGHWAY 12: SONOMA'S TOWNS IN BRIEF

As you approach the Wine Country from the south, you must first pass through the **Carneros District,** a cool, windswept region that borders San Pablo Bay and marks the entrance to both Napa and Sonoma valleys. Until the latter part of the 20th century, this mixture of marsh, sloughs, and rolling hills was mainly used as sheep pasture. (*Carnero* means "sheep" in Spanish.) After experimental plantings yielded slow-growing yet high-quality grapes—particularly chardonnay and pinot noir—several Napa Valley and Sonoma Valley wineries expanded their plantings here, eventually establishing the Carneros District as an American viticultural appellation. Although about a dozen wineries are spread throughout the region, there are no major towns or attractions—just plenty of gorgeous scenery as you cruise along Highway 121, the major junction between Napa and Sonoma.

At the northern boundary of the Carneros District, along Highway 12, is the centerpiece of Sonoma Valley: the midsized town of **Sonoma,** which owes much of its appeal to Mexican general Mariano Guadalupe Vallejo. Vallejo fashioned this pleasant, slow-paced community after a typical Mexican village—right down to its central plaza, Sonoma's geographical and commercial center. The plaza sits at the top of a T formed by Broadway (Hwy. 12) and Napa Street. Most of the surrounding streets form a grid pattern around this axis, making Sonoma easy to navigate. The plaza's Bear Flag Monument marks the spot where the crude Bear Flag was raised in 1846, signaling the end of Mexican rule; the symbol was later adopted by the state of California and placed on its flag. The 8-acre park at the center of the plaza, complete with two ponds that are populated with ducks and geese, is perfect for an afternoon siesta in the cool shade. About 7 miles north of Sonoma on Highway 12 is the town of **Glen Ellen,** which, though just a fraction of the size of Sonoma, is home to several of the valley's finest wineries, restaurants, and inns. Aside from the addition of a few new restaurants, this charming Wine Country town hasn't changed much since the days when Jack London settled on his Beauty Ranch, about a mile west. Other than the wineries, you'll find few real signs of commercialism; the shops and restaurants, located along one main winding lane, cater to a small, local clientele—that is, until the summer tourist season, when traffic nearly triples on the weekends. If you're as yet undecided about where you want to set up camp during your visit to the Wine Country, I highly recommend this lovable little town.

A few miles north of Glen Ellen along Highway 12 is the tiny town of **Kenwood,** the northernmost outpost of Sonoma Valley. Though the Kenwood Vineyards wines are well known throughout the United States, the town itself consists of little more than a few restaurants, wineries, and modest homes recessed into the wooded hillsides. The nearest lodging, the luxurious Kenwood Inn & Spa, is located about a mile south. Kenwood makes for a pleasant day trip—lunch at Café Citti, a tour of Chateau St. Jean, dinner at Kenwood Restaurant & Bar—before returning to Glen Ellen or Sonoma for the night.

A few miles beyond Kenwood is **Santa Rosa,** the county seat of Sonoma, home to more than 150,000 residents, and the gateway to Northern Sonoma wine country. Historically, it's best known as the hometown of horticulturist Luther Burbank, who produced more than 800 new varieties of fruits, vegetables, and plants during his 50-year tenure here. Today, it's a burgeoning city. Unless you're armed with a map, however, it's best to avoid exploring the large, sprawling area and its rural surroundings, as it's easy to get lost.

VISITOR INFORMATION

While you're in Sonoma, stop by the **Sonoma Valley Visitors Bureau,** 453 1st St. E., Sonoma, CA 95476, in the Carnegie Library Building (© **707/996-1090;** www.sonomavalley.com). It's open daily from 9am to 6pm in summer and from 9am to 5pm in winter. An additional **visitors bureau** is located a few miles south of the square, at 25200 Arnold Dr. (Hwy. 121), Sonoma, CA 95476, at the entrance to Viansa Winery; it's open daily from 9am to 4pm, and from 9am to 5pm in summer.

TOURING SONOMA VALLEY BY BIKE

Sonoma and its neighboring towns are so small, close together, and relatively flat that it's not difficult to get around on two wheels. In fact, if you're not in a great hurry, there's no better way to tour Sonoma Valley than via bicycle. You can rent a bike from the **Goodtime Bicycle Company** ☎ (© 888/525-0453 or 707/938-0453; www.goodtimetouring.com). The staff will happily point you to easy bike trails, or you can take an organized excursion to Kenwood-area wineries, south Sonoma wineries, or even Northern Sonoma's Russian River and Dry Creek areas. Goodtime also provides a gourmet lunch featuring local Sonoma products. If you purchase wine along the way, Goodtime will carry it for you and help with shipping arrangements. Lunch rides start at 10:30am and end around 3:30pm. The cost, including food and equipment, is $125 per person (that's a darn good deal). Rentals cost $25 a day, and include helmets, locks, everything else you'll need, and delivery and pickup to and from local hotels.

Mountain bikes, helmets, and locks are also available for rent from **Sonoma Valley Cyclery**, 20093 Broadway, Sonoma (© 707/935-3377), for $35 a day. Hybrid bikes (better for casual wine-tasting cruisers) are $25 per day, helmet and lock included.

FAST FACTS: Sonoma Valley

Hospitals The **Sonoma Valley Hospital**, 347 Andrieux St. (© 707/935-5000), in downtown Sonoma, is a district hospital that provides inpatient, outpatient, and extended care to the public. Its emergency room is supported by state-of-the-art equipment and is staffed 24 hours a day by physicians and nurses who are specifically trained in emergency treatment. SVH also has an intensive care unit and surgical services.

Santa Rosa Memorial Hospital, 1165 Montgomery Dr. in Santa Rosa (© 707/546-3210), about a 30-minute drive north from Sonoma, offers 24-hour emergency service as well as complete inpatient and outpatient services, a cardiac center, pediatric services, and a dental clinic.

Information See "Visitor Information," above.

Newspapers & Magazines The main newspaper in Sonoma Valley is the *Press Democrat,* a *New York Times* publication that is printed daily and distributed at newsstands throughout

Sonoma, Lake, Napa, and Mendocino counties. Sonoma now offers two local papers: The *Sonoma Index Tribune,* published twice a week and available at newsstands around town, covers regional news, events, and issues; *The Sun,* and its sister paper *El Sol de Sonoma,* out on Thursdays, stick to local news and events with a hipper viewpoint. Also available around town is the *Sonoma Valley Visitors Guide,* a slender free publication that lists just about every sightseeing, recreation, shopping, lodging, and dining option in the valley, as well as a winery map.

Pharmacy The pharmacy at **Longs Drugs,** 201 W. Napa St., Sonoma (© **707/938-4734**), is open Monday through Friday from 9am to 9pm, Saturday 10am to 7pm and Sunday from 10am to 6pm. If you prefer a more personable place to get your prescription filled, try **Pharmaca Integrative Pharmacy,** 303 W. Napa St., Sonoma (© **707/938-1147**). Although it's a national chain, Pharmaca maintains a down-home feel, and offers a full range of traditional medicines and prescriptions, as well as a wide variety of homeopathic remedies, and a very knowledgeable staff trained in both that is always available for a consultation. They also have a great variety of small gifts, beauty products, cards, and magazines. Delivery available. Open Monday through Friday 9am to 7pm, Saturday 9am to 6pm, and Sunday 10am to 6pm.

Police For the local police, call © **707/996-3602,** or in an emergency, call © **911.**

Post Offices In **downtown Sonoma,** the post office is at 617 Broadway, at Patton Street (© **707/996-9311**). The **Glen Ellen** post office is at 13720 Arnold Dr., at O'Donnell Lane (© **707/ 996-9233**). Both branches are open Monday through Friday from 8:30am to 5pm.

Shipping Companies See "The Ins & Outs of Shipping Wine Home," in chapter 3.

Taxis Call **A-C Taxi** at © **707/526-4888** or **Vern's Taxi** at © **707/ 938-8885.**

2 Touring the Wineries

Sonoma Valley is currently home to more than 40 wineries (including California's first winery, Buena Vista, founded in 1857) and 13,000 acres of vineyards, which produce roughly 40 types of wine.

Unlike the rigidly structured tours at many of Napa Valley's corporate-owned wineries, tastings and tours on the Sonoma side of the Mayacamas Mountains are low-key, often free, and include plenty of friendly banter between the winemakers and their guests.

The towns and wineries covered below are organized geographically from south to north, starting at the intersection of Highway 37 and Highway 121 in the Carneros District and ending in Kenwood. The wineries here tend to be a little more spread out than they are in Napa Valley, but they're easy to find. Still, it's best to decide which wineries you're most interested in and devise a touring strategy before you set out so you don't find yourself doing a lot of backtracking. (For more on this, see "Strategies for Touring the Wine Country," in chapter 3; and check out the map "Sonoma Valley Wineries" on p. 125 to get your bearings.)

Below is a great selection of Sonoma Valley wineries. If you'd like a complete list of local wineries, be sure to pick up one of the free guides to the valley available at the **Sonoma Valley Visitors Bureau** (see "Visitor Information," above).

THE CARNEROS DISTRICT

Roche   The first winery you'll encounter as you enter Sonoma Valley, Roche (pronounced *Rosh*) is typical of the area—a small, family-run operation that focuses on four varietals and has very limited distribution. (Roche wines, in fact, are sold exclusively through the tasting room.) Situated atop a gently sloping knoll, the ranch-style winery and surrounding 2,200 acres of vineyards and estate are owned by Genevieve and Joe Roche, who originally bought the property with no intention of starting a winery. But in the early 1980s, a colleague suggested that they experiment with a few vines of chardonnay—and the results were so impressive that they decided to go into business making estate-grown chardonnay, pinot noir, merlot, and syrah.

The Roches produce only about 6,000 to 10,000 cases per year, some of which are bought before the wine even hits the bottle. Tastings are complimentary for nonreserve wines, and prices range from $10 for a Tamarix pinot noir blend to $43 for the unfiltered estate reserve pinot noir. Picnic tables overlooking the valley and San Pablo Bay are available, though you'd probably prefer lunching at neighboring Viansa Winery and Italian Marketplace (see below).

28700 Arnold Dr. (Hwy. 121), Sonoma. ℂ **800/825-9475** or 707/935-7115. www. rochewinery.com. Daily 10am–6pm (5pm in winter). Tours available by appointment.

Sonoma Valley Wineries

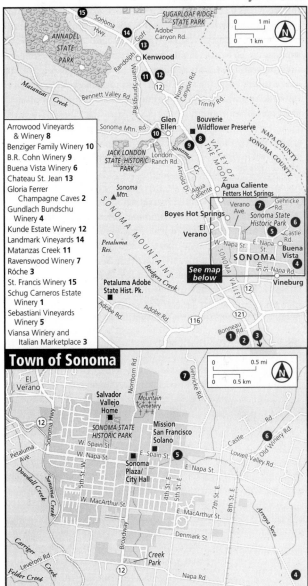

Arrowood Vineyards
  & Winery **8**
Benziger Family Winery **10**
B.R. Cohn Winery **9**
Buena Vista Winery **6**
Chateau St. Jean **13**
Gloria Ferrer
  Champagne Caves **2**
Gundlach Bundschu
  Winery **4**
Kunde Estate Winery **12**
Landmark Vineyards **14**
Matanzas Creek **11**
Ravenswood Winery **7**
Róche **3**
St. Francis Winery **15**
Schug Carneros Estate
  Winery **1**
Sebastiani Vineyards
  Winery **5**
Viansa Winery and
  Italian Marketplace **3**

Town of Sonoma

Viansa Winery and Italian Marketplace ⊛ *Finds*   This sprawling Tuscan-style villa perches atop a knoll overlooking the entire lower Sonoma Valley. Viansa is the brainchild of Sam and Vicki Sebastiani, who left the family dynasty to create their own temple to food and wine. (*Viansa* is a contraction of "Vicki and Sam.") While Sam, a third-generation winemaker, runs the winery, Vicki manages the marketplace, a large room crammed with a cornucopia of high-quality preserves, mustards, olive oils, pastas, salads, breads, desserts, Italian tableware, cookbooks, and wine-related gifts.

The winery, which sells its varietals exclusively at the winery and through their extensive mail-order business called the Tuscan Club, has established a favorable reputation for its Italian varietals such as muscat canelli, sangiovese, and nebbiolo. Five-dollar tastings are poured at the east end of the marketplace, and the self-guided tour includes a trip through the underground barrel-aging cellar adorned with colorful hand-painted murals. Free guided tours are held daily at 11am and 2pm.

Viansa is also one of the few wineries in Sonoma Valley that sells deli items—the focaccia sandwiches are delicious. You can dine alfresco while you admire the bucolic wetlands view.

25200 Arnold Dr. (Hwy. 121), Sonoma. ⓒ **800/995-4740** or 707/935-4700. www. viansa.com. Daily 10am–5pm. No appointment needed for the self-guided tour.

Gloria Ferrer Champagne Caves ⊛ *Finds*   When you have had it up to here with chardonnays and pinots, it's time to pay a visit to Gloria Ferrer, the grande dame of the Wine Country's sparkling-wine producers. Who's Gloria? She's the wife of José Ferrer, whose family has made sparkling wine for 5 centuries. The family business, Freixenet, is the largest producer of sparkling wine in the world; Cordon Negro is its most popular brand. That equals big bucks, and certainly a good chunk went into building this palatial estate. Glimmering like Oz high atop a gently sloping hill, it overlooks the verdant Carneros District. On a sunny day, enjoying a glass of dry brut while soaking in the magnificent views is a must.

If you're unfamiliar with the term *méthode champenoise,* be sure to take the free 30-minute tour of the fermenting tanks, bottling line, and caves brimming with racks of yeast-laden bottles. Afterward, retire to the elegant tasting room, order a glass of one of seven sparkling wines ($4–$10 a glass) or tastes of their eight still wines ($2 to $3 per taste), find an empty chair on the veranda, and say, "Ahhh. *This* is the life." There are picnic tables, but it's usually too windy for comfort, and you must buy a bottle (from around $18 to $40) or glass of sparkling wine to reserve a table.

23555 Carneros Hwy. (California 121), Sonoma. ℭ **707/996-7256.** www.gloria ferrer.com. Daily 10am–5:15pm. Tours daily; call day of visit to confirm schedule.

Schug Carneros Estate Winery   A native of Germany's Rhine River valley, Walter Schug (pronounced *Shewg*) comes from a long line of pinot noir vintners. After graduating from the prestigious German wine institute of Geisenheim in 1959, he came to California and worked as winemaker for Joseph Phelps, where he established his reputation as one of California's top cabernet sauvignon and Riesling producers. In 1980, he launched his own label from a vineyard he tended at Phelps, and he left soon afterward to build Schug Carneros Estate Winery. Since then, Schug's wines have achieved world-class status, and an astounding amount of his wine is sent overseas.

The winery is situated on top of a rise overlooking the surrounding Carneros District, a prime region for cool-climate grapes such as chardonnay and pinot noir (Schug's predominant wines). Its post-and-beam architecture reflects the Schug family's German heritage; the tasting room, however, is quite ordinary and small, designed more for practicality than pomp and circumstance (a radical contrast to neighboring Viansa and Gloria Ferrer). Typical of Sonoma wineries, there's no tasting fee for new releases (reserve tasting $5), and bottle prices are all quite reasonable, ranging from $15 for a Sonoma Valley sauvignon blanc to $50 for a Heritage reserve cabernet. The winery has new picnic facilities, but picnicking can be breezy when the winds upwell from the neighboring dairy farm. More fun: *pétanque* courts, Carneros views, and cave tours by appointment.

602 Bonneau Rd. (west of Hwy. 121), Sonoma. ℭ **800/966-9365** or 707/939-9363. www.schugwinery.com. Daily 10am–5pm. Tours by appointment only.

SONOMA

Gundlach Bundschu Winery 🦊🦊   If it looks like the people working here are actually enjoying themselves, that's because they are. Gundlach Bundschu (pronounced *Gun*-lock *Bun*-shoe) is the quintessential Sonoma winery—nonchalant in appearance but obsessed with wine: The GB clan are a nefarious lot, infamous for wild stunts such as holding up Napa's Wine Train on horseback and—egad!—serving Sonoma wines to their captives; the small tasting room looks not unlike a bomb shelter, the Talking Heads is their version of Muzak, and the "art" consists of a dozen witty black-and-white posters promoting GB wines.

This is the oldest continually family-owned and -operated winery in California, going into its sixth generation since Jacob Gundlach harvested his first crop in 1858. Drop in to sample chardonnay, pinot noir, merlot, cabernet, and more. Prices for the 14 distinct wines range from $20 per bottle for the Mountain Cuvee to $70 for the Vintage reserve cabernet sauvignon. Tastings are $5 and tours, which include a trip into the 430-foot cave, are held regularly on weekends on the hour from 12–3pm, and by appointment on weekdays.

Gundlach Bundschu has the best picnic grounds in the valley, though you have to walk to the top of Towles' Hill to earn the sensational view. They also have great activities (Midsummer Mozart Festival, film fests), so call or check the website if you want to join the fun.

2000 Denmark St. (off 8th St. E.), Sonoma. ☎ **707/938-5277**. www.gunbun.com. Daily 11am–4:30pm. Tours last 10–20 min. and are offered Sat–Sun on the hour 12–3pm; by appointment on weekdays.

Sebastiani Vineyards & Winery   The name Sebastiani is practically synonymous with Sonoma. What started in 1904, when Samuele Sebastiani began producing his first wines, has in three generations grown into a small empire, producing some 200,000 cases a year. After a few years of seismic retrofitting, a face-lift, and a temporary tasting room, the original 1904 winery is now open to the public with more extensive educational tours ($5 per person), an 80-foot S-shaped tasting bar, and lots of shopping opportunities in the gift shop. In the contemporary tasting room's minimuseum area you can see the winery's original turn-of-the-20th-century crusher and press, as well as the world's largest collection of oak-barrel carvings, crafted by bygone local artist Earle Brown. If it's merely wine that interests you, you can sample an extensive selection of wines for a price that ranges from complimentary to $18 for the fancy stuff, the latter of which includes a keepsake glass. Bottle prices are reasonable, ranging from $13 to $75. A picnic area adjoins the cellars; a far more scenic spot is across the parking lot in Sebastiani's Cherryblock Vineyards.

389 4th St. E., Sonoma. ☎ **800/888-5532** or 707/933-3200. www.sebastiani.com. Daily 10am–5pm. Tours: winter daily 11am and 3pm, summer 11am, 1pm, and 3pm.

Buena Vista Winery   Count Agoston Haraszthy, the Hungarian émigré who is universally regarded as the father of California's wine industry, founded this historic winery in 1857. A close friend of General Vallejo, Haraszthy returned from Europe in 1861 with 100,000 of the finest vine cuttings, which he made available to all growers.

Although Buena Vista's winemaking now takes place at an ultramodern facility in the Carneros District, the winery maintains a tasting room inside the restored 1862 Press House. The beautiful stone-crafted room brims with wines, wine-related gifts, and accessories.

Tastings are $5 for four wines, $10 for a flight of three library wines. You can take the self-guided tour any time during operating hours; a "Historical Tour and Tasting," offered daily at 11am and 2pm, details the life and times of Count Haraszthy and includes a viticultural tour and wine and food pairing. If you drop by on a Saturday you can also opt for the $35 wine and cheese tasting. After tasting, grab your favorite bottle, a selection of cheeses from the Sonoma Cheese Factory, salami, bread, and spreads (all available in the tasting room), and plant yourself at one of the many picnic tables in the lush, verdant setting.

18000 Old Winery Rd. (off E. Napa St., slightly northeast of downtown), Sonoma. ℂ 800/926-1266 or 707/265-1472. www.buenavistawinery.com. Nov–May daily 10am–5pm; June–Oct 10am–5:30pm.

Ravenswood Winery   Compared to old heavies like Sebastiani and Buena Vista, Ravenswood is a relative newcomer to the Sonoma wine scene. Nevertheless, it quickly established itself as the sine qua non of zinfandel, the versatile red grape that's known in these parts for being big, ripe, juicy, and powerful. The first winery in the United States to focus primarily on zins, which make up about three-quarters of its 700,000-case production, Ravenswood underscores zin's zest with their motto, "No Wimpy Wines." But they also produce merlot, cabernet sauvignon, Rhone varietals, and a small amount of chardonnay.

The winery is smartly designed—recessed into the hillside to protect its treasures from the simmering summers. Tours ($10 per person) follow the winemaking process from grape to glass, and include a visit to the aromatic oak-barrel aging rooms. You're welcome to bring your own picnic basket to any of the tables, but if you're coming on the weekend from Memorial Day to Labor Day, consider joining one of their famously fun barbecues (call for details). Regardless, tastings are $5 for four wines, which is refundable with purchase.

18701 Gehricke Rd. (off Lovall Valley Rd.), Sonoma. ℂ 888/NO-WIMPY or 707/933-2332. www.ravenswood-wine.com. Labor Day to Memorial Day 10am–4:30pm; Memorial Day to Labor Day 10am–5pm. Tours by reservation only at 10:30am.

GLEN ELLEN

B. R. Cohn Winery   You may not have heard of Bruce Cohn, but you've certainly heard of the Doobie Brothers, the San Francisco band he managed to fame and fortune. He used part of his share of that fortune to purchase this wonderfully bucolic estate with its whitewashed farmhouse and groves of rare olive trees. Cohn, a native of Sonoma County, started making his own wine in 1984 and was an immediate success. The tasting room showcases framed gold and platinum albums and is home to the friendly and informative staff who pours $5 tastings (applied toward purchase) of cabernet, pinot noir, chardonnay, syrah (new as of 2003), zinfandel, sauvignon blanc, rosé, Bruce's own SyrCab (get it?) and an occasional merlot. Bottle prices range from the mid-teens to $150, and the winery often sells selections that aren't available elsewhere. The winery also specializes in award-winning (and pricey) "gourmet" olive oils and hand-crafted vinegars. There are a few picnic tables on the property, but it's not a bad idea to bring along a blanket and relax on the terraced hills of plush lawn overlooking the vineyards.

15000 Sonoma Hwy. (Hwy. 12, just north of Madrone Rd.), Glen Ellen. © **800/330-4064**, ext. 24 or 707/938-4064. www.brcohn.com. Daily 10am–5pm. Tours by appointment.

Arrowood Vineyards & Winery   Richard Arrowood had already established a reputation as a master winemaker at Chateau St. Jean when he and his wife, Alis Demers Arrowood, set out on their own in 1986. Their picturesque winery stands on a gently rising hillside lined with perfectly manicured vineyards. Tastings take place in the Hospitality House, the newer of Arrowood's two stately gray-and-white buildings. They're fashioned after New England farmhouses, complete with wraparound porches. Richard's focus is on making world-class wine with minimal intervention, and his results are impressive: More than one of his current releases has scored over 90 points in *Wine Spectator.* Mind you, excellence doesn't come cheap: A taste here is $5 or $10 for four limited-production wines, but if you're curious about what near-perfection tastes like, it's well worth it. *Note:* No picnic facilities are available here.

14347 Sonoma Hwy. (California 12), Glen Ellen. © **707/935-2600**. www.arrowood vineyards.com. Daily 10am–4:30pm. Tours by appointment only, daily at 10:30am and 2:30pm.

Benziger Family Winery ⟨ *Finds*   A visit here confirms that this is indeed a family winery. At any given time, two generations of Benzigers (*Ben*-zig-ers) may be running around tending to chores, and they instantly make you feel as if you're part of the clan. The pastoral, user-friendly property features an exceptional self-guided tour of the certified biodynamic winery ("The most comprehensive tour in the wine industry," according to *Wine Spectator*), gardens, and a spacious tasting room staffed by amiable folks. The $10 45-minute tram tour, pulled by a beefy tractor, is both informative and fun. It winds through the estate vineyards and into caves, and ends with a tasting. ***Tip:*** Tram tickets—a hot item in the summer—are available on a first-come, first-served basis, so either arrive early or stop by in the morning to pick up afternoon tickets.

Tastings of the standard-release wines are $5. Tastes that include several limited-production wines or reserve or estate wines cost $10. The winery offers several scenic picnic spots.

1883 London Ranch Rd. (off Arnold Dr., on the way to Jack London State Historic Park), Glen Ellen. ✆ 800/989-8890 or 707/935-3000. www.benziger.com. Tasting room daily 10am–5pm. Tram tours daily (weather permitting) $10 adults and $5 children at 11:30am, noon, 12:30, 1:30, 2:30, and 3:30pm.

KENWOOD

Kunde Estate Winery   Expect a friendly, unintimidating welcome at this scenic winery, run by five generations of the Kundes since 1904. One of the largest grape suppliers in the area, the Kunde family (pronounced *Kun*-dee) has devoted 800 acres of its 2,000-acre ranch to growing ultrapremium-quality grapes, which it provides to many Sonoma and Napa wineries. This abundance allows the Kundes to make nothing but estate wines (wines made from grapes grown on the Kunde property, as opposed to also using grapes purchased from other growers).

The tasting room is located in a spiffy 17,000-square-foot wine-making facility, which features specialized crushing equipment that enables the winemaker to run whole clusters to the press—a real advantage in white-wine production. Tastings of four estate releases are $5 (refunded with purchase) and reserve tastings will set you back $10; bottle prices range from $15 for a Magnolia Lane sauvignon blanc to $50 for a Drummond Vineyards cabernet sauvignon; most labels sell in the high teens. The tasting room also has a gift shop and large windows overlooking the bottling room and tank room.

The tour of the property's extensive wine caves includes a history of the winery. Private tours are available by appointment, but most folks are happy to just stop by for some *vino* and to relax at one of the many patio tables placed around the man-made pond. Animal lovers will appreciate Kunde's preservation efforts: The property has a duck estuary with more than 50 species (which can be seen by appointment only).

10155 Sonoma Hwy., Kenwood. ☎ **707/833-5501.** www.kunde.com. Tastings daily 10:30am–4:30pm. Cave tours Tues–Thurs 11am, Fri–Mon on the hour 11am–3pm.

Kenwood Vineyards Kenwood's history dates from 1906, when the Pagani brothers made their living selling wine straight from the barrel and into the jug. In 1970 the Lee family bought the property and dumped a ton of money into converting the aging winery into a modern, high-production facility (most of it cleverly concealed in the original barnlike buildings). Since then, Kenwood has earned a solid reputation for consistent quality with each of its varietals: cabernet sauvignon, chardonnay, zinfandel, pinot noir, merlot and, most popular, sauvignon blanc—a crisp, light wine with hints of melon.

Although the winery looks rather modest in size, its output is staggering: nearly 500,000 cases of ultrapremium wines fermented in steel tanks and French and American oak barrels. Popular with collectors is winemaker Michael Lee's Artist Series cabernet sauvignon, a limited production from the winery's best vineyards, featuring labels with original artwork by renowned artists. The tasting room, housed in one of the old barns, offers complimentary tastes, $2 to $5 tastings of private reserve wines, and gift items for purchase. *FYI:* The Lees no longer own the winery.

9592 Sonoma Hwy. (California 12), Kenwood. ☎ **707/833-5891.** www.kenwood vineyards.com. Daily 10am–4:30pm. No tours.

Chateau St. Jean ☆ *Finds* Chateau St. Jean is notable for its exceptionally beautiful buildings, expansive landscaped grounds, and gourmet marketlike tasting room. Among California wineries, it's a pioneer in vineyard designation—the procedure of making wine from, and naming it for, a single vineyard. A private drive takes you to what was once a 250-acre country retreat built in 1920; a well-manicured lawn overlooking the meticulously maintained vineyards is now a picnic area, complete with a fountain and picnic tables.

In the huge tasting room—where there's also a charcuterie shop and plenty of housewares for sale—you can sample Chateau St. Jean's wide array of wines. They range from chardonnays and cabernet sauvignon to fumé blanc, merlot, Johannesburg Riesling, and gewürztraminer. Tastings are $5 per person; $10 per person for reserve wines.

8555 Sonoma Hwy. (California 12), Kenwood. ☎ **800/543-7572** or 707/833-4134. www.chateaustjean.com. Tasting daily 10am–5pm. Tours 11am and 3pm. At the foot of Sugarloaf Ridge, just north of Kenwood and east of Hwy. 12.

St. Francis Winery   Although St. Francis Winery makes a commendable chardonnay, zinfandel, and cabernet sauvignon, it's their highly coveted merlot that they're best known for. Winemaker Tom Mackey, a former high-school English teacher from San Francisco, has been hailed as the "Master of Merlot" by *Wine Spectator* for his uncanny ability to craft the finest merlot in California.

If you've visited this winery and haven't been here in a while, don't follow your memory to the front door. In 2001, St. Francis moved a little farther north to digs bordering on the Santa Rosa County line. The original property was planted in 1910 as part of a wedding gift to Alice Kunde (scion of the local Kunde family) and christened St. Francis of Assisi in 1971 when Joe Martin and Lloyd Canton—two white-collar executives turned vintners—completed their long-awaited dream winery. Today the winery still owns the property, but there's new history in the making at their much larger facilities, which include a tasting room and upscale gift shop. Tastings are $10 for four current releases. The $20 for reserve tasting is paired with food, served in the private reserve tasting room, and requires an appointment. Now that St. Francis is planning more special activities, it's worthwhile to call or check their website for their calendar of events.

100 Pythian Rd. (California 12/Sonoma Hwy.), Santa Rosa (at the Kenwood border). ✆ 800/543-7713 or 707/833-4666. www.stfranciswinery.com. Daily 10am–5pm.

Landmark Vineyards   One of California's oldest exclusively chardonnay estates was first founded in 1972 in the Windsor area of Northern Sonoma County. When new housing development started encroaching on the winery's territory, proprietor Damaris Deere W. Ethridge (great-great-granddaughter of John Deere, the tractor baron) moved her operation to Northern Sonoma Valley in 1990. The winery, which produces about 27,000 cases annually, is housed in a modest, mission-style building set on 11 acres of vineyards. The tasting room offers complimentary samples of current releases and pours reserve tastings for $10. (Note the wall-to-wall mural behind the tasting counter painted by noted Sonoma County artist Claudia Wagar.) Wine prices range from $15 for the Courtyard chardonnay to $45 for a reserve pinot noir.

The winery has a pond-side picnic area, as well as what is probably the only professional bocce court in the valley (yes, you can play, and yes, they provide instructions). Also available from Memorial Day to Labor Day are free Belgian horse–drawn wagon tours through the vineyards, offered every Saturday from 11:30am to 3pm.

101 Adobe Canyon Rd. (just east of Hwy. 12), Kenwood. ℂ **800/452-6365** or 707/ 833-1144. www.landmarkwine.com. Daily 10am–4:30pm. Tours available by appointment.

3 More to See & Do

If you tire of visiting Sonoma Valley wineries, you can explore the valley's numerous other sites and attractions. The majority of activities are centered around the town of Sonoma, which is small enough to explore on foot. (The picturesque town plaza is truly worth checking out.) If the weather's warm, I strongly recommend a guided tour of Sonoma Valley via horseback or bicycle, two of the best things to do in the Wine Country (p. 138 and 122).

THE CARNEROS DISTRICT

BIPLANE RIDES   For the adrenaline junkie in your group, **Vintage Aircraft Company** ⍣ will help you lose your lunch on one of its authentic 1940 Boeing-built Stearman biplanes. Rides range from the scenic (a leisurely flight over Sonoma Valley) and aerobatic (loops, rolls, and assorted maneuvers) to—drumroll, please—the kamikaze, an intensely bowel-shaking aerobatic death wish that's (and I quote) "not for the faint of heart." For two people, prices start at $190 for the scenic, $250 for the kamikaze and $295 for the explorer, an extended ride over Napa and Sonoma or the Coast. They now also offer Warbird plane rides ranging from $250 to $550. Vintage Aircraft Company is at the Sonoma Valley Airport, 23982 Arnold Dr. (on Hwy. 121, across from Gloria Ferrer Champagne Caves), Sonoma Valley (ℂ **707/938-2444;** www.vintage aircraft.com). Closed Tuesdays. Call for reservations.

A GARDEN TOUR   Garden lovers should pull over for a $9 gander at the latest downtown Sonoma addition, the **Cornerstone Festival of Gardens,** 23570 Arnold Drive, Sonoma (ℂ **707/933-3010;** kids 4 to 12 are $3 and kids under 4 are free; locals, senior, and student discounts available). Modeled in part after the International Garden festival at Chaumont-sur-Loire in France's Loire Valley and the Grand-Métis in Quebec, Canada, the nine-acre property is the first gallery-style garden exhibit in the United States and includes a series of 15 ever-changing gardens designed by famed landscape architects and designers. With a recently added children's garden featuring a brightly painted water tower, sand moat, and buckets of plastic plumbing fittings, this is a great spot if you're traveling with a family. And on the first and third Saturday of each month, they host a children's craft area in a barn from 11am to 3pm. If you work up an appetite, stop by the **Market Café** for light breakfast, pastries, and espresso drinks or their seasonal lunch menu including soup, salads, and sandwiches. If you get inspired, you can load up on loot here that will help your own garden grow—from furniture and gifts to plants, garden art, and books. The gardens are open daily 10am to 5pm from April 1 to December 19; tours by appointment during winter; the shops and cafe are open year round.

SONOMA

The best way to learn about the history of Sonoma is to follow the self-guided *Sonoma Walking Tour* map, provided by the Sonoma League for Historic Preservation. Tour highlights include General Vallejo's 1852 Victorian-style home; the Sonoma Barracks, erected in 1836 to house Mexican army troops; and the Blue Wing Inn, an 1840 hostelry built to accommodate travelers—including John Fremont, Kit Carson, and Ulysses S. Grant—and new settlers while they erected homes in Sonoma. You can purchase the map for $2.75 at the **Sonoma Valley Visitors Bureau** (see "Visitor Information," earlier in this chapter) as well as at the Sonoma Barracks, which is next door to the Mission.

Also worth a look is the **Mission San Francisco Solano de Sonoma,** located on Sonoma Plaza, at the corner of 1st Street East and Spain Street (© **707/938-9560**). Founded in 1823, this was the northernmost—and last—mission built in California. It also was the only mission established on the northern coast by the Mexican government, which wanted to protect its territory from expansionist Russian fur traders. It's now part of Sonoma State Historic Park. Admission is $2 for adults, free for children 17 and under. It's open daily from 10am to 5pm except New Year's Day, Thanksgiving, and Christmas.

It may not be all bells and whistles for adults, but add steam, and that's exactly what **Train Town** is for tots. In this 10-acre mini-amusement park the theme is locomotion—as in train rides around the wooded property, over bridges, and past doting parents. Other attractions include a petting zoo, Ferris wheel, and carousel. Train Town is on Broadway, between MacArthur Street and Napa Road, Sonoma (© **707/938-3912;** www.traintown.com). The train keeps a-rolling Friday through Sunday from 10am to 5pm September 1 through May and daily 10am to 5pm June through Labor Day. Train rides cost $3.75 each, and the other attractions are $1.75 per person.

Moments **The Super Spa**

The **Sonoma Mission Inn, Spa & Country Club,** 18140 Sonoma Hwy., Sonoma (© **800/862-4945** or 707/938-9000; www.fairmont.com/sonoma), has always been the most complete—and the most luxurious—spa in the entire Wine Country. With its recent $20-million, 43,000-square-foot facility, this super spa is now one of the best in the country. The Spanish mission–style retreat offers more than 50 spa treatments, ever-popular natural mineral baths, and virtually every facility and activity imaginable. You can pamper yourself silly: Take a sauna or herbal steam, have a facial set to music, indulge in a grape-seed body wrap, relax with a massage, go for a dip in the outdoor pool, or soak away your worries in the celestial indoor mineral pool area—the list goes on and on (and, alas, so will the bill). You can also work off those wicked Wine Country meals with aerobics, weights, and cardio machines; get loose in a yoga class; or just lounge and lunch by the pool. There is a catch, however: Since the renovations, the spa has become "private," which means you must be a guest to reap the relaxation rewards. However, they do offer personalized day spa packages, which range in price from $159 to $459 depending on what you request and include use of the pool, classes, and hot tub. If you don't mind splurging and are a fan of luxury living, you'll agree that the Sonoma Mission Inn Spa is one of the best ways to unwind in the Wine Country.

SHOPPING Most of Sonoma's shops, which offer everything from food and wine to clothing and books, are located around the plaza. **The Mercado,** a small shopping center at 452 1st St. E., houses several good stores that sell unusual wares. The **Arts Guild of Sonoma,** 140 E. Napa St. (© 707/996-3115), showcases the works of local artists in a wide variety of styles and media. It's open Sunday, Monday, Wednesday and Thursday from 11am to 5pm, Friday and Saturday from 11am to 9pm. Admission is free. For the closest thing to a trendy city boutique, check out **The Loop,** on the square at 461 1st St. W. (© **707/939-8400**). They carry names you've heard before (Think Diane von Furstenberg and Citizen of

Humanity.) and some you haven't heard yet, plus accessories, bath products, and a sprinkling of local artists' work. It's open Monday through Saturday 10am to 6pm, Sunday 11am to 5pm. Not for the claustrophobic, **Sign of the Bear,** on the square at 435 1st St. W. (© 707/996-3722), is filled to the brim with every possible kitchen gadget available—and I do mean *every,* with 17,000 available items ranging from three cent replacement corks to cookware sets that'll set you back close to a grand. The staff is incredibly enthusiastic and always on hand to help with any questions. They're open 10am to 6pm daily, closed major holidays. For interesting, funky gifts with an international flair stop by **Baksheesh** at 423 1st St. W. (© 707/ 939-2847), where you'll find handcrafted goods made by artisans in the developing world who would otherwise be unemployed. Check out the kids' offerings; they're a welcome departure from the usual plastic characters you'll find elsewhere. Open Monday through Saturday 10am to 6pm and Sunday noon to 6pm. Just off the square in the historic Torres House is **Etre** ✪, 156 E. Napa St. (© 707/ 939-2700), a chic "home emporium and apothecary" carrying everything from luxuriously soft linens to heavenly soaps to antiques to women's accessories and great gifts. Open Monday and Wednesday through Saturday from 11am to 6pm and Sunday 11am to 5pm. Closed Tuesday.

Another good stop along the plaza is **Wine Exchange** ✪, 452 1st St. E. (© 707/938-1794), which carries more than 700 domestic wines, books on wine, wine paraphernalia, olive oils, and a small selection of cigars. It's a great place to begin your wine experience: You can browse though the numerous racks of bottles and ask questions of the wine-savvy staff. Even the beer connoisseur who's feeling displaced in the Wine Country will be happy at Wine Exchange, where you can find close to 300 beers from around the world. There are $1 wine and beer tastings daily at the small bar in back, which is occupied most evenings by a gaggle of friendly locals. Wine Exchange is open daily from 10am to 6pm. Shipping is available anywhere in the United States.

THE LOCAL FARMER'S MARKET   Obsessed with farm-fresh produce, Sonomans host a year-round **Sonoma Valley Farmer's Market** every Friday morning from 9am to noon at Depot Park on 1st Street West (just north of E. Spain St.). Dozens of growers offer fresh fruits, vegetables, flowers, homemade jams, honey, barbecued turkey, baked goods, and handmade crafts from local artists. It's such a popular gathering place for locals and visitors alike that they added a Tuesday-night market from 5:30pm to dusk April through October. The Tuesday market is held at the plaza in front of City Hall. (There's also a Saturday morning market from 9am to noon on the corner of Oakmont Drive and White Oak in Santa Rosa, about 5 min. north of Kenwood.)

GLEN ELLEN

Hikers, mountain bikers, horseback riders, and picnickers will enjoy a day spent at **Jack London State Historic Park** *ƒ*, 2400 London Ranch Rd., off Arnold Drive (*©* 707/938-5216). On its 800-plus acres, which were once home to the renowned writer, you'll find 10 miles of trails, the remains of London's burned-down dream house (as well as some preserved structures), and plenty of ideal picnic spots. An on-site museum, called the House of Happy Walls, was built by Jack's wife to display a collection from the author's life. The grounds are open 9:30am to 5pm daily; the museum is open daily from 10am to 5pm. Admission to the park is $6 per car, $5 per car for seniors 62 and over. Pick up the $1 self-guided tour map on arrival to get acquainted with the grounds. In summer, golf-cart rides also are offered from noon to 4pm on weekends for those who don't want to hoof it.

SHOPPING   Gourmands might want to stop by **The Olive Press,** 14301 Arnold Dr., in Jack London Village (*©* **800/9-OLIVE-9** or 707/939-8900). With olive trees abounding in the area and the locals' penchant for gourmet foods, it's no surprise that fresh-pressed olive oil has become a lucrative business in this neck of the woods. Everyone from large commercial outfits to small-volume growers and hobbyists can pile their olives in the hopper and watch the state-of-the-art, Italian-made olive press in action, as it conveys the fruit up a belt, cleans it, and begins the pressing process. There's also a nifty tasting bar and retail shop, but don't expect a bargain here; even if you bring your own bottle, a gallon of oil can go for $128. (You'd be surprised how many olives it takes to make a gallon.) The Press also carries numerous varieties of extra virgin flavored and infused olive oils, cured olives, and olive-related foods, gifts, and books. Open daily from 10am to 5pm.

HORSEBACK RIDING   Long before Sonoma Valley became part of the Wine Country, it was better known as cattle country—and there's no better way to explore the land's old roots than with a guided horseback tour provided by the **Triple Creek Horse Outfit** (*©* **707/933-1600;** www.triplecreekhorseoutfit.com), which will lead you on a leisurely stroll—with the occasional trot thrown in for thrills. April through October, you can take a memorable ride through the beautiful Jack London State Historic Park. The ride takes you past vineyards owned by London's descendants, across meadows blanketed with lupine, around a lake originally dammed by London, and up to enjoy Sonoma Mountain's panoramic views. Triple Creek also offers regular, sunset, and full-moon rides at Sugarloaf Ridge at the northern end of Sonoma Valley; a route that also winds through deep, shady forests and up to ridge tops with spectacular 360-degree views. A third itinerary, through the Bothe-Napa Valley State Park, takes you along Ritchey Creek through a shady redwood and Douglas fir forest. Two-hour rides start at $70, and 1-hour rides start at $60. Call for additional information and prices.

GOLF   Thanks to the valley's mild climate, golf is a year-round pursuit. At the northern end of Sonoma Valley is the semiprivate **Oakmont Golf Club,** 7025 Oakmont Dr., off the Sonoma Highway, Santa Rosa (© **707/539-0415;** www.oakmontgc.com), which has two 18-hole championship courses, both designed by Ted Robinson, as well as a driving range and a clubhouse. The par 63 East course is considered the most challenging, and the par 72 West course is for higher-handicapped golfers. Greens fees are $32 Monday through Thursday, $37 Friday, and $50 weekends and holidays; carts are $14 per rider. Reservations are recommended at least a day in advance on weekdays, and at least a week in advance on weekends, but walk-ins are welcome too.

Originally designed by Sam Whiting in 1926, the **Sonoma Golf Club,** 17700 Arnold Dr., off Boyes Drive (pro shop © **707/996-0300**), was completely remodeled in 1991 by Robert Muir Graves. It is only accessible if you're a member, or are staying at the Fairmont Sonoma Mission Inn (p. 140). Its par 72, 18-hole, 7,069-yard championship course is mostly flat, with several tight doglegs around an armada of redwoods and oaks. The clubhouse was completely renovated in 2005 and there are also locker rooms and a driving range available. Greens fees ($160 daily; packages available through the hotel) include a cart and use of the driving range. A strict dress code is enforced.

If you're a beginner or just want to bone up on your irons game, **Los Arroyos Golf Club,** 5000 Stage Gulch Rd. off Arnold Drive, a short drive from downtown Sonoma (pro shop © **707/938-8835**), is for you. The small 9-hole course is fairly flat and inexpensive—$12 for 9 holes and $17 for eighteen holes on weekdays; weekends it's $14 and $20. Pull carts are an extra $2; club rentals are also available. It's open on a first-come, first-play basis from 7am until one hour before dusk. Senior discounts available.

4 Where to Stay

When planning your trip, keep in mind that during the high season—between April and November—most hotels charge peak rates and sell out completely on weekends; many have a 2-night minimum. Always ask about discounts, particularly during midweek, when most hotels and B&Bs drop their rates by as much as 30%. During the off season, you will have far better bargaining power and may be able to get a room at almost half the summer rate.

The accommodations listed below are arranged first by area and then by price, using the following categories: **Very Expensive,** more than $250 per night; **Expensive,** $200 to $250 per night; **Moderate,** $150 to $200 per night; and **Inexpensive,** less than $150 per night. (Sorry, the reality is that anything less than $150 a night qualifies as inexpensive 'round these parts.)

HELP WITH RESERVATIONS If you are having trouble finding a room, try calling the **Sonoma Valley Visitors Bureau** (② 707/996-1090; www.sonomavalley.com), which can refer you to a lodging that has a room to spare (but won't make reservations for you). The **Bed and Breakfast Association of Sonoma Valley** (② 800/969-4667; www.sonomabb.com) can refer you to one of its member B&Bs, inns, cottages, or vacation rentals and can make reservations for you as well.

SONOMA
VERY EXPENSIVE

Fairmont Sonoma Mission Inn & Spa 🎔🎔🎔 As you drive through Boyes Hot Springs, you may wonder why someone decided to build a multimillion-dollar spa resort in this ordinary little town. There's no view to speak of, and it certainly isn't within walking distance of any wineries or fancy restaurants. So what's the deal? It's the naturally heated artesian mineral water, piped from directly underneath the spa into the temperature-controlled pools and whirlpools. Set on 12 meticulously groomed acres, the Sonoma Mission Inn consists of a massive three-story replica of a Spanish mission (well, aside from the pink paint job) built in 1927, an array of satellite wings housing numerous superluxury suites and world-class spa facilities. It's a popular retreat for the wealthy and well known, so

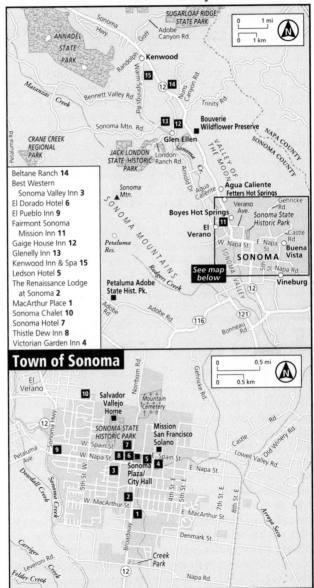

Sonoma Valley Accommodations

Beltane Ranch **14**
Best Western
  Sonoma Valley Inn **3**
El Dorado Hotel **6**
El Pueblo Inn **9**
Fairmont Sonoma
  Mission Inn **11**
Gaige House Inn **12**
Glenelly Inn **13**
Kenwood Inn & Spa **15**
Ledson Hotel **5**
The Renaissance Lodge
  at Sonoma **2**
MacArthur Place **1**
Sonoma Chalet **10**
Sonoma Hotel **7**
Thistle Dew Inn **8**
Victorian Garden Inn **4**

Town of Sonoma

don't be surprised if you see a famous face. (I bumped into Tiffani-Amber Thiessen of *Beverly Hills 90210* in the spa dressing room during my last visit.) Big changes have occurred here since the resort changed ownership in 2000. It has gained 60 suites, updated its spa to the tune of $20 million, and just finished a $62 million renovation, which included completely redoing the Heritage Rooms in understated country elegance. Fancier digs include more modern rooms with plantation-style shutters, ceiling fans, down comforters, and oversize bath towels. The Wine Country rooms have king-size beds, desks, refrigerators, and huge limestone and marble bathrooms; some offer wood-burning fireplaces, too, and many have balconies. For the ultimate in luxury, the opulently appointed Mission Suites are the way to go. Golfers will be glad to know the resort also has the Sonoma Golf Club, home to the PGA championship every October.

Corner of Boyes Blvd. and California 12 (P.O. Box 1447), Sonoma, CA 95476. © 800/257-7544 or 707/938-9000. Fax 707/938-4250. www.fairmont.com/sonoma. 226 units. $199–$1,000 double. AE, DC, MC, V. Valet parking is free for day use (spa goers) and $14 for overnight guests. From central Sonoma, drive 3 miles north on Hwy. 12 and turn left on Boyes Blvd. **Amenities:** 2 restaurants; 2 large heated outdoor pools; golf course; health club and spa (see box, "The Super Spa," on p. 136 for the complete rundown); Jacuzzi; sauna; bike rental; concierge; business center; salon; free wine tasting (4:30-5:30pm); room service (6am–11pm); babysitting; same-day laundry service/dry cleaning. *In room:* A/C, TV, dataport, minibar, hair dryer, iron, safe, high-speed Internet access ($13 per day), complimentary bottle of wine upon arrival.

Ledson Hotel 🕿🕿 Sonoma Square's hottest, chicest abode might look like a historic landmark, but this two-story, six-room luxury inn was brand-spanking new when it debuted in 2003. The regal brick hotel with ornate railings and an antiquated aura is the realized dream of vintner Steve Ledson who wanted to create the ultimate luxury hotel that gave a nod to the past through decor and a wink at the future with amenities. The result is six ultra-opulent rooms adorned with period furnishings, lots of rich fabrics, hardwood floors, Italian marble, fresh flowers, king-size beds, whirlpool tubs, fireplaces, balconies, surround-sound television and digital music, high-speed Internet access, and a welcoming of in-room wine and cheese. Alas, there are no public areas to speak of; you actually enter through a side door or through the hotel's restaurant, Harmony Club, which takes up the entire first floor, opens onto the plaza, and is a great wine bar and restaurant serving up tasty, albeit expensive French-inspired cuisine, Ledson wines, and live jazz.

480 1st St. E. (at the plaza), Sonoma CA 95476. © **707/996-9779**. Fax 707/996-9776. www.ledsonhotel.com. 6 units. $350–$395. Rates include full breakfast served in the Harmony Club. AE, DISC, MC, V. **Amenities:** Restaurant and wine bar. *In room:* A/C, TV, dataport, whirlpool tub, hair dryer, iron, digital music with surround sound.

MacArthur Place 🐞🐞   A highly recommended alternative to the Fairmont Sonoma Mission Inn & Spa (see above) is this much smaller and more intimate luxury property and spa located 4 blocks south of Sonoma's plaza. Once a 300-acre vineyard and ranch, MacArthur Place has since been whittled down to a 5½-acre "country estate" replete with landscaped gardens and tree-lined pathways, various free-standing accommodations, and a spa and heated swimming pool and whirlpool. Most of the individually decorated guest rooms are Victorian-modern cottages scattered throughout the resort; all are exceedingly well stocked with custom linens, oversize comforters, and original artwork. The newer suites come with fireplaces, porches, wet bars, six-speaker surround sound, and whirlpool tubs that often have shutters opening to the bedroom. Everyone has access to complimentary wine and cheese in the evening and the DVD library anytime. The full-service spa offers a fitness center, body treatments, skin care, and massages. Within the resort's restored century-old barn is Saddles, Sonoma's only steakhouse specializing in grass-fed beef, organic and sustainably farmed produce, and whimsically classy Western decor. An array of other excellent restaurants—as well as shops, wineries, and bars—is a short walk away. In fact, that's where MacArthur Place has Sonoma Mission Inn beat: Once you park your car here, you can *leave* it parked during a good part of your stay. *Note:* All rooms are nonsmoking.

29 E. MacArthur St., Sonoma, CA 95476. © **800/722-1866** or 707/938-2929. www.macarthurplace.com. 64 units. Sun–Thurs $299–$499 double; Fri–Sat $349–$550 double. Rates include continental breakfast. AE, MC, V. Free parking. **Amenities:** Restaurant and bar specializing in martinis; outdoor heated pool; exercise room; full-service spa; outdoor Jacuzzi; steam room; rental bikes; concierge; limited room service; massage; laundry service; same-day dry cleaning. *In room:* A/C, TV/DVD, dataport, hair dryer, iron, wireless Internet access ($10 per day), wet bar and coffeemaker in suites.

EXPENSIVE

Best Western Sonoma Valley Inn 🧒   There are just two reasons to stay here: 1) It's the only place left with a vacancy or 2) you're bringing the kids along. Otherwise, unless you don't mind staying in a rather drab room with thin walls and small bathrooms, you're probably going to be a little disappointed. Kids, on the other hand, will love this place: There's plenty of room to run around, plus a large heated outdoor pool, gazebo-covered spa, and sauna to play in. The rooms *do* come with a lot of perks, such as continental breakfast delivered to your room each morning, a gift bottle of white Sonoma Valley wine (chilling in the fridge), and satellite TV with HBO. Most rooms have either a balcony or a deck overlooking the inner courtyard. The inn is also in a good location, just a block from Sonoma's plaza.

550 2nd St. W. (1 block from the plaza), Sonoma, CA 95476. ℂ **800/334-5784** or 707/938-9200. Fax 707/938-0935. www.sonomavalleyinn.com. 80 units. $114–$361 double. Rates include continental breakfast. AE, DC, DISC, MC, V. **Amenities:** Heated outdoor pool; exercise room; Jacuzzi; sauna; steam room; free wireless Internet access. *In room:* A/C, TV, dataport, fridge, coffeemaker, hair dryer, iron.

El Dorado Hotel 🐸🐸   This 1843 mission revival building may look like a 19th-century Wild West relic from the outside, but inside it's all 21st-century deluxe. Each modern, handsomely appointed guest room has French windows and tiny balconies. Some rooms offer lovely views of the plaza; others overlook the private courtyard and heated lap pool. All rooms (except those for guests with disabilities) are on the second floor and were upgraded in 2004. The four rooms on the ground floor are off the private courtyard, and each has a partially enclosed patio. Though prices reflect its prime location on Sonoma Square, this is still one of the more charming options within its price range.

405 1st St. W., Sonoma, CA 95476. ℂ **800/289-3031** or 707/996-3030. Fax 707/ 996-3148. www.hoteleldorado.com. 27 units. Summer $170–$190 double; winter $135–$155 double. AE, MC, V. **Amenities:** Restaurant; heated outdoor pool; free access to nearby health club; concierge; room service (11:30am–10pm); laundry service; dry cleaning. *In room:* A/C, TV/DVD, dataport, fridge, hair dryer, iron, CD player.

The Renaissance Lodge at Sonoma 🐸🐸   Not surprisingly, a large-scale hotel finally made its way to downtown Sonoma. The good news is that this one, which is privately owned but operated by Marriott, takes into account its surroundings, offering some country charm in its 182 rooms. At the center of this resort is a U-shaped building with a classic big-hotel lobby, the Carneros restaurant with decent food and city-slick ambience, and a large courtyard swimming pool with plenty of lounge chairs. The very tasteful and spacious accommodations in the main building are decorated in various shades of earth tones and come complete with prints by local artists, artistic lighting fixtures, balconies or patios, and some fireplaces and tubs with shutters that open from the lovely bathroom to the bedroom. The two-story cottages along the property are especially appealing because they're surrounded by trees, flowers, and shrubs and offer a sense of seclusion. All rooms have great robes and bath amenities. The full-service spa, where I've consistently had one of the best massages of my life, makes excellent use of its outdoor public space, with a number of small pools surrounded by lush plants. And as a bonus after your treatment, you get to hang around the pool all day if you want to.

1325 Broadway, Sonoma, CA 95476. ✆ **888/710-8008** or 707/935-6600. Fax 707/935-6829. www.thelodgeatsonoma.com. 182 units. $159–$349 double. AE, MC, V. **Amenities:** Restaurant; large heated outdoor pool; health club and spa; Jacuzzi; concierge; business center; limited room service; in-room massage. *In room:* A/C, TV w/pay movies, dataport, wet bar in suites and some rooms, coffeemaker, hair dryer, iron.

MODERATE

El Pueblo Inn Located on Sonoma's main east-west street, 8 blocks from the center of town, this isn't Sonoma's fanciest hotel, but it did just undergo renovations, is well cared for, and offers some of the best-priced accommodations around. The rooms here are pleasant enough, with individual entrances, post-and-beam construction, exposed brick walls, light-wood furniture, and geometric prints. A new addition in 2002 resulted in 20 new larger rooms with high ceilings, DVDs, and fireplaces in some rooms. They also recently made each room open to a courtyard with a fountain. Their new reception area doubles as a breakfast room for their continental breakfast and leads to a small meeting room. Reservations should be made at least a month in advance for the spring and summer months.

896 W. Napa St., Sonoma, CA 95476. ✆ **800/900-8844** or 707/996-3651. Fax 707/935-5988. www.elppuebloinn.com. 53 units. May–Oct $120–$280 double; Nov–Apr $110–$195 double. AE, DC, DISC, MC, V. Corporate, AAA, and senior discounts available. **Amenities:** Seasonal heated outdoor pool; Jacuzzi; fitness room; in-room massage. *In room:* A/C, TV, DVD (newer rooms only), fridge, coffeemaker and biscotti, hair dryer, iron, high-speed Internet access.

Sonoma Chalet ⚜ This is one of the few accommodations in Sonoma that's truly secluded; it's on the outskirts of town, in a peaceful country setting overlooking a 200-acre ranch. The accommodations, housed in a Swiss-style farmhouse and several cottages, have all been delightfully decorated by someone with an eye for color and a concern for comfort. You'll find claw-foot tubs, country quilts, Oriental carpets, comfortable furnishings, and private decks; some units have wood stoves or fireplaces. The two least expensive rooms share a bathroom, and the cottages offer the most privacy. A breakfast of fruit, yogurt, pastries, and cereal is served either in the country kitchen or in your room. If you like country rustic, you'll like the Sonoma Chalet.

18935 5th St. W., Sonoma, CA 95476. (C) **800/938-3129** or 707/938-3129. www. sonomachalet.com. 7 units, including 3 cottages. Apr–Oct $110–$225 double; Nov–Mar $110–$195 double. Rates include continental breakfast. AE, MC, V. **Amenities:** Hot tub. *In room:* A/C, coffeemaker in cottages, hair dryer, iron on request, no phone.

Sonoma Hotel ᐟ This cute little historic hotel on Sonoma's tree-lined town plaza emphasizes 19th-century elegance and comfort. Built in 1880 by German immigrant Henry Weyl, it has attractive guest rooms decorated in early California style, with French country furnishings, wood and iron beds, and pine armoires. In a bow to modern luxuries, recent additions include private bathrooms, cable TV, phones with dataports, and (this is crucial) air-conditioning. Perks include fresh coffee and pastries in the morning and wine in the evening. The lovely restaurant, The Girl & the Fig (p. 153) serves California-French cuisine. *Tip:* For a quieter stay, request a room that doesn't front on the street.

110 W. Spain St., Sonoma, CA 95476. (C) **800/468-6016** or 707/996-2996. Fax 707/ 996-7014. www.sonomahotel.com. 16 units. Summer $110–$245 double; winter $95–$195 double. 2-night minimum required for summer weekends. Rates include continental breakfast and evening wine. AE, DC, MC, V. *In room:* A/C, TV, dataport.

Thistle Dew Inn After 24 years as a Sonoma resident, Gregg Percival decided to join the ranks in the hospitality industry, and along with his sister, Jan Rafiq, bought the this historic Sonoma inn in 2003. Five rooms—all with private baths, queen-size beds, and phones with voice mail—are split between two homes, one built in 1869 and the other 1910. Both are handsomely furnished with an impressive collection of original Arts and Crafts furniture. If you're looking to save a few bucks, opt for the room in the main house; otherwise, you'll want one of the four larger and quieter rooms in the rear house. Each of the rooms in the rear house has its own deck overlooking the garden and is furnished with either a gas fireplace, a two-person whirlpool tub, or both.

Luxury perks at Thistle Dew Inn include a full breakfast (most popular are the Dutch babies—German pancakes with ricotta cheese and jams), which can be delivered to your room for an additional fee; afternoon hors d'oeuvres on request; free use of bicycles and utensil-filled picnic baskets; and use of the garden hot tub. You're bound to like the location—just half a block from Sonoma's plaza.

171 W. Spain St., Sonoma, CA 95476. © 800/382-7895 or 707/938-2909. Fax 707/938-2129. www.thistledew.com. 5 units. $165–$300 double; check their website for specials. Rates include full breakfast and afternoon hors d'oeuvres. AE, DISC, MC, V. **Amenities:** Hot tub; free bikes; TV in sitting room. *In room:* A/C.

INEXPENSIVE

Victorian Garden Inn 🌟🌟   Here, proprietor Donna Lewis runs what is easily the cutest B&B in Sonoma Valley. A small picket fence, a wall of trees, and an acre of gardens enclose an adorable Victorian garden brimming with violets, roses, camellias, and peonies, all shaded under flowering fruit trees. It's truly a marvelous sight in the springtime. The guest units—three in the century-old water tower and one in the main building (an 1870s Greek Revival farmhouse), as well as a cottage—continue the Victorian theme, with white wicker furniture, floral prints, padded armchairs, and clawfoot tubs. The most popular units are the Top o' the Tower and the Woodcutter's Cottage. Each has its own entrance and a garden view; the cottage boasts a sofa and armchairs set in front of the fireplace. After a hard day of wine tasting, spend the afternoon cooling off in the pool or on the shaded wraparound porch, enjoying a mellow merlot while soaking in the sweet garden smells. *New parents, take note:* The property recommends you leave young tots behind.

316 E. Napa St., Sonoma, CA 95476. © 800/543-5339 or 707/996-5339. Fax 707/996-1689. www.victoriangardeninn.com. 3 units, 1 cottage. $139–$259 double. Rates include continental breakfast. AE, DC, MC, V. **Amenities:** Outdoor pool; hot tub; concierge; business center with free Internet access; laundry service. *In room:* A/C, fireplaces in some rooms.

GLEN ELLEN
VERY EXPENSIVE

Gaige House Inn 🌟🌟🌟 *(Finds)*   Owners Ken Burnet, Jr., and Greg Nemrow run Wine Country's finest B&B. Here you'll find a level of service, amenities, and decor normally associated with four-star resorts—minus the snobbery. Every nook and cranny of the 1890 Queen Anne–Italianate building and garden annex is swathed with fashionable articles found during the owners' world travels. Spacious rooms offer everything you could want—firm mattresses, wondrously silky-soft Mascioni linens, and premium comforters gracing the beds; even the furniture and artwork are the kind you'd like to take home with you. All 23 rooms, artistically decorated in a plantation theme with Asian and Indonesian influences (trust me, they're beautiful), have king- or queen-size beds; four rooms have Jacuzzi tubs, one has a Japanese soaking tub, and the superfancy eight new spa garden suites have, among other delights, granite soaking tubs. For chilly country nights, fireplaces (in 17 rooms) definitely come in handy. Bathrooms are equally luxe, range in size, and are stocked with Aveda products and slippers. Attention to detail means you'll be treated to a robe I liked so much I had to buy it. For the ultimate retreat, reserve one of the suites, which have patios overlooking a stream or private gardens.

But wait, it gets better. Behind the inn is a 3-acre oasis with perfectly manicured lawns and gardens, a 40-foot-long heated pool, and an achingly inviting creek-side hammock shaded by a majestic Heritage oak. Evenings are best spent in the reading parlor, sipping premium wines. Appetizers at wine hour might include freshly shucked oysters or a sautéed scallop served ready-to-slurp on a Chinese soupspoon. Breakfast is a momentous event, accented with herbs from the inn's garden and prepared by a chef who cooked at the James Beard House in 2001. On sunny days, the meal can be served at individual tables on the large terrace.

Greg and Ken also manage two long-term rentals (private guesthouses on private estates) for those who want more privacy and fewer services

13540 Arnold Dr., Glen Ellen, CA 95442. © **800/935-0237** or 707/935-0237. Fax 707/935-6411. www.gaige.com. 23 units. Summer $275–$375 double, $395–$550 suite; winter $150–$275 double, $325–$525 suite. Rates include full breakfast and evening wines. AE, DC, DISC, MC, V. **Amenities:** Large heated pool; in-room massage; free wireless Internet access. *In room:* A/C, TV/DVD, dataport, hair dryer, iron, safe, fridge in some rooms, DSL Internet access.

INEXPENSIVE

Beltane Ranch ⚡ *Finds* The word *ranch* conjures up a big ol' two-story house in the middle of hundreds of rolling acres, the kind of place where you laze away the day in a hammock watching the grass grow or pitching horseshoes in the garden. Well, friend, you can have all that and more at the well-located Beltane Ranch, a century-old buttercup-yellow manor that's been everything from a bunkhouse to a brothel to a turkey farm. You simply can't help but feel your tensions ease away as you prop your feet up on the shady wraparound porch overlooking the quiet vineyards, sipping a cool, fruity chardonnay while reading *Lonesome Dove* for the third time. Each room is uniquely decorated with American and European antiques; all have sitting areas and separate entrances. A big and creative country breakfast is served in the garden or on the porch overlooking the vineyards. For exercise, you can play tennis on the private court or hike the trails meandering through the 105-acre estate. The staff here is knowledgeable and helpful. *Tip:* Request one of the upstairs rooms, which have the best views.

11775 Sonoma Hwy./Hwy. 12. (P.O. Box 395) Glen Ellen, CA 95442. © **707/996-6501.** www.beltaneranch.com. 5 units, 1 cottage. $140–$190 double; $220 cottage. Rates include full breakfast. No credit cards; personal checks accepted. **Amenities:** Outdoor, unlit tennis court. *In room:* No phone.

Glenelly Inn and Cottages ⭐   Perhaps the best thing about this rustic retreat is its reasonable rates. But equally important, this former railroad inn, built in 1916, is positively drenched in serenity. Located well off the main highway on an oak-studded hillside, the peach-and-cream inn comes with everything you would expect from a country retreat. Long verandas offer Adirondack-style chairs and views of the verdant Sonoma hillsides; breakfast is served beside a large cobblestone fireplace; and bright units contain old-fashioned claw-foot tubs, Scandinavian down comforters, and ceiling fans (though cottages have whirlpool tubs and A/C). Downsides include thin walls, the usual laugh lines that come with age, and depending on your perspective, lack of TV and phone. However, the staff understands that it's the little things that make the difference; hence the firm mattresses, good reading lights, and a simmering hot tub in a grapevine- and rose-covered arbor. All rooms, decorated with antiques and country furnishings, have terry robes and private entrances. Top picks are the Vallejo and Jack London family suites, both with large private patios, although I also like the rooms on the upper veranda—particularly in the spring, when the terraced gardens below are in full bloom. The new freestanding garden cottages (the best option) are for those who want to splurge, and come with fireplaces, TV/VCRs, CD players, coffeemakers, and fridges.

5131 Warm Springs Rd. (off Arnold Dr.), Glen Ellen, CA 95442. © **707/996-6720.** Fax 707/996-5227. www.glenelly.com. 10 units. $150–$185 double/suite; $250 cottage. Rates include full breakfast. AE, DISC, MC, V. **Amenities:** Outdoor Jacuzzi; free Internet access at computer stations; TV in common room.

KENWOOD
VERY EXPENSIVE

Kenwood Inn & Spa ⭐⭐   Inspired by the villas of Tuscany, the Kenwood Inn's honey-colored Italian-style buildings, flower-filled flagstone courtyard, and pastoral views of vineyard-covered hills are enough to make any northern Italian homesick. The friendly staff and luxuriously restful surroundings made this California girl feel right at home. What's not to like about a spacious room lavishly and exquisitely decorated with imported tapestries, velvets, and antiques, plus a fireplace, balcony (except on the ground floor), feather bed, CD player, and down comforter? With no TV in the rooms, relaxation is inevitable—especially if you book treatments at the spa, which gets creative with its rejuvenating program. A minor caveat is road noise, which you're unlikely to hear from your room but can be slightly audible over the tranquil pumped-in music around the courtyard and decent-size pool. Longtime guests will be surprised to find more bodies around the pool—18 guest rooms and an adjoining building joined this slice of pastoral heaven in June 2003. Anyone with a hefty credit card limit can buy complete seclusion by renting the inn's new nearby and very private two-bedroom villa.

An impressive three-course gourmet breakfast is served in the courtyard or in the Mediterranean-style dining room.

10400 Sonoma Hwy., Kenwood, CA 95452. ℂ **800/353-6966** or 707/833-1293. Fax 707/833-1247. www.kenwoodinn.com. 30 units. Apr–Oct $400–$725 double; Nov–Mar $375–$675 double, $800–$1,000 villa. Rates include gourmet breakfast and bottle of wine. 2-night minimum on weekends. AE, MC, V. **Amenities:** 2 heated outdoor pools; full-service spa; concierge. *In room:* Hair dryer, iron, CD player, high-speed Internet access.

5 Where to Dine

In the past decade, Sonoma Valley has experienced a culinary revolution. In response to the saturation of restaurants in the Bay Area, both budding and renowned chefs and restaurateurs have pulled out their San Francisco stakes and resettled in Sonoma Valley to craft culinary art from the region's bounty of organic produce and meats. The result is something longtime locals never dared to dream of when it came to fine dining in Sonoma: a choice.

Granted, the restaurants in Sonoma Valley—both in quality and quantity—pale in comparison to those found in Napa Valley, but the overall dining experience is splendid regardless. Even the big players are forced to concede to Sonoma's small-town code by keeping their restaurants simple and unpretentious; hence, the absence of ostentatious eateries such as Napa's Tra Vigne and Pinot Blanc.

As you travel through the valley, you'll find a few dozen modestly sized and privately owned cafes, often run by husband-and-wife teams who pour their hearts and bank accounts into keeping their businesses thriving during the off season. In fact, don't be surprised if the person waiting your table is also the owner, chef, host, sommelier, and retired professor from Yale. It's this sort of combination

Dining in the Town of Sonoma

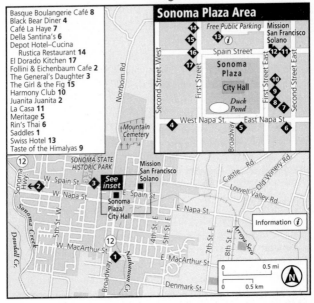

Basque Boulangerie Café **8**
Black Bear Diner **4**
Café La Haye **7**
Della Santina's **6**
Depot Hotel–Cucina
　Rustica Restaurant **14**
El Dorado Kitchen **17**
Follini & Eichenbaum Cafe **2**
The General's Daughter **3**
The Girl & the Fig **15**
Harmony Club **10**
Juanita Juanita **2**
La Casa **11**
Meritage **5**
Rin's Thai **6**
Saddles **1**
Swiss Hotel **13**
Taste of the Himalyas **9**

that often makes dining in Sonoma a very personable experience and one that you'll relish long after you leave the Wine Country.

The restaurants listed below are classified first by town, then by price, using the following categories: **Expensive,** dinner from $50 per person; **Moderate,** dinner from $35 to $50 per person; and **Inexpensive,** dinner less than $35 per person. These categories reflect prices for an appetizer, a main course, and a dessert.

Note: Though Sonoma Valley has far fewer visitors than Napa Valley, its restaurants are often equally crowded, so be sure to make reservations as far in advance as possible. Also bear in mind that the food in the Wine Country is usually served in large portions and washed down with copious amounts of wine—enough so that I make a point of eating at only one restaurant a day, lest I explode.

SONOMA
EXPENSIVE

Santé Restaurant ✿ EUROPEAN/CALIFORNIA　One of the fanciest restaurants in Sonoma Valley, Santé Restaurant has long suffered from a solid reputation for serving high-caliber spa cuisine. Although still billed as "a salute to your health," they've moved away from "spa" and in 2005 chef Joe Brown left the Ritz Carlton in Half Moon Bay to take over as chef de cuisine. Alas, dining here has yet to prove itself a worthy diversion, unless it's one from your suite at the Sonoma Mission Inn and because you don't want to get in the car to dine. Selections from the seasonally changing menu might include skate wing with confit, leeks and a brown butter vinaigrette, roasted pheasant with royal trumpet mushroom and chestnut puree, and red wine poached organic beef tenderloin with potato rosti and rutabaga Bordelaise. Service is professional yet friendly, and the wine list is extensive and expensive.

At Fairmont Sonoma Mission Inn, 18140 Sonoma Hwy., Sonoma. ✆ 707/938-9000. Reservations recommended. Appetizers $17; main courses $35; desserts $15; fixed-price menu $65. AE, DC, MC, V. Daily 6:30–9:30pm.

MODERATE

Cafe La Haye ✿✿ ECLECTIC Well-prepared and wholesome food, an experienced waitstaff, friendly owners, a soothing atmosphere, and reasonable prices—including a modestly priced wine list—make La Haye a favorite. In truth, everything about this cafe-like restaurant is charming. The atmosphere within the small split-level dining room, pleasantly decorated with hardwood floors, an exposed-beam ceiling, and revolving contemporary artwork, is smart and intimate. The vibe is small business—a welcome departure from Napa Valley's big-business restaurants. The straightforward, seasonally inspired cuisine, which chefs bring forth from the tiny open kitchen, is delicious and wonderfully well priced. Although the menu is small, it offers just enough options. Expect a risotto special; pasta such as fresh tagliarini with butternut squash, prosciutto, sage, and garlic cream; and pan-roasted chicken breast, perhaps with goat cheese–herb stuffing, caramelized shallot jus, and fennel mashed potatoes. Meat eaters are sure to be pleased with filet of beef seared with black pepper–lavender sauce and served with Gorgonzola-potato gratin; and no one can resist the creative salads.

140 E. Napa St., Sonoma. ✆ 707/935-5994. Reservations recommended. Main courses $14–$24. AE, MC, V. Tues–Sat 5:30–9pm.

Depot Hotel–Cucina Rustica Restaurant NORTHERN ITALIAN Michael Ghilarducci has been the chef and owner here for nearly two decades, which means he's either independently wealthy or a darned good cook. Fortunately, it's the latter. A block north of the plaza in a handsome 1870 stone building, the Depot Hotel offers pleasant outdoor dining in an Italian garden, complete with a reflecting pool and cascading Roman fountain. The menu is unwaveringly Italian, featuring classic dishes such as spaghetti Bolognese and veal alla parmigiana. Start with the bounteous antipasto misto, and end the feast with a dish of Michael's handmade Italian ice cream and fresh-fruit sorbets.

241 1st St. W. (off Spain St.), Sonoma. © 707/938-2980. www.depothotel.com. Reservations recommended. Main courses lunch $10–$16, dinner $14–$22. AE, DISC, MC, V. Wed–Fri 11:30am–2pm; Wed–Sun 5–9pm.

El Dorado Kitchen 😋😋 MEDITERRANEAN-INSPIRED BISTRO With a Napa Valley pedigree, El Dorado Kitchen is upping the ante for Sonoma dining. Part owner and executive chef Ryan Fancher, who worked at Napa's famed French Laundry and Auberge du Soleil, brings a much-needed dose of modern, casual fare to the center of town with a seasonal menu that shows off Fancher's talent at elevating everyday lunch options. Take grilled cheese and tomato soup for example. He gives the comfort classic dignity with griddled prosciutto and Vermont cheddar alongside San Marzzano tomato soup. A simple twist like balsamic aioli turns a regular BLT into a sandwich you just can't put down. The fine cooking of Italy is reminisced, by way of India with a dash of Californian ingenuity, with the curry fritto misto (lightly battered apples, cauliflower, and fall squash served with curry salt and aioli). There are also several nods to the French, among them a charcuterie plate and a Caesar Provençal (i.e., added olives). Dinner entrees include delicate Pacific salmon with white bean cassoulet, prosciutto and sage and succulent lamb loin with rosemary polenta, pequillo peppers, Swiss chard and niçoise olive sauce. House cocktails, which also trot the globe, range from the Cuban mojito to spiked Thai iced tea. It all comes together in the open, airy dining room, which is sleek and comfortable, if not overly cozy. Added bonuses: El Dorado Kitchen's prices are surprisingly reasonable and portions are generous.

405 1st St. W., Sonoma. © 707/996-3030. Reservations recommended. Lunch $7–$15; dinner $8–$25. Daily 11:30am–2:30pm and 5:30–10pm.

The Girl & The Fig 😋😋 COUNTRY FRENCH Well established in its downtown Sonoma digs (it used to be in Glen Ellen), this modern, attractive, and cozy eatery, with lovely patio seating, is the home for Sondra Bernstein's (The Girl) beloved restaurant. Here the cuisine, orchestrated by chef de cuisine Matt Murray, is nouveau country with French nuances, and yes, figs are sure to be on the menu in one form or another. The wonderful winter fig salad contains arugula, pecans, dried figs, Laura Chenel goat cheese, and fig-and-port vinaigrette. Murray uses garden-fresh produce and local meats, poultry, and fish whenever possible, in dishes such as grilled pork chops or duck confit. For dessert, try lavender crème brûlée, a glass of Jaboulet muscat, and a sliver of raclette from the cheese list. Sondra knows her wines, features Rhone varietals, and will be happy to choose the best accompaniment for your meal. Looking for brunch? Head here on Sunday when it's served until 3pm.

110 W. Spain St., Sonoma. ✆ **707/938-3634.** www.thegirlandthefig.com. Reservations recommended. Main courses $13–$24. AE, DISC, MC, V. Mon–Sat 11:30am–11pm; Sun 10am-11pm.

Harmony Club ☆ *Finds* CONTINENTAL   The most welcome addition to Sonoma's dining scene in 2003, the Harmony Club is not just a looker, with its elegant Italianate dining room with dark woods, high ceilings, marble flooring, and a wall of giant doors opening to sidewalk seating and Sonoma's plaza. It also delivers in food and live entertainment. Drop in for a seasonal menu, which features hearty winter rib-grippers such as veal osso bucco with creamy roast garlic mushroom polenta and braised greens or somewhat lighter warm-weather fare such as cumin-crusted ahi tuna with beluga lentils, roasted vegetables, and red wine sauce. Go for sidewalk seating during warmer weather (they also have heat lamps), sit inside, or hang at the carved wood bar. Either way you'll want to face the piano when the nightly performer is tinkling the keys and singing jazz standards. Alas, the only letdown is the wine list, which leaves little in the way of options since this spot, owned by Steve Ledson of Ledson Winery, naturally features only Ledson wines.

480 1st St. E. (at the plaza), Sonoma. ✆ **707/996-9779.** Reservations accepted. Entrees $14–$26. AE, MC, V. Wed–Mon 11:30am–10pm.

Meritage ☆☆ SOUTHERN FRENCH/NORTHERN ITALIAN   Learning from the previous occupants' mistakes—that Sonoma ain't New York and shouldn't treat its customers that way—chef-owner Carlo Cavallo eliminated the big-city attitude and prices at his restaurant without diminishing style, service, or quality. The former executive chef for Giorgio Armani, Cavallo combines the best of southern French and northern Italian cuisines (hence "Meritage," after a blend made with traditional Bordeaux varieties), giving Sonomans yet another reason to eat out. The menu, which changes twice daily, is a good read: foie gras ravioli with sage truffle sauce; seafood stew with tiger prawns, Manila clams, mussels, and mixed fresh fish in a spicy tomato saffron broth; and wild boar chops in white truffle sauce with mashed potatoes. Shellfish fans can't help but love the oyster raw bar and options of fresh crab and lobster. They also have a new martini bar. A lovely garden patio is prime positioning for sunny breakfasts and lunches and summer dinners. Such edible enticement—combined with reasonable prices, excellent service, a stellar wine list, cozy booth seating, a handsome dining room, and Carlo's practiced charm—make Meritage a trustworthy option.

165 W. Napa St., Sonoma. $\textcircled{C}$ **707/938-9430**. www.sonomameritage.com. Reservations recommended. Main courses $13–$30. AE, MC, V. Wed–Mon 11:30am-9:30pm.

Saddles AMERICAN STEAK HOUSE   You won't find any culinary trailblazing here, but you will get fresh, innovative versions of your favorite comfort foods amidst environs that could inspire a hearty "giddy-up." With firelight dancing on the walls, murals of horses, wainscoting painted to look like a picket fence, and yes, well-worn saddles perched around the entrance, this place does things on a scale that would make any cowboy proud. Get the night going with one of their signature martinis, offered in either 6- or put-you-under-the-table 10-ounce servings. (Try the Jolly Rancher—Absolut citron vodka and sour apple liqueur.) Break into a dining trot with a selection from the extensive wine list and an order of cornmeal haystack onion rings with blue cheese aioli. Then get your taste buds galloping with ribs, chicken, burgers, fish, pasta, or one of the fourteen choices of red meat. (Try the buttery, tender Niman Ranch filet mignon.) Most steaks are served a la carte, but you can add standards such as freshly made creamed spinach and potatoes au gratin. Don't declare, "whoa," before trying the caramel apple crisp with vanilla ice cream or cheesecake with fresh berries.

29 E. MacArthur St., Sonoma $\textcircled{C}$ **707/933-3191**. Reservations recommended. Main courses $9.95–$49. Sun–Thurs 5:30pm–9pm; Fri–Sat 5:30pm–9:30pm.

Swiss Hotel $\textcircled{R}$ CONTINENTAL/NORTHERN ITALIAN   With its slanting floors and beamed ceilings, the historic Swiss Hotel, located right in the town center, is a Sonoma landmark and very much the local favorite for fine food served at reasonable prices. The turn-of-the-20th-century oak bar at the left of the entrance is adorned with black-and-white photos of pioneering Sonomans. The bright white dining room and sidewalk patio seats are pleasant spots to enjoy lunch specials such as penne with chicken, mushrooms, and tomato cream; hot sandwiches; and California-style pizzas fired in a wood-burning oven. But the secret spot is the very atmospheric back garden patio, a secluded oasis shaded by a wisteria-covered trellis and adorned with plants, a fountain, gingham tablecloths, and a fireplace. Dinner might start with a warm winter salad of radicchio and frisée with pears, walnuts, and bleu cheese. Main courses run the gamut; I like the linguine and prawns with garlic, hot pepper, and tomatoes; the filet mignon wrapped in bleu-cheese crust; and roasted rosemary chicken. The food may not knock your socks off, but it's all very simply satisfying.

18 W. Spain St. (at 1st St. W.), Sonoma. *C* **707/938-2884.** Reservations recommended. Main courses lunch $8.50–$16, dinner $10–$24. AE, MC, V. Daily 11:30am–2:30pm and 5–9:30pm. (Bar daily 11:30am–2am.)

INEXPENSIVE

Basque Boulangerie Café BAKERY/DELI If you prefer a lighter morning meal and strong coffee, stand in line with the locals at the Basque Boulangerie Café, the most popular gathering spot in Sonoma Valley. Most everything—sourdough Basque breads, pastries, quiche, soups, salads, desserts, sandwiches, cookies—is made in-house and made well. Daily lunch specials, such as a grilled-veggie sandwich with smoked mozzarella cheese ($4.95), are listed on the chalkboard out front. Seating is scarce, and if you can score a sidewalk table on a sunny day, consider yourself one lucky person. A popular option is ordering to go and eating in the shady plaza across the street. The cafe also sells wine by the glass, as well as a wonderful cinnamon bread by the loaf that's ideal for making French toast.

460 1st St. E., Sonoma. *C* **707/935-7687.** Menu items $3–$10. Credit cards accepted with a $5 minimum, local checks only. Daily 7am–6pm.

Della Santina's *★★* TUSCAN For those of you who just can't swallow another expensive, chichi California meal, follow the locals to this friendly, traditional Italian restaurant. How traditional? Ask father-and-son team Dan and Robert: When I last dined here, they pointed out Signora Santina's hand-embroidered linen doilies as they proudly told me about her Tuscan recipes. (Heck, even the dining room looks like an old-fashioned, elegant Italian living room.) And their pride is merited: Every dish my party tried was refreshingly authentic and well flavored, without overbearing sauces or one *hint* of California pretentiousness. Be sure to start with traditional antipasti, especially sliced mozzarella and tomatoes, or delicious White Beans–Sunday. The nine pasta dishes are, again, wonderfully authentic. (Gnocchi lovers, rejoice!) The spit-roasted meat dishes are a local favorite (although I found them a bit overcooked); for those who can't choose between chicken, pork, turkey, rabbit, or duck, there's a selection that offers a choice of three. Don't worry about breaking your bank on a bottle of wine, because many choices here go for under $40. Portions are huge, but be sure to save room for a wonderful dessert.

133 E. Napa St. (just east of the square), Sonoma. © 707/935-0576. Reservations recommended. Main courses $10–$20. AE, DISC, MC, V. Daily 11:30am–3pm and 5–9:30pm.

Follini & Eichenbaum Café DELI When I'm looking for picnic goods, a deliciously fresh and inexpensive meal, or a kid-friendly spot for the family meal—indoors or out—this is one of my top picks. Jules Abate joined her aunts (Follini and Eichenbaum) in Sonoma to bring her unique take on "Jewish-Italian deli" food to Sonoma. Yes, that means there's good hot pastrami in Sonoma. But there's also a large selection of fresh salads, unusual sodas and chips, and habit-forming homemade chocolate chip cookies.

You can also drop by any morning for coffee and pastries, but on Sundays the offerings tempt further, with a brunch buffet that includes potato pancakes, deep-dish quiches, eggs Benedict, breads, baked goods, salads and desserts, plus a lot more. Oy! So many choices.

19100 Arnold Dr., Sonoma © 707/996-3287. Reservations recommended for brunch. Sandwiches and entrees $4.95–$9.95. Mon–Fri 6am–2:30pm; Sat 8am–2:30pm; Sun brunch 10am–2pm.

Juanita Juanita MEXICAN Everyone loves this roadside shack hawking fresh Mexican specialties and hearty sides of who-gives-a-heck attitude. Lines out the door during weekends prove the point. But if you've gotta have a killer quesadilla, nachos, enchiladas, tacos, and their very fabulous "plate" specials (think grilled chicken with chipotle cream sauce on a bed of spinach and avocado with rice, beans, and tortillas) it's worth the wait. Besides, the place is fun. Here the decor and vibe is about as casual as you can get. Plop down at the counter, pull up a chair at one of the mix-and-match tables, or grab a table on the patio, kick up your heels, dig into the plastic bucket of tortilla chips and side o' salsa, sip on an ice cold beer, and revel in the oh-so-Sonoma-casual vibe as you fill up on the huge portions. Kids dig the place, too, and have their own specialties offered at pint-sized prices of $4.

19114 Arnold Dr. (just north of W. Napa St.), Sonoma. © 707/935-3981. www. juanitajuanita.com. No reservations. Main courses $6.50–$12. No credit cards. Daily 11am–8pm.

Rin's Thai ⚓ THAI   When valley residents or visitors get a hankering for pad thai, curry chicken, or *tom yam* (classic spicy soup), they head to this adorable little restaurant just off Sonoma Plaza. The atmosphere itself—contemporary, sparse, yet warm environs within an old house—is tasty and the staff is extremely accommodating. After you settle into one of the well-spaced tables within or on the outside patio (weather permitting), go for your favorites— from satay with peanut sauce and cucumber salad or salmon with grilled veggies to yummy *gai kraprao* (minced chicken, chiles, basil, and garlic sauce) or char-broiled vegetables or ribs with chile-garlic dipping sauce. They've got it all covered, including that oh-so-sweet Thai iced tea, fried bananas with coconut ice cream, and fresh mango with sticky rice (seasonal).

139 E. Napa St. (just east of the plaza), Sonoma. ⓒ **707/938-1462**. www.rinsthai. com. Reservations recommended. Main courses lunch $8.25–$13, dinner $8.25–$11. MC, V. Sun–Thurs 11:30am–9pm; Fri–Sat until 9:30.

Taste of the Himalayas NEPALESE/INDIAN   You might wonder how this group of Nepalese friends (including a Sherpa!), ended up in this small restaurant just off the square in Sonoma, but then you taste their food and you're just happy they did. If you're looking for something other than the usual pizzas, pastas and burritos, this is your spot. Just what does a Nepalese meal entail? Start with crisp *samosas* (a mild blend of potatoes and peas served with mint sauce,) or *momos* (small steamed dumplings stuffed with either lamb or veggies). Move on to entrees such as curry or Tandoori dishes, which wash down nicely with Indian Taj Mahal beer. All entrees come with a delicious bowl of mild *daal bhat,* the traditional Indian lentil soup, your choice of basmati rice or *naan,* and casual but attentive service.

464 1st St. E., Sonoma ⓒ **707/996-1161**. Reservations recommended. Main courses $10–$18. Daily 11am–3pm and 5–10pm.

GLEN ELLEN
MODERATE

the fig café & wine bar ⚓⚓ NEW AMERICAN   The Girl & the Fig's (p. 153) sister restaurant is more casual than its downtown Sonoma sibling. But don't let the bucolic neighborhood vibe, airy environs and soothing sage and mustard color scheme fool you. From his open kitchen, chef de cuisine Bryan Jones brings you the kind of rustic sophistication more commonly associated with urban restaurants. Start with a thin-crust pizza, fried calamari with spicy lemon aioli, a cheese plate, or the signature fig and arugula salad,

Café Citti **4**

Fig Cafe & Wine Bar **2**

Glen Ellen Inn
Restaurant **2**

Kenwood
Restaurant & Bar **3**

Santé Restaurant **1**

Wolf House **2**

move on to braised pot roast with mashed potatoes and vegetables or mussels in a garlic, leek, and tarragon sauce with fries, and finish with a chocolate brownie with vanilla ice cream. *A perk:* The "Rhone Alone" wine selections are available by the flight, glass, or bottle; free corkage.

13690 Arnold Dr. (at Madrone Rd.), Glen Ellen. © **707/938-2130.** www.thefig cafe.com. Reservations not accepted. Main courses $10–$17. AE, DISC, MC, V. Sun–Thurs 5:30–9pm; Fri–Sat 5–9:30pm; brunch offered Sat–Sun 9:30am–2pm.

Glen Ellen Inn Restaurant ✿ CALIFORNIA   Christian and Karen Bertrand have made this place so quaint and cozy that you feel as if you're dining in their home, and that's exactly the place's charm. Garden seating is the favored choice on sunny days, but the covered, heated patio is also always welcoming. The first course from Christian's open kitchen might be a wild-mushroom-and-sausage purse served in brandy cream sauce or warm goat-cheese croquettes. Main courses, which change with the seasons, range from linguine with artichoke hearts and feta to stellar late-harvest ravioli stuffed with pumpkin, walnuts, and sun-dried cranberries on a bed of butternut squash. Other favorites include marinated pork tenderloin on smoked mozzarella polenta, topped with roasted pepper–onion compote and utterly tender Nebraska corn-fed filet mignon in a foie gras–brandy reduction sauce. On my last visit, the Sonoma Valley mixed-green salad, seared ahi tuna, and homemade French vanilla ice cream floating in bittersweet caramel sauce made a lovely meal. The 550-selection wine list offers numerous bottles from Sonoma, as well as more than a dozen wines by the glass. *Tip:* There's a small parking lot behind the restaurant.

13670 Arnold Dr. (at O'Donnell Lane), Glen Ellen. © **707/996-6409.** www.glen elleninn.com. Reservations recommended. Main courses $16–$24. AE, DISC, MC, V. Mon–Tues 11:30am–2:30pm; Mon–Thurs 5:30-9pm; Fri–Sun 11:30am–9:30pm. Closed 1 week in Jan. New full bar.

Wolf House ✿ ECLECTIC   The most polished-looking dining room in Glen Ellen is elegant yet relaxed whether you're seated in the handsome dining room—smartly adorned with maple floors, gold walls, dark-wood wainscoting, and a corner fireplace—or outside on the multilevel terrace under the canopy of trees with serene views of the adjacent Sonoma Creek. The lunch menu adds fancy finishes to old favorites such as the excellent chicken Caesar salad, fresh grilled ahi tuna niçoise sandwich, or a juicy half-pound burger with Point Reyes Original Blue cheese. During dinner, skip the soggy sparkling-wine battered prawns with upland cress salad and head straight for seared Roasted Liberty farms duck breast with pecan and dried cherry strudel with sautéed cider cabbage and braised kumquat demi, or pan-seared day boat scallops with heirloom tomatoes and avocado-cucumber emulsion. The reasonably priced wine list offers many by-the-glass options as well as a fine selection of Sonoma wines. Locals love the brunch, complete with huevos rancheros, Dungeness crab cake Benedict, omelets, and brioche French toast. During my visits, service was rather languid, but well meaning.

13740 Arnold Dr. (at London Ranch Rd.), Glen Ellen. © **707/996-4401.** www.jack londonlodge.com/rest.html. Reservations recommended. Main courses brunch and lunch $8–$15, dinner $15–$25. AE, MC, V. Brunch Sat–Sun 10am–3pm; lunch Mon–Fri 11am–3pm; dinner nightly 5:30–9:30pm.

KENWOOD
MODERATE
Kenwood Restaurant & Bar ✿✿ CALIFORNIA/CONTINEN
TAL   This is what Wine Country dining should be—but often, disappointingly, is not. From the terrace of the Kenwood Restaurant, diners enjoy a view of the vineyards set against Sugarloaf Ridge

as they imbibe Sonoma's finest at umbrella-covered tables. On nippy days, you can retreat inside to the Sonoma-style roadhouse, with its shiny wood floors, pine ceiling, vibrant artwork, and cushioned rattan chairs at white cloth–covered tables. Regardless of where you pull up a chair, expect first-rate cuisine, perfectly balanced between tradition and innovation, complemented by a reasonably priced wine list. Great starters are Dungeness crab cake with herb mayonnaise; superfresh sashimi with ginger, soy, and wasabi; and a wonderful Caesar salad. The main dish might be poached salmon in creamy caper sauce or prawns with saffron Pernod sauce. But the Kenwood doesn't take itself too seriously: Great sandwiches and burgers are also available.

9900 Sonoma Hwy. (just north of Dunbar Rd.), Kenwood. ✆ **707/833-6326**. www. kenwoodrestaurant.com. Reservations recommended. Main courses $13–$28. MC, V. Wed–Sun 11:30am–9pm.

INEXPENSIVE

Café Citti NORTHERN ITALIAN   If you're this far north into the Wine Country, then you're probably doing some serious wine tasting. If that's the case, then you don't want to spend half the day at a fancy, high-priced restaurant. What you need is Café Citti (pronounced *Cheat*-ee), a roadside do-it-yourself Italian trattoria that is both good and cheap. You order from the huge menu board displayed above the open kitchen. Afterward, you grab a table (the ones on the patio, shaded by umbrellas, are the best on warm afternoons), and a server will bring your meal. It's all hearty, home-cooked Italian. Standout dishes are the green-bean salad, tangy Caesar salad, focaccia sandwiches, and roasted rotisserie chicken stuffed with rosemary and garlic. The freshly made pastas come with a variety of sauces; try the zesty marinara. Wine is available by the bottle, and the espresso is plenty strong. Everything on the menu board is available to go, which makes Café Citti an excellent resource for picnic supplies.

9049 Sonoma Hwy., Kenwood. ✆ **707/833-2690**. Main courses $7–$22. Lunch daily 11am–3:30pm; dinner Sun–Thurs 5–8:30pm, Fri–Sat 5–9pm.

6 Where to Stock Up for a Picnic & Where to Enjoy It

Sure, Sonoma has plenty of restaurants, but when the weather's warm there's no better way to have lunch in the Wine Country than by toting a picnic basket to your favorite winery and basking in the sweet Sonoma sunshine. Even Sonoma's central plaza, with its many picnic tables, is a good spot to set up a gourmet picnic. But first you need grub, so for your picnicking pleasure, check out Sonoma's top spots for stocking up for an alfresco fete.

If you want to pick up some specialty fare on your way into town, stop at **Angelo's Wine Country Deli,** 23400 Arnold Dr. (© 707/ 938-3688), where you'll find all types of smoked meats, special salsas, and homemade mustards. The deli is known for its half-dozen types of homemade beef jerky. It's open in summer daily from 9am to 6pm; off season daily from 9am to 5pm.

The venerable **Sonoma Cheese Factory** ✛, on the plaza at 2 W. Spain St. (© 707/996-1931), offers award-winning house-made cheeses and an extraordinary variety of imported meats and cheeses. The factory also sells salads, pâté, and homemade Sonoma Jack cheese. Good, inexpensive sandwiches are also available, such as New York steak or sausage. The factory is open Monday through Friday from 8:30am to 5:30pm and Saturday and Sunday from 8:30am to 6pm.

At 315 2nd St. E., a block north of East Spain Street, is the **Vella Cheese Company** ✛ (© 800/848-0505 or 707/938-3232), established in 1931. The folks at Vella pride themselves on making cheese into an award-winning science, and their best-known beauty, the Monterey Dry Jack, continues to garner blue ribbons. Other cheeses range from flavorful High Moisture Jack to a razor-sharp Raw Milk Cheddar. Vella has also become famous for its Oregon Blue, made at its southern Oregon factory—it's rich, buttery, and even spreadable, one of the few premier bleus produced in this country. Any of these fine, handmade, all-natural cheeses can be shipped directly from the store. Hours are Monday through Saturday from 9am to 6pm.

Being born into a famous food family might be daunting for some, but not for Ditty Vella (yes, *that* Vella family, see above). She followed her father's advice to "Eat well, eat slowly, but above all, eat cheese!" and opened the **Cheesemaker's Daughter,** just off the square at 127 E. Napa St. (© 707/996-4060; www.cheesemakers daughter.com). Of course her small store features a few Vella cheeses, but the majority of her dairy delights are American and European artisanal cheeses along with other gourmet foods and drinks. Stop by to taste from her selection and you'll find a friendly, knowledgeable staff who clearly loves cheese too. The store is open Tuesday through Saturday from 10am to 6pm and Sunday from 10am to 5pm.

Finally, someone has opened an eatery on the eastern side of town. Since **Nonna's Eastside Market,** at 1190 E. Napa St. (*©* **707/933-3000;** www.nonnaseastsidemarket.com), opened in 2005, it has become known as the perfect place to stop for a picnic lunch, a coffee and pastry, or basic groceries while en route to downtown Sonoma via 8th Street East or the wineries of the Carneros region. Drop by anytime between 7am and 7pm.

Other highly recommended picnic outfitters include **Basque Boulangerie Cafe** (p. 156), **Follini & Eichenbaum** (p. 157) in Sonoma, **Café Citti** in Kenwood (see "Where to Dine," above), and **Viansa Winery & Italian Marketplace,** which makes fabulous focaccia sandwiches—and has a lovely picnic area for noshing on them, too (p. 126).

Gundlach Bundschu (p. 127), located on the outskirts of Sonoma, also has a wonderful picnic area perched on the side of a small hill overlooking the Sonoma countryside (though you'll have to earn the sensational view by making the trek to the top). On the opposite side of the valley, my favorite picnic picks are **Chateau St. Jean**'s (p. 132) big, beautiful lawn overlooking the vineyards (bring a blanket); the blissfully quiet pond-side picnic area at **Landmark Vineyards** (p. 133), which also sports a bocce court; and **Bartholomew Park,** 1000 Vineyard Lane, Sonoma, (*©* **707/935-9511**), where oak tree-shaded rolling lawns overlook the valley—and are kid friendly.

6

Northern Sonoma County

Most visitors to Northern California Wine Country relegate their vacation time to Napa Valley or Sonoma Valley. But insiders have long known that the best of both worlds can be found in Northern Sonoma. Here, amidst hundreds of acres of vineyards, are family-owned wineries, adorable B&Bs, charming towns, friendly residents, classic river fun in summertime, and of course more than your share of outstanding food and wine experiences. Add to that the best shopping (in Healdsburg) and less traffic on the charming country roads and in the tasting rooms and you might begin to understand why this region is a bona fide hot spot right now.

1 Orientation & Getting Around

Northern Sonoma spans a substantial area covering around a million acres, 50,000 of which are dedicated to vines. With more than 150 wineries and 1,000 growers, there's more than enough to explore here. Fortunately, the area is relatively easy to navigate—provided you have a decent map.

Unlike Napa Valley, where all the action is strewn across a narrow valley along or just off two major roads, and contrary to Sonoma Valley, which is relatively compact, Northern Sonoma is downright vast, with more than one major hub and attractions branched off in virtually every direction. What this part of paradise does have in common with its neighboring regions is proximity: While you're destined to add some miles to the odometer to get from one area to the other, it doesn't really matter where you decide to call your temporary home because, bustling and traffic-laden Highway 101 aside, all the drives are so pleasant they're attractions in themselves. That said, each area does have its own distinct flavor and instant access to specific attractions, so read up and decide what works best for you.

NORTHERN SONOMA'S TOWNS IN BRIEF

Not all the region's towns are described below. Instead we're highlighting those most important for the visitor.

The commercial center of the region, **Santa Rosa** is also the gateway to Northern Sonoma wine country. About as far away from a quaint country town as you can get yet minutes from vineyards and 55 miles from San Francisco, this major city with more than 150,000 residents still feels surprisingly small town and rural. What it does ante up on the cosmopolitan front is worth exploring—including a symphony, performing arts center where major talents are booked each year, lots of golf, theater productions, and a slew of restaurants. As the gateway to Northern Sonoma wine country, it's also got a lot of well-priced accommodations, which can be quite a draw for those who don't want to fork over a small fortune to stay in a just-okay frilly B&B or can't find lodging elsewhere.

Farther north, the **Russian River Valley wine region** is also home to the funky riverside town of **Guerneville.** Though it's a good 20 minutes west of the Highway 101 thoroughfare, it does offer relatively easy access to the region's wineries. However, this town of around 2,600 residents, which was explored by the Russians in the 1840s and became one of the busiest logging centers in the West in the 1880s, is now known for its casual cabin-like resort communities flanking the Russian River and its summertime popularity among the gay and lesbian community, who flock here and spend their days idling on inner tubes, canoeing, car camping, or hiking redwood trails. Accommodations here tend to be old and funky, like the town and homes around it, but the relaxed summertime feel is pure old-fashioned fun. (Think scorching afternoons, cut-off shorts, and popsicles.) That said, if it's the ultimate Wine Country vibe you're after, you won't find it here, except for at the town's eastern entrance, which is home to Korbel Champagne Cellars.

North of the Russian River area is the greatly heralded wine region known as **Dry Creek** as well as the undisputed hub of Northern Sonoma wine country, the town of **Healdsburg.** A mere 30- to 45-minute drive from either valley (and 1½ hours from San Francisco) and just north of burgeoning suburb Santa Rosa, its centerpiece historic square, which has been the heart of the town since its inception in 1857, captures the quaint shopping and dining experiences of downtown Sonoma's plaza (only better in both areas). Its rural roads and country B&Bs have the same genuine backcountry appeal as its surrounding wineries, while the abundance of Victorian architecture gives it a bit of old-world charm. But recently, Healdsburg has become a bona fide alternative Napa Valley highlife due to the arrival of a few very sophisticated restaurants and hotels. (The wine scene here was already exceptional.) Adding to its intrinsic allure, the town is surrounded by all the premier viticultural areas, allowing for easy access to Russian River, Dry Creek, Alexander Valley, and Chalk Hill. What more could you ask for?

When you take the Highway 101 turnoff to downtown **Geyserville** and arrive in the tiny two-block town, you might wonder why you even made the detour. But not so fast. The draw here isn't the commercial center, but the winery-dense area surrounding it. Known as Alexander Valley, it attracts wine lovers from the world over.

VISITOR INFORMATION

Northern Sonoma doesn't have one major convention and visitors bureau representing the entire region. Fortunately, if you visit www.sonoma.com, it will direct you to the various visitors bureaus. However, there's plenty of information available should you contact the following sources. The **Santa Rosa Convention & Visitors Bureau,** 9 4th St., Santa Rosa, CA 95401 (© **800/404-7673** or 707/577-8674), can give you the scoop on all things Santa Rosa, as well as a bit about the areas and wineries to the north. Or you can get information by visiting www.visitsantarosa.com.

Farther north, if you roll into downtown Healdsburg off of Highway 101, you'll pass the **Healdsburg Chamber of Commerce and Visitors Bureau** (217 Healdsburg Ave., Healdsburg; © **800/648-9922** from within California or 707/433-6935; www.healdsburg. com). It's definitely worth a pit stop to get brochures and answers to any questions from their very helpful staff.

FAST FACTS: Northern Sonoma

Hospitals **Santa Rosa Memorial Hospital** (1165 Montgomery Dr., Santa Rosa; © **707/546-3210**) and **Healdsburg District Hospital** (1375 University St., Healdsburg; © **707/431-6300**) offer emergency services available round the clock.

Information See "Visitor Information," above.

Newspapers/Magazines The most widely distributed newspaper in the area is Santa Rosa's *The Press Democrat*. To learn about Healdsburg happenings you can turn to the weekly *Healdsburg Tribune*.

Pharmacies **Longs Drug** stores pepper this area. Two locations include 2771 4th St., Santa Rosa (© **707/528-1151**), open from Monday through Saturday from 9am to 7pm and Sunday 10am to 6pm, and 9030 Brooks Rd. S. and Healdsburg, (© **707/433-3357**), open Monday through Friday 9am to 8pm, Saturday and Sunday 10am to 6pm.

Police Call © **707/528-5222** for nonemergencies; in an emergency call © **911**.

Post Offices Each town has its own post office. In Healdsburg, go to 404 Center St., (© **707/433-8142**).

Shipping Companies See "The Ins & Outs of Shipping Wine Home," in chapter 3.

Taxis Call **Healdsburg Taxi Cab** at © **707/433-7088**.

2 Touring the Wineries

Touring Northern Sonoma is very different from the winery-hopping in Napa and Sonoma valleys. Here sipping destinations are scattered every which way over a vast landscape of tiny towns surrounded by open land and miles of vineyards. And they're tucked away on one-lane roads that would be impossible to find if it weren't for the periodic white arrow signs pointing you in the right direction. They are also far more mom-and-pop, which means it's very likely you'll rub elbows with winemaker/owners as you taste at their bars. Alas, this piece of paradise is quickly being touted as the next hot vacation spot, so there are more cars on the roads and in the parking lots than there used to be. But it's still less crowded than the alternatives, and if it's a genuine country wine-tasting experience you're after, there is no better option than to fill up the tank and hit the roads here. Of course, you should chart your path—or at least attempt to—before going. But keep in mind that the diversions you'll stumble upon along the way are likely to slow you down—in a good way. (For more on this, see "Strategies for Touring the Wine Country," in chapter 3.)

The towns and wineries listed below are organized geographically, from the city of Santa Rosa in the south to Geyserville in the north. Bear in mind that because the wineries are scattered all over the place, the order in which they're listed is not necessarily the best path to follow. To save time, plan your wine tour while looking at a map and charting the most logical path.

Also, there's no way I could cover even close to all the wineries in the region, so be sure to stop by the Healdsburg Chamber of Commerce and Visitors Bureau (217 Healdsburg Ave., Healdsburg; © 800/648-9922 within California or 707/433-6935; www. healdsburg.com) for a more complete list.

SANTA ROSA

Matanzas Creek *Finds* It's not technically in Sonoma Valley, but if there's one winery that's worth a detour, it's Matanzas (pronounced Mah-*tan*-zas) Creek. After a scenic 20-minute drive, you'll arrive at one of the prettiest wineries in California, blanketed by fields of lavender (usually in bloom near the end of June), and surrounded by rolling hills of well-tended vineyards.

The winery has a rather unorthodox history. In 1978, Sandra and Bill MacIver, neither of whom had any previous experience in winemaking or business, set out with one goal in mind: to create the finest wines in the country. Actually, they overshot the mark. With the release of their Journey 1990 chardonnay, they were hailed by wine critics as the proud parents of the finest chardonnay ever produced in the United States, comparable to the finest white wines in the world.

This state-of-the-art, environmentally conscious winery produces chardonnay, sauvignon blanc, merlot, syrah, and cabernet, all of which you can taste for $5. Prices for current releases are, as you would imagine, at the higher end ($20–$45). Also available for purchase is culinary lavender from Matanzas Creek's own lavender field, the largest outside Provence. Purchase a full glass of wine and bring it outside to savor as you wander through these wonderfully aromatic gardens. Picnic tables hidden under groves of oak have pleasant views of the surrounding vineyards. On the return trip, be sure to take the Sonoma Mountain Road detour for a real backcountry experience.

6097 Bennett Valley Rd. (off Warm Springs Rd.), Santa Rosa. © **800/590-6464** or 707/528-6464. www.matanzascreek.com. Daily 10am–4:30pm. Tours by appointment only at 10:30am and 2:30pm weekdays and 10:30am Saturday. From Hwy. 12 in Kenwood or Glen Ellen, take Warm Springs Rd.; turn off on Bennett Valley Rd.; the drive takes 15–20 min.

Kendall-Jackson Wine Center *Finds* Just north of Santa Rosa in Fulton is the region's most big-business winery and the best bet for tasters who want some education and winery grandeur with their chardonnay. Though it's right off the highway, KJ is a 120-acre

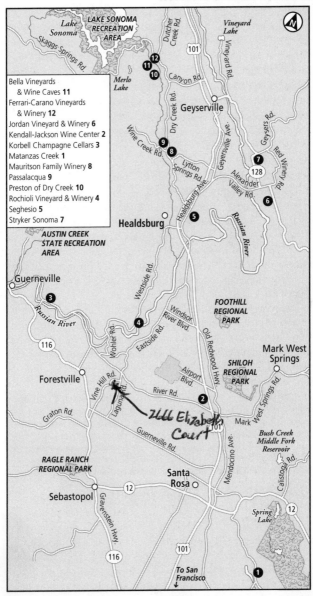

LAKE SONOMA RECREATION AREA

Lake Sonoma

Skaggs Springs Rd.

Vineyard Lake

101

Dutcher Creek Rd.

Canyon Rd.

Vineyard Rd.

11 **12**

10

Merlo Lake

Dry Creek Rd.

Geyserville

Geysers Rd.

Red Winery Rd.

Wine Creek Rd.

9

8

Lytton Springs Rd.

Geyserville Ave.

7

128

Alexander Valley Rd.

6

Healdsburg Ave.

5

Healdsburg

Russian River

| Bella Vineyards |
| & Wine Caves **11** |
| Ferrari-Carano Vineyards |
| & Winery **12** |
| Jordan Vineyard & Winery **6** |
| Kendall-Jackson Wine Center **2** |
| Korbell Champagne Cellars **3** |
| Matanzas Creek **1** |
| Mauritson Family Winery **8** |
| Passalacqua **9** |
| Preston of Dry Creek **10** |
| Rochioli Vineyard & Winery **4** |
| Seghesio **5** |
| Stryker Sonoma **7** |

AUSTIN CREEK STATE RECREATION AREA

Guerneville

3

Russian River

116

Westside Rd.

Wohler Rd.

4

Windsor River Blvd.

Eastside Rd.

FOOTHILL REGIONAL PARK

Old Redwood Hwy.

Forestville

Vine Hill Rd.

Graton Rd.

Laguna Rd.

Airport Blvd.

River Rd.

2

SHILOH REGIONAL PARK

Mark West Springs

Mark West Springs Rd.

1466 Elizabeth Court

101

Guerneville Rd.

Bush Creek Middle Fork Reservoir

Calistoga Rd.

RAGLE RANCH REGIONAL PARK

Santa Rosa

Mendocino Ave.

Sebastopol

12

Gravenstein Hwy.

Spring Lake

12

116

101

To San Francisco

1

world in itself, complete with truly stunning gardens, including acres of organic herbs, vegetables, flowers, a culinary and wine sensory garden, plenty of picnic spots, demonstration vineyards, occasional culinary programs to complement wine tastings from the brand's vast selections (and sister wineries), and gift-shop browsing. Tastings range from $2 for current releases to $10 for reserve wines, but check the "tasting room" section of their website—when I last looked they offered a coupon for a free reserve tasting for two.

5007 Fulton Rd., Fulton. ℂ **707/571-8100.** www.kj.com. Daily 10am-5pm. From Hwy. 101 N. take the River Rd. exit, turn left at the stoplight to go over the freeway, turn right onto Fulton Rd., go ½ mile, and it's on your left.

GUERNEVILLE/RUSSIAN RIVER VALLEY

Korbel Champagne Cellars   Okay, so technically they don't make—or cellar—"champagne" since they're not located in the region of the same name in France. But that doesn't stop visitors from sipping bubbly, getting a good buzz, and having a great time here. Set in a redwood grove at the eastern edge of the town of Guerneville, Korbel is a winemaking relic with more than 120 years of history under its grape-growing belt. You can peruse the ivy-draped brick winery and its stunning gardens, take an informative tour that explains their production process, and grab picnic snacks at their Delicatessen and Market. A bottle of bubbly will set you back $10 to $30, while tastes and tours are free. From mid-April through mid-October flower lovers should detour to browse the Antique Rose Gardens' 250 varieties of antique roses. To confirm tour times call ℂ **707/824-7316.**

13250 River Rd. (at the eastern entrance of downtown), Guerneville, ℂ **707/824-7000.** www.korbel.com. Tasting room 9am–5pm May 1–Sept 30; 9am–4:30pm Oct 1–Apr 30. Tours in winter are daily, every hour on the hour 10am–3pm; in summer, Mon–Fri every 45 min. from 10am–3:45pm; weekends and holidays at 10am, 11am, and noon, then every 45 min. until 3:45pm. Rose Garden tours are available mid-Apr through mid-Oct Tues–Sat at 11am, 1pm, and 3pm. From Hwy. 101 take the River Rd. exit, turn left (westbound) onto River Rd. and follow it for 13 miles.

HEALDSBURG/DRY CREEK VALLEY/ ALEXANDER VALLEY

Find out more about the region and its wineries by visiting the Winegrowers of Dry Creek Valley's website at www.wdcv.com and the Alexander Valley Winegrowers website at http://alexander valley.org.

Mauritson Family Winery   Mauritson Vineyards boasts a lineage that dates back to the 1870s, but until the late 1990s, they only sold grapes to their Sonoma neighbors. That's when current owner

The Ways of Wine Clubs

If you're particularly fond of a winery's products, you might consider joining their wine club. Most wineries have such a program and membership essentially means that you're committing to paying a certain amount of money over the course of the year to receive their new releases— and sometimes a library wine thrown in for good measure and good drinking—via the mail. But that's not all. Usually, club membership includes a variety of bonuses—free tasting and tour privileges at the winery, discounts on wine and merchandise, a newsletter subscription, exclusive invitations to winery events both at the winery and around the country, and an array of other perks ranging from annual throw-down release parties to European cruises (a la Domaine Carneros). It's worth mentioning that even with an invitation most private parties cost a fee (often worth it—Northern California wineries definitely know how to party!) and that due to state laws, wineries can only ship to areas that allow for direct shipments of alcohol. But if you can swing it, it's worth considering.

and winemaker Clay Mauritson—who had a marketing degree and had honed his sales and winemaking skills at neighboring vineyards Kenwood, Taft, and Dry Creek—jumped into making wines under his own label. Their wines include selections from the small Rock-pile appellation. Only designated an official appellation since 2002, this 15,400-acre ridge above Lake Sonoma grows grapes at the fog line at 800 feet or higher above sea level. (Think tannic wines with an oomph.) Don't be surprised if you encounter Clay's friendly yellow Lab, SoHo, in the tasting room; his beloved pup-cum-greeter is the Mauritson wine club's namesake—The SoHo Club.

2859 Dry Creek Rd., Healdsburg. ✆ **707/431-0804.** www.mauritsonwines.com. Daily 10am–5pm.

Passalacqua A romantic rural vision with a white wisteria-draped trellis, rows of old vines, umbrella-shaded tables on a patio overlooking vineyards, and a modest, welcoming tasting room pouring free samples, this family-owned winery, which was previously Pezzi King, has long been a vision of idyllic wine country. But since young Jason Passalacqua bought it a few years ago, a lot has changed, especially regarding winemaking since Margaret Davenport, a veteran from Clos du Bois, was appointed winemaker. Along with overseeing the development of on-site production facilities, she garnered recognition for the winery when her 2002 Dry Creek Old Vine zinfandel made the *San Francisco Chronicle*'s top 100 wine list for 2004 and her 2001 cabernet sauvignon was awarded Double Gold and Best of Class in the *San Francisco Chronicle*'s 2005 wine judging competition. Drop by, absorb the afternoon sun on the patio, and see for yourself why I consider this a worthy stop.

3805 Lambert Bridge Rd. (at Dry Creek Rd.), Healdsburg, ✆ 877/825-5547. Daily 11am–5pm. From Hwy. 101 take Dry Creek Rd. west, and turn left on Lambert Bridge Rd.

Rochioli Vineyard & Winery ✎ There are two things that I love about this tasting room. The first is that it's all about the wine—no fancy logo shirts for sale, no tours and no hard-selling or snobby staff. In fact the only extra embellishments the simple room and its surroundings have are rotating local art and crafts and a few picnic tables on the patio. The second thing is the wine itself. Rochioli (pronounced "*Ro*-kee-*o*-lee") makes *really* good sauvignon blanc, chardonnay, and pinot noir. It's so good that at certain times of year they must limit the sales of their total annual production of 10,000 cases of estate wines (that means their own grapes grown on their 161 acres) in order to make sure people like you get to buy a bottle when you drop buy. Thus, keep in mind that no matter how much you beg, the staff will only sell you a limited amount of what's currently available (ranging from 1 bottle to a case depending on how much they have left), which will set you back anywhere from $24 to $30 per bottle.

6192 Westside Rd. (near Sweetwater Springs Rd.), Healdsburg. ✆ 707/433-2305. Daily 11am–4pm.

Ferrari-Carano Vineyards & Winery ✎ The hands-down winner for Most Stunning Landscaping goes to this spot known for producing everything from fumé blanc to zinfandel. Come during spring and the air is sweet with aromas drifting form the abundant wisteria and the grounds are in bloom with literally thousands of tulips. Come any time of year to meander the formal Asian garden—abounding with rhododendron, Japanese arched bridges, boxwood, maples, magnolia, and roses—not to mention taste wines and scan quintessential wine country views. Alas, the tasting room and gift shop is a little more big-business than country with plenty of logo items and fine wines to taste and carry. If you're interested in the tour, which previews the winery and its production process and is offered Monday through Saturday at 10am only, make a reservation—it's required and can be made by calling ℂ 800/831-0381, extension 251. Prices are $5 for a selection of four current releases, $10 for reserve wines.

8761 Dry Creek Rd., Healdsburg. ℂ 707/433-6700. www.ferrari-carano.com. Daily 10am–5pm. Tours Mon–Sat 10am with a reservation. From Hwy. 101 take Dry Creek Rd. exit headed west and go 9 miles.

Bella Vineyards & Wine Caves 🍷🍷 Do yourself a favor—call ahead for a cave tour at Bella. No, not a vineyard tour, a cave tour. Why? Because you'll see mysterious arched doors built into the hillside when you pull up to the unassuming, barnlike tasting room, and after a few sips of hearty, spicy old vine zinfandel you'll ask the staff about the doors. They tell you the doors, flanked by old olive trees, are caves housing barrels and underground functions rooms. During your tour, you'll feel warm and cozy thanks to well-placed mood lighting and big, sturdy wood tables filling the winding caverns. You'll be so happy you stopped by this small family-run winery (named Bella as an ode to the owners' two young daughters), located in the heart of Dry Creek Valley, that you'll leave plotting a way to schedule your next underground party at the Bella wine caves.

9711 West Dry Creek Rd, Healdsburg. ℂ 866/572-3552 or 707/473-9171. www. bellawinery.com. Daily 10am–5pm.

Preston of Dry Creek 🍷🍷 Preston's wines are fine, but what makes this one of my favorite stops in all of Northern Sonoma is everything else about the place—the winding dirt road that leads to the parking lot; the rustic grassy area outside with picnic tables, well-established wisteria, games of bocce ball; and the supercute tasting room and store, which is located in a Victorian farmhouse and comes complete with all the charm you'd expect from such a structure. Follow the neon sign's direction and "drink zin," but also dabble in the broad selection of Rhone varietals made here—including mourvedre, viognier, Rousanne, Barbera, and syrah. By the way, you can taste more of owner Lou Preston's passions here. Organic vegetables grown on the property and bread baked in the property's custom wood-fired brick oven are sold here daily. The bread sells out quickly, however, so arrive early to indulge.

6192 Westside Rd. (near Sweetwater Springs Rd.), Healdsburg. ℂ 707/433-2305. http://prestonofdrycreek.com. Daily 10am–4pm. From Hwy. 101, take the Dry Creek

Rd. exit headed west, turn left at the Lambert Bridge, turn right on W. Dry Creek Rd., turn right onto Westside Rd.

Seghesio   Unlike the many small, boutique wineries dotting this area, you might be familiar with Seghesio's wines—their zinfandels make it to many out-of-state liquor stores and they enjoy enough press attention to warrant countrywide recognition. While their light wood and modern tasting room offers a window into their winemaking facility, it is otherwise nothing to go gaga over—plus their staff was a tad stuffy on my visit. But the pungent, well-structured zins made the visit worth it, as does the tasting room's location adjacent to the center of Healdsburg (a 10-min. walk)—a great stop as you stroll around the main plaza in town. Tastings are $5.

14730 Grove St., Healdsburg. ✆ **707/433-3579**. www.seghesio.com. Daily 10am–5pm.

Jordan Vineyard & Winery ✿   For the ultimate in classic, refined Wine Country opulence—with a serious and stately tour and tasting to match—make a reservation to visit Jordan's stunning estate. Inspired by the grand chateaux of southwestern France, owner and oil magnate Tom Jordan's vine-covered winery was founded in 1972. Only a small portion of the property, which spans more than 1,500 acres, is committed to actual vines—cabernet sauvignon, merlot, and chardonnay. Though you may stop by to purchase wine Monday through Saturday, you must make a reservation to take the tour, during which you'll see that here literally every detail is attended to—from the winery construction to way the beautiful and shiny stainless steel tanks line the fermentation room to the patio seating under great oak trees on the patio to the manicured grounds. Raucous revelers may want to skip this one, as the vibe here is composed and sophisticated. But those who want to feel a bit of the Wine Country high life *and* enjoy some darn tasty chardonnay and cabernet sauvignon should detour here and take the complimentary tour, which ends with a tasting in the formal library—where you'll also catch glimpses of Tom's wife Sandra's elegant and expensive home and entertaining products, which are available for sale.

1474 Alexander Valley Rd., Healdsburg. ✆ **800/654-1213** or 707/431-5250. www.jordanwinery.com. Mon–Fri 8am–5pm; Sat 9am–4pm. From Hwy. 101, take Dry Creek Rd. exit, turn left at 2nd traffic light onto Healdsburg Ave., go 2 miles and turn right onto Alexander Valley Rd., go 1½ miles, and turn right to enter the estate.

Stryker Sonoma ✿   Stryker Sonoma has attitude. A friendly, young attitude. This attitude is an extension of founders Pat Stryker and Craig and Karen McDonald. You'll feel it when you arrive at this boutique winery's slatted-wood walkway, march up to the sleek and polished curved bar, gaze up at the lofted wood ceiling, order a taste of zin, and gaze out at the vines through floor-to-ceiling windows. If you tire of the view, cross the mahogany-stained cement floor and peer through the windows overlooking the barrel room below. You won't see Stryker wines on the shelves of the wine shops: Stryker only sells out of its tasting room, online, and, per winemaker Tim Hardin, "to a few local restaurants we like." Like many vineyards in the Alexander Valley, you won't pay a tasting fee here. Cheers to that.

5110 Hwy. 128, Geyserville. © 707/433-1944. Fax 707/433-1948. www.stryker sonoma.com. Jan–Mar Thurs–Sun 10:30am–5pm, Mon–Wed by appointment; Apr–Dec daily 10:30am–5pm.

3 More to See & Do

Believe it or not, you can get tired of tasting wine all day every day—your liver is likely to beg for respite. Luckily, there's more extracurricular activity here than in both Napa and Sonoma valleys.

SANTA ROSA

Though you won't be surrounded by vineyards and countryside, a visit to downtown Santa Rosa has its perks.

FARMER'S MARKET Anyone interested in rubbing elbows with the locals, snatching up farm-fresh produce, and taking in a little entertainment a la musicians and street performers should meander the **Farmer's Market.** Each Wednesday night from 5pm to 8:30pm from mid-May through August on 4th Street between B and D streets. (© 707/524-2123; www.srdowntownmarket.com). You can also browse fresh fruits and vegetables on Wednesday and Saturday mornings, year-round, from 8:30am to noon at the Veteran's Building east parking lot (1351 Maple Ave.). Call © 707/ 522-8629 for more information.

GARDEN TOUR For plants to look at rather than eat, head to **Luther Burbank Home and Gardens** (at Santa Rosa and Sonoma aves.; © 707/524-5445; http://lutherburbank.org). The one-plus-acre public garden showcases medicinal herbs, cutting flowers, roses, and ornamental grasses as well as the home and history of Luther Burbank (1849-1926), a botanist and scientist famed for inventing new fruits, plants, and flowers who is regarded as the father of modern plant breeding. The museum shop is open and tours are given

April through September, Tuesday through Sunday from 10am to 4pm. You can opt for the docent-led tour of the gardens, home and greenhouse, offered every half-hour, or the self-guided audio tour (using an MP3 player). The tours costs $4 for adults, $3 for seniors 65 and older and youth 12 to 18, and free to children under 12. You can of course also just drop by the gardens. They're open daily year-round from 8am to dusk. For more information contact ℂ **707/524-5445.**

GOLF   If golf is your game, you'll find two 18-hole courses at the southern Santa Rosa border just north of Sonoma Valley at the **Oakmont Golf Club,** 7025 Oakmont Dr. (ℂ **707/539-0415;** www.empiregolf.com). Green fees are $32 Monday through Thursday, $37 Friday, and $50 weekends and holidays; carts cost $14 per rider. **The Fountaingrove Club** (ℂ **707/521-3214;** www.fountain grovegolf.com) is a substantial step up. A private club set among 170 acres dotted with oak trees and backed by rolling hills, it's got a challenging championship 18-hole course that's accessible to members of other private clubs with reciprocal fees. If you fall into that category, it'll cost you $95 on weekdays and $125 on weekends and holidays—including a cart and range balls.

HOT-AIR BALLOONING   If you're interested in a quintessential Wine Country experience, drop a good deal of dough on an early morning **hot-air balloon ride.** But this one isn't for late sleepers. The adventure begins by meeting your balloon and pilot at the crack of dawn at Sonoma County Airport, outside of Santa Rosa. From there you travel to the best launch site given the conditions. (If weather's bad they're sure to cancel.) Then you're off on a one-hour ride, drifting over the countryside and finishing with a champagne brunch—after both of your feet are back on the ground. Fares are $195 per adult, $155 for teens 13 to 18, and $130 for children 6 to 12. For more information call **Up & Away** at ℂ **800/711-2998** or 707/836-0171 or visit www.up-away.com.

AFRICAN-STYLE SAFARI   Looking for something totally wild to do during your vacation? Head to **Safari West** (3115 Porter Creek Rd.; ℂ **800/616-2695** or 707/579-2551; www.safariwest. com), a wildlife reserve that's about as close as you can get to an African adventure without boarding an overseas flight. Aboard an open-air safari vehicle (not unlike the ones I traveled in during a visit to Kenya), you'll tour the grounds and get up close and personal with the likes of giraffes, gazelles, ostrich, cheetahs, zebras, and antelope during the 3-hour tour. Monday through Thursday prices are $52 for adults, $28 children 3 to 12; Friday through Sunday it's $60 per adult and $25 for kids. For the full experience you can even opt for a tented camp experience. Reservations are required for day and overnight adventures. Call for details and seasonal hours.

MUSEUMS   For indoor entertainment for the whole family, consider the **Charles M. Schulz Museum,** 2301 Hardies Lane (© 707/ 579-4452; www.charlesmschulzmuseum.org), which features cartoons of the famous local cartoonist's Peanuts characters (the most famous of which is Snoopy). It's open Monday and Wednesday through Friday from noon to 5pm and Saturday and Sunday from 10am to 5pm. Prices are $8 for adults and $5 for seniors and youth under 18. You can also get cultured at the **Museum of Contemporary Art at the Luther Burbank Center for the Arts,** 50 Mark West Springs Rd. (© 707/527-0297; www.lbc.net), which has ever-evolving exhibits showcasing the works of some of America's most promising contemporary artists. It's open Wednesday through Saturday from 10am to 4pm and Sunday from 1pm to 4pm. Outdoor sculptural exhibits can be viewed daily from 9am to 9pm. Entrance fees are $2 for adults and free for youth under 16. It's also home to the area's premier concert hall where world-class acts, such as Seal and Diana Krall, perform to a full house.

GUERNEVILLE

The town closest to the Russian River may be short on wineries, but it's long on outdoor fun.

CANOEING   One of my all-time favorite summertime excursions—canoeing—can be embarked upon from the tiny area of Forestville, adjacent to Guerneville. At **Burke's Canoes,** 8600 River Rd., at Mirabel Rd. (© 707/887-1222; www.burkescanoetrips. com), it's an all-day adventure. You simply pack a lunch (ideally wrapped in a waterproof bag), park the car, leave all your valuables in the trunk, pay $55 (cash only) for a canoe that can comfortably fit three adults (the minimum required is two adults), throw on a bathing suit, sunscreen, and a life vest and launch yourself onto the Russian River. It's a leisurely paddle downstream, with the occasional tricky turn—especially during early summer when the water is higher. During the 10-mile journey, you'll pass beaches that beg for you to pause and bask, redwood trees, and kids jumping off rocks and rope swings, before arriving at a well-marked beach where Burke's staff will pick you up and take you back to your car. Though you can make the journey in about 3 hours, you're more likely to spend 4 or 5 with pit stops to swim, eat, and laze. Definitely reserve your canoe in advance. This is a popular activity. Also, Burke's welcomes good swimmers only—and children over 5 years of age.

BEACHING IT   Should you be more of a landlubber, you can also simply spread a towel and picnic feast at **Johnson's Beach** (near downtown Guerneville, off Church St.; ℂ **707/869-2022;** www. johnsonsbeach.com), a river resort with a big stretch of pebbly sand and snack bar that's popular with frolicking families. You can also rent a kayak, canoe, or paddleboat here from May to October. Don't come for an early morning or evening dip—the resort is only open from 10am to 6pm daily.

HORSEBACK RIDING   Another exceptional way to experience the natural beauty of this region is on **horseback.** Longtime residents Laura and Jonathan Ayers are behind the **Armstrong Woods Pack Station** (ℂ **707/887-2939;** http://redwoodhorses.com), which offers guided trail rides through old-growth redwood forests. All rides include instruction and a rest or lunch stop on top of a ridge with fabulous valley views. You can saddle up year-round, weather and trail conditions permitting. Prices start at $70 per adult and $60 per child for a 2½ hour ride.

To find out more about the Russian River area and its activities, contact the **Russian River Chamber of Commerce Visitors Center** (16209 1st St., at the historic bridge, Guerneville; ℂ **877/644-9001** or 707/869-90000; www.russianriver.com).

HEALDSBURG

SHOPPING   One of the town's greatest attractions is its centerpiece square. The **shop-lined plaza** has been the heart of the town since 1857, when Ohio-born gold miner Harmon Heald built a few businesses around it, just a few blocks off the main route between San Francisco and the northern gold country. Today it continues to be the region's epicenter, luring locals with coffee and legendary sticky buns at **Downtown Bakery & Creamery,** 308 A Center St. (ℂ **707/431-2719;** www.downtownbakery.net), and everyone with outstanding boutique shopping and dining.

BICYCLING   Rather than driving from winery to winery, consider maneuvering on two wheels along the quiet country roads. **Wine Country Bikes** (ℂ **866/922-4537;** www.winecountrybikes. com) offers day rentals (with maps) and guided tours. A road bike goes for $55 per day and includes a helmet, lock, bag, and route suggestions. An all-day tour goes for $119 per person and includes a picnic lunch, wine tasting, and a van to lug any goodies you buy along the way.

4 Where to Stay

The accommodations listed below are arranged first by area and then by price, using the following categories: **Very Expensive,** more than $250 per night; **Expensive,** $200 to $250 per night; **Moderate,** $150 to $200 per night; and **Inexpensive,** less than $150 per night.

As I already mentioned, remember that during the high season—between June and November—most hotels charge peak rates and sell out completely on weekends; many have a 2-night minimum. Always ask about discounts. During the off season, you have far better bargaining power and may be able to get a room at almost half the summer rate.

RESERVATIONS SERVICES   For more lodging options, check http://Sonoma.com and http://winecountry.com.

SANTA ROSA
INEXPENSIVE
Sandman Motel   What sets this very clean motel apart from others in the basic-abode category are an abundance of perks and thoughtful touches. Sure you'll find the usual classic motel-style furnishings (dark woods, bright-print bedspreads, framed prints) and expected extras such as refrigerators and coffeemakers. But you'll also get access to their large heated outdoor pool and Jacuzzi, be surrounded by well-maintained and surprisingly lush landscaping, and have the option of indulging in their free breakfast bar, which includes a make-your-own waffle station. An astoundingly cheap price makes it that much better—and a very wise choice for the touring visitor since it's likely you'll only be in your room to sleep off the day's overindulgence. You'll have to drive another 15 minutes (or more with traffic) on Highway 101 to get to the heart of this region's wine country, but the truth is, you'll have to drive no matter where you stay and unless you want to pay a premium for fancier digs or old-fashioned B&B hospitality, you're not likely to find a better deal in this expensive area. *Tip:* Skip dining at adjoining Carrow's; it's basic cheap chain food.

3421 Cleveland Ave. (at Piner Rd.), Santa Rosa, CA 95403. © **707/544-8570.** 136 units. $82–$92 double, $133 suite. Rates include extensive breakfast bar. AE, DC, DISC, MC, V. **Amenities:** Restaurant; heated outdoor pool; Jacuzzi; exercise room; laundry room. *In room:* A/C, TV, dataport, fridge, coffeemaker, hair dryer, iron.

FORESTVILLE

The Farmhouse Inn & Restaurant ★★   The Farmhouse Inn, located in a speck of a town just outside of Guerneville, may be more famous for its destination restaurant than its rooms, but that doesn't mean the accommodations here aren't praiseworthy. In fact, the inn has been named one of the nation's top 30 by *Travel + Leisure* magazine. Run by the Bartolomei family, who are fourth-generation Forestvilleans, the 6-acre rural property is lined with superbly spacious and charming cottages. Each looks English country from the outside and creatively cozy from within. Exceedingly spacious rooms are individually decorated with colorful walls adorned with whimsical sayings, surprise amenities like saunas, whirlpool tubs, a fireplace, and quality bath products, and a good dose of solitude. Common areas include a truly beautiful and a superb European country–style restaurant complete with excellent wine list and polished service, heated outdoor pool, and a demonstration vineyard and rose garden.

7871 River Rd., Forestville, CA 95436. ℰ **800/464-6642** or 707/887-3300. www.farmhouseinn.com. 8 units. $195–$299 double. AE, MC, V. **Amenities:** Restaurant; unheated outdoor pool; spa; concierge; limited room service; massage; wireless Internet connections. *In room:* TV/VCR w/cable, fridge, coffeemaker (available upon request), hair dryer, iron.

GUERNEVILLE

Gentrification hasn't caught up with the laid-back river life of this town. Thus, most of the options in Guerneville are on the old-school funky side. However, you can find more choices than are listed here if you visit the area's visitor center website, which offers an array of accommodations, ranging from camping to vacation rentals. See http://russianriver.com for details and options.

Applewood Inn & Restaurant ★   By far the most elegant option in the area, this sweet, expanded 1922 California Mission Revival mansion celebrates country living with 19 well-appointed rooms within three buildings and one of the area's better restaurants. Though it's a 2-minute drive to downtown, its location, tucked away on 6 acres of forested hillside, makes a visit to this Mediterranean-style compound feel like a completely different destination than the funky, bustling river town in which is resides. Add to that individually decorated rooms with antiques, lively colors, and benefits like down comforters, Italian linens, spa toiletries, and the included full breakfast and you're not likely to mind that the hotel does indeed show its age in some areas (lack of central heating is a

Northern Sonoma Accommodations

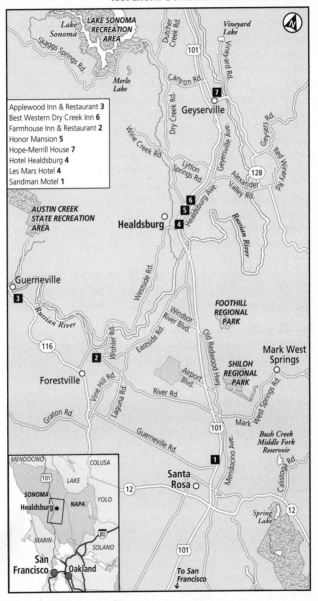

Applewood Inn & Restaurant **3**
Best Western Dry Creek Inn **6**
Farmhouse Inn & Restaurant **2**
Honor Mansion **5**
Hope-Merrill House **7**
Hotel Healdsburg **4**
Les Mars Hotel **4**
Sandman Motel **1**

good example). You can opt for one of the Historic Belden House rooms with country charm or one of the "newer" rooms, which lean more modern and have fireplaces and small private decks or court-yards. Outside, you'll find an outdoor pool (heated spring through fall), a hot tub (heated year-round), and an organic garden where tonight's dinner might be growing right now. Keep in mind that it's about a 15-minute drive on country roads to get to the winery-dense area of Dry Creek.

13555 Hwy. 116, Guerneville, CA 95446. ⓒ 800/555-8509 or 707/869-9093. www.applewoodinn.com. 19 units. $185–$345. Rates include full breakfast. AE, MC, V. **Amenities:** Restaurant; pool (heated for part of the year); Jacuzzi; concierge; in-room massage. *In room:* A/C in "studio" rooms, TV (some with VCR), hair dryer, robes, wireless Internet.

HEALDSBURG
VERY EXPENSIVE
Les Mars Hotel 🏵🏵   One block off Healdsburg Square, the exte-rior of Northern Sonoma's most luxurious inn is so understated that you're likely to pass it. But inside the three-floor hotel there's no mistaking the opulence. The lobby alone smacks of old-world French luxury accommodations with light Venetian plaster and travertine marble accented by a dramatic wrought-iron-wrapped staircase—and a small subtly placed elevator. The 16 individually decorated rooms are equally plush. Swathed in creams and warm beiges and furnished with hand-selected 18th and 19th century European antiques, they're equipped with the likes of a canopy bed with Italian linens, a large TV and DVD player, a marble bathroom with a whirlpool soaking tub and walk-in shower, and personal touches at every turn, and they feel more like a rich friend's home than a hotel. Each morning guests are treated to a continental break-fast in the wood-paneled library, and during evenings they have easy access to the region's finest restaurant, Cyrus, which adjoins the hotel. Without a doubt this is the finest place to stay in the region.

27 North St. (at Healdsburg Ave.), Healdsburg, CA 95448. ⓒ 877/431-1700 or 707/433-4211. www.lesmarshotel.com. 16 units. $495–$995 double. Rate includes continental breakfast. AE, DISC, MC, V. **Amenities:** Restaurant; heated outdoor pool; exercise room; concierge; dry cleaning (same-day weekdays only); wireless Internet in lobby and library. *In room:* A/C, TV/DVD, hair dryer, iron (on request), safe, stereo, high-speed Internet.

EXPENSIVE
Honor Mansion 🏵🏵🏵 *Finds*   Guests who stay at this small luxury inn don't want to leave their rooms—a jaunt to one of the nearby vineyards or a stroll up to the main square of town might be in

order, but then it's back to the mansion. Maybe it's the fluffy featherbeds, winter and summer bathrobes, or delicious toiletries. If you are in one of the particularly splendid units boasting a claw-foot tub, cozy gas fireplace, or a private deck with a Jacuzzi, you might only get up to help yourself to the decanter of sherry placed in each room. Be sure to indulge in breakfast, a decadent, two- to three-course affair (think Mexican eggs, baked blintz, or soufflé French toast and espresso chocolate chip muffins) served in the parlor of this 1883 Italianate Victorian or on the redwood deck overlooking the pond (check out the koi). As if this isn't enough, you'll also find bocce and tennis courts, a huge lap pool, a croquet lawn, afternoon wine and cheese, a 24-hour self-serve espresso and cappuccino machine in the main building, and a never-ending supply of cookies. Add in the hospitality of owners Cathi and Joe Fowler, two gems making you feel right at home, and you'll be booking your next stay the day you leave.

14891 Grove St., Healdsburg, CA 95448. ⓒ **800/554-4667** or 707/433-4277. Fax 707/431-7173. www.honormansion.com. $190–$325 doubles; $300–$550 suites. DISC, MC, V. Rates include full breakfast and evening wine and cheese. **Amenities:** Outdoor pool; tennis court; croquet lawn; putting green. *In room:* TV w/movie library, hair dryer, iron.

Hotel Healdsburg 🥝🥝   The first "upscale" property to debut in Healdsburg when it opened in 2001, this home away from home across the street from the plaza is a visitor favorite because it not only has spacious, comfortable rooms adorned with country-chic furnishings (You'll find no doilies and lace here!), but it also has amenities associated with a true hotel. Want to spend the day spaing it? You're golden. Lounge by a heated pool? No problem. Linger on an oversize couch over the morning paper in front of a roaring fire in the lobby? Sure thing. Dine at a refined restaurant? With Dry Creek Kitchen (p. 189) fronting the hotel, you're already there. Rooms are minimalist-refined (think Pottery Barn) with angular, modern dark-wood furnishings, big fluffy beds, oversize bathrooms with glass walk-in showers (some with soaking tubs), and in many cases, balconies. Though they're comfy enough to linger in, there's good reason not to: The region's best shopping is outside your door around Healdsburg's historic plaza. An added bonus for the business-minded traveler (or anyone who wants to send an e-mail) is that each floor has a computer with Internet access that's free to use. Yes, it costs a pretty penny to stay here, but you might be able to find a deal on their website, where they often post promotions and packages.

25 Matheson St. (at the square), Healdsburg, CA 95448. © **800/889-7199** or 707/431-2800. Fax 707/431-0414. www.hotelhealdsburg.com. 55 units. $250–$495 double, $425–790 junior and one-bedroom suites. Rates include a "country harvest" breakfast. AE, MC, V. **Amenities:** Restaurant; cafe; bar; heated outdoor pool; spa; Jacuzzi; concierge; limited room service; laundry service; same-day dry cleaning; wireless Internet in lobby. *In room:* A/C, TV/DVD, fridge, coffeemaker, hair dryer, iron, safe, CD player.

MODERATE

Best Western Dry Creek Inn   It's not exactly a romantic Wine Country getaway, but anyone looking for a wonderfully clean and affordable place to crash after a day of wining and dining will be very happy here—especially considering all the extras. Along with basic motel-style rooms you'll find a complimentary bottle of Sonoma wine upon check in, a small fridge for chilling your chardonnay and picnic items, and even a tiny fitness room for working off the pounds you're inevitably putting on. Add to that coffeemakers, free high-speed Internet access, and the great promotions featured on their website and you've found one of Wine Country's best bargains. Yes, it's still expensive, but get used to it—that's Healdsburg for you.

198 Dry Creek Rd, Healdsburg, CA 95448. © **800/222-5784** or 707/433-0300. www.drycreekinn.com. **Amenities:** Restaurant; small heated outdoor pool; exercise room; coin-op washers and dryers. *In room:* A/C, TV w/pay movies, fridge, coffeemaker, hair dryer, iron, free high-speed Internet.

GEYSERVILLE
MODERATE

Hope-Merrill House   If your dream Wine Country vacation includes a stay in a comfy and quiet B&B with old-fashioned charm, look no further. Located in the less-trodden area of Geyserville, but a few minutes from all the winery action, this beautifully restored 1870 Eastlake Stick-style Victorian home has three things going for it: value, an attractive and unique setting, and a gracious and helpful staff. Manicured landscaping surrounds the Sonoma historic landmark, which is characterized by bay windows and a veranda on the outside and wainscoting and gorgeous silk-screened wallpaper hark the antiquated style of living from within. Each of the eight rooms is individually decorated with private baths and queen-size beds. If it's available and you're in a splurging mood, go for the Sterling Suite, which boasts a fireplace, private entrance, and private garden patio. A hearty breakfast is included in the rates. By the way, if they're sold out they can direct you to their sister property, another "Painted Lady" construction, located across the street.

21253 Geyserville Ave., (at School House Lane), Geyserville, CA 95441. © 800/
825-4233 or 707/857-3356. www.hope-inns.com. 8 units. $129–$250 double;
rates include breakfast. AE, MC, V. **Amenities:** Pool (heated May–Oct), courtesy
computer on verandah, wi-fi, TV in living room, courtesy phone. *In room:* A/C, TV
(one room), no phone.

5 Where to Dine

No area in Wine Country has seen more culinary growth over the
past few years than Northern Sonoma. But even before the true destination dining rooms arrived, this region was still a fantastic place
to dine—thanks to sweet little country restaurants and a few more
contemporary staples. But now you've got even more options. Outstanding sushi, chic small plates, truly world-class experiences,
excellent baked goods—they're all here, and all yours, provided you
make a reservation.

The restaurants listed below are classified first by town, then by
price, using the following categories: **Expensive,** dinner from $50
per person; **Moderate,** dinner from $35 to $50 per person; and
Inexpensive, dinner less than $35 per person. These categories
reflect prices for an appetizer, a main course, and a dessert.

SANTA ROSA
MODERATE

Hana Japanese Restaurant 🐠🐠 SUSHI/JAPANESE Chef-
owner Ken Tominaga has become so well known for his fantastically
fresh sushi and beautifully composed Japanese-inspired dishes that
Napa residents happily make regular one-hour pilgrimages to grab a
seat at this strip mall dining room and sushi bar located in a Santa
Rosa suburb. With matter-of-fact decor and casual, friendly service,
it's the menu that truly dazzles. The extensive selection of superfresh raw fish—including rare finds like Japanese *shimaaji* (striped
jack) and *kohoada* (shad). More elaborate offerings such as Hawai-
ian-style ahi poke, buttery monkfish liver, creamy uni custard,
grilled Kobe steak with miso–green onion sauce, and sake-braised
black pork belly are edible heaven, especially when accompanied by
one of the excellent sakes or a German Riesling. Anyone averse to
raw fish can choose from the extensive menu of classics (tempura or
teriyaki) to exceptional juicy steaks or grilled salmon. For the ultimate experience, give chef Ken a budget and let him make a multi-
course meal for you. It's likely to be one of the most memorable
meals you'll have in these parts.

101 Golf Course Dr. (in the DoubleTree Plaza), Rohnert Park. © **707/586-0270.** www.hanajapanese.com. Reservations recommended. Sushi $3.50–$12; main courses $6.50–$24 lunch, $13–$34 dinner. AE, DC, DISC, MC, V. Mon–Thurs 11:30am–2:30pm and 5–9pm; Fri–Sat 11:30am–2:30pm and 5–9:30pm; Sun 5–9pm.

Zazu 🐸🐸 AMERICAN/ITALIAN   You'll feel like you're on the road to nowhere while driving here, but it's common knowledge that this is a destination restaurant where chefs/owners Duskie Estes and John Stewart take roadhouse dining to gastronomic heights within their long, crooked, and quaintly quirky-shaped room. The cozy, warmly lit room with comfy banquettes and myriad strategically placed mirrors is the perfect setting for the couple's creative and playful American and Northern Italian–inspired menu featuring extremely generous portions of homey comfort foods. The menu might include seared duck with steamed romano beans, and is very likely to showcase the house staple of tender balsamic pork shoulder with creamy buttermilk mashed potatoes. Regardless, save room for dessert. Keeping with the kickback spirit, they tend to be reminiscent of childhood favorites—only more decadent. Trust me: You'll be hard-pressed to pass on messy-fun chocolate fondue with homemade Nutter Butter–like cookies. An added bonus is the well-priced Sonoma-centric wine list.

3535 Guerneville Rd. (about 5 miles west of Hwy. 101), Santa Rosa. © **707/523-4814.** www.zazurestaurant.com. Reservations recommended. Main courses $17–$21. AE, DISC, MC, V. Wed–Mon 5:30–9:30pm.

Syrah   Josh Silvers likes to play with sexy, unconventional food pairings in his Santa Rosa restaurant, an urban space where hanging copper pots, exposed pipes, and oak-colored wood beams coexist—think urban loft meets mountain lodge. The menu is divided into smaller plates and larger plates, perfect for any size appetite, but your biggest challenge is choosing among selections like seared Sonoma foie gras served with a grapefruit and orange crêpes suzette, prosciutto-wrapped prawns with tabbouleh and mint pesto, and day boat scallops flanked by cauliflower couscous and preserved Meyer lemon and zucchini broth. You might want to chill out in the cozy digs, relinquish the power of choice, and open your palate to Chef Silvers's whim by just opting for the tasting menu (4 courses for $55, 7 for $75; with wine parings, $75 and $105, respectively).

205 5th St. (in the City 205 Building), Santa Rosa. © **707/568-4002.** www.syrah bistro.com. Main courses $15–$24, chef's tasting menu $54. AE, DC, MC, V. Mon–Fri 11:30am–2:00pm, 5:30–9:30pm weeknights, until 10:30 weekends.

Northern Sonoma Dining

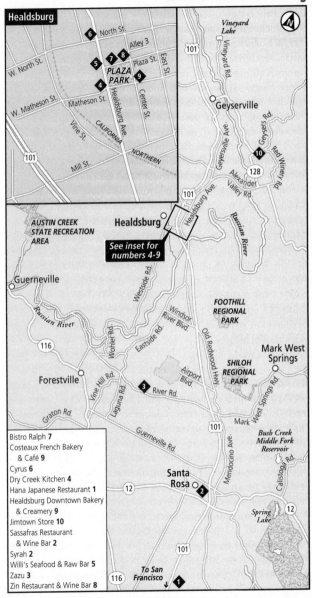

Bistro Ralph **7**
Costeaux French Bakery
  & Café **9**
Cyrus **6**
Dry Creek Kitchen **4**
Hana Japanese Restaurant **1**
Healdsburg Downtown Bakery
  & Creamery **9**
Jimtown Store **10**
Sassafras Restaurant
  & Wine Bar **2**
Syrah **2**
Willi's Seafood & Raw Bar **5**
Zazu **3**
Zin Restaurant & Wine Bar **8**

INEXPENSIVE

Sassafras Restaurant & Wine Bar 🍴 *Kids*   Modern American chef Jack Mitchell makes it impossible not to want to book a reservation here. Never mind that the ambience is more open and vibrant with new flooring and fresh Tuscan brown walls since it has recently been redone. Or that Mitchell uses the best local artisan products to whip up deliciously affordable and creative offerings from the huge seasonal menu. (Think Dungeness crab cakes with apple-fennel slaw, curry aioli, and pomegranate; organic heirloom tomatoes with olive vinaigrette, pear, and candied walnuts.) Even if you overlook the award-winning Northern California–centric wine list with 40 wines by the glass and 200 by the bottle, you'll still be inclined to head this way. Why? Perhaps because of the full bar and happening happy hour Monday through Friday from 4:30 to 6:30pm when drinks go for $2 to $4 and a tasty happy hour menu features small plates and flatbread pizzas ranging from $4 to $10. Or the kids menu with grilled cheese, corn dogs, and chicken breast— all with fries and topping out at $5. Regardless of what attracts you, you'll be glad you came.

1229 N. Dutton Ave. (north of College Ave.). © **707/578-7600**. www.sassafras restaurant.com. Main courses $9–$15 lunch, $16–$24 dinner. AE, DISC, MC, V. Lunch Mon–Fri 11:30am–5:30pm; dinner daily 5:30–9pm.

HEALDSBURG
EXPENSIVE

Cyrus 🌟🌟🌟 *Finds*   Without question, this newcomer of 2005 is Sonoma County's finest fine-dining restaurant. Run by veteran San Francisco maitre d' Nick Peyton and heralded chef Douglas Keane, it's truly a gastronome's dream destination: Romantic Burgundy, France–inspired interior, an intimate and friendly yet somewhat formal atmosphere, and to-die-for seasonal "contemporary luxury" cuisine (read: French-inspired with seasonal and global influences). Within the intimate vaulted room with warm lighting, and colors of deep chocolate and gold brightened by ruffled white curtains an evening appropriately starts, if your heart desires, with selections from carts showcasing caviar (measured to order on a scale against tiny gold bars) and champagne. It continues with a menu of build-your-own fixed-price three-, four-, or five-course options, which might include heavenly seared foie gras with fig compote, crispy potato, and balsamic reduction; roasted quail with black mission figs and mushrooms, and glazed pork belly with braised lettuce and fried green tomato. Everything is as stunning to look at as it is to taste, and if there's any question this restaurant wants to perfect the dining experience, consider this: The chef's personal line is listed on the website for those who want to discuss special dietary requests. FYI, there's also a small bar for impromptu snacking and sipping.

29 North St. (at Healdsburg Ave.). © **707/433-3311.** www.cyrusrestaurant.com. Reservations required. 3 courses $58; 4 courses $69; 5 courses $80. AE, MC, V. Daily 5:30–9:30pm.

Dry Creek Kitchen 𝓻𝓻 CONTEMPORARY AMERICAN Since its inception in 2001, the restaurant of famed chef Charlie Palmer (of Aureole in New York City and Las Vegas) has had three chefs at the helm—with ups and downs to match. But for the moment the third, 27-year-old Michael Voltaggio, is the culinary charm. Flanked by square-front windows and striated glass that gives shaded glimpses into the kitchen, the vaulted restaurant's white-tablecloth ambience is relaxed by rural touches like a long centerpiece wooden table and breadsticks protruding from pilsner glasses. But Voltaggio's cuisine, which emphasizes local seasonal produce, herbs, poultry, and meats, definitely underscores formality. His langoustine "cappuccino"—a demitasse cup of langoustine broth with two plump lobster fritters and flavorful dots of vanilla mango sauce, three-spice, and lime *fleur de sel*—is magnificent. Sea bass and potato ballotine, a headless skinless fish bundled in thin potato slices with the tail peeking out, shows the kitchen's well-measured use of restraint with each delicately flavored bite. For perfect pairings, turn to the list featuring 600 Sonoma wines. (And should you like to bring your own, you won't have to pay a corkage fee if it's made from 100% Sonoma fruit!—Maximum is two bottles.) Alas, prices are big-city, but if you're up for the ultimate splurge, this is a fine option, although my favorite is definitely nearby Cyrus.

317 Healdsburg Ave. (at the square). © **707/431-0330.** www.charliepalmer.com. Reservations recommended. Lunch and dinner main courses $22–$34. AE, DISC, MC, V. Lunch Fri–Sun noon–2:30pm; dinner Sun–Thurs 5–9:30pm, Fri–Sat 5–10pm.

Zin Restaurant & Wine Bar Locals and visitors flock to this downtown Healdsburg hot culinary outpost, where talented, innovative young chefs fuse big-city ideas with country-comfort dishes. The seasonal menu does the Wine Country norm, pairing a top-notch wine list with local foods and produce. I loved the sautéed shrimp with a smoky tomato sauce atop crispy white corn grits followed by signature dish Coq au "Zin," chicken braised in red wine with applewood-smoked bacon, roasted mushrooms, and pearl onions, served over celery-root mashed potatoes. Non-meat eaters beware: On my January visit, the winter menu featured few vegetarian options, and only one main fish entree. But don't fret: You can make a fine meal out of a few apps, and you'll have plenty of choices when you get to their exceptional Dry Creek, Russian River, and Alexander Valley–focused wine list (15 to 17 picks by the glass, around 100 by the bottle). I was lulled by the velvety '02 Stryker Sonoma old vine zinfandel, bottled just up the road.

344 Center St., Healdsburg. © **707/473-0946.** www.zinrestaurant.com. Main courses $15–$30. AE, DISC, MC, V. Daily 11:30–2pm and 5:30–10pm.

MODERATE

Bistro Ralph ⚘ CALIFORNIA   Located on the square and looking rather industrial-chic amidst its country-town environs, this longtime standby is a prime pick for a fresh, tasty meal in an upbeat and casual environment. Whether in the narrow dining room with high ceilings, concrete floors, and stainless steel embellishments around the open kitchen and bar or on the small sidewalk patio, diners have come to feast on chef/owner Ralph Tingle's deliciously simple fare showcasing local ingredients. Though the menu changes weekly, with seasonal dishes such as sautéed mahi mahi with hedgehog mushrooms, there are some standards that would inspire protest if taken off the list—osso buco with saffron risotto, for example. Lunch goes lighter with upscale salads and sandwiches.

109 Plaza St. (at Healdsburg Ave.). © **707/433-1380.** Reservations recommended. Main courses $9.50–$15 lunch, $17–$25 dinner. MC, V. Mon–Sat 11:30am–2:30pm and 5:30–9:30pm.

Willi's Seafood & Raw Bar ⚘ SEAFOOD/LATIN-INSPIRED AMERICAN   This relative newcomer underscores Healdsburg's evolution from down-home dining rooms to festive, modern restaurants with city-slick bars and menus. With urban-Caribbean decor, an exotic selection of international small plates (think ceviches, skewers, New England-style "rolls," and a crazy-good array of other options), and 40 mostly local wines (all of which are available by the glass, carafe, and full bottle), Willi's slick but relaxed surroundings and unconventional fare are a far cry from the area's traditional joints. But that's a good thing—especially if you're in the mood for delicate flash-fried calamari appetizer with orange chili gremolata, outstanding sliced hanger steak drizzled with chimichurri sauce atop a bed of cucumber salad, or caramelized eggplant and French green beans with roasted garlic vinaigrette. Add to that heated sidewalk seating and a fun and friendly bar scene (with a full bar) and reasonable prices and you've got one of downtown's hottest attractions.

403 Healdsburg Ave., (at North St.). ℭ **707/433-9191.** www.willisseafood.net. Reservations recommended for parties of 8 or more. Small plates $4–$14. DISC, MC, V. Wed–Mon 11:30am–9pm; Fri–Sat 11:30am–10pm.

INEXPENSIVE

Costeaux French Bakery & Café *Value* BAKERY/CAFE   Swing by this simple, quaint bakery in the heart of Healdsburg for breakfast, lunch, or a coffee and pastry. Owned by Karl and Nancy Seppi for over 25 years, this family-operated gem churns out sandwiches made with homemade artisanal bread, hearty soups (the French onion is to die for), imaginative salads (daily specials include pistachio pasta and cherry tomato with fresh herbs), and insane cakes to satisfy any sweet tooth. (The caramel macadamia nut tart is crowned with Belgian chocolate; the pink champagne unites rum custard, whipped cream, and chocolate.) Wash it all down with glass of local zinfandel, a Pabst Blue Ribbon, or root beer, and contemplate which winery to hit next.

417 Healdsburg Ave., Healdsburg. ℭ **707/433-1913.** Fax 707/433-1955. www. costeaux.com. Main courses $4.25–7.95 breakfast, $4.95–$8.50 lunch. MC, V. Tues–Sat 6:30am–6pm; Sun 6:30am–4pm; closed Mon.

Healdsburg Downtown Bakery & Creamery ✦ BAKERY   If you want a local experience along with your morning jolt of caffeine, head to the pastry party happening every morning fronting Healdsburg's plaza. Inside crowds form to mingle over the baked goods by Kathleen Stewart, who used to work at Berkeley's famed restaurant Chez Panisse. Along with your standard lattes and the like you can load up on outstanding breads, focaccia, legendary cinnamon rolls, cakes, and during summer homemade ice cream and sherbets. A bonus for anyone who previously visited and experienced the inevitable standing room only, in 2005 they added 20 closely packed family-style seats, breakfast items ranging from eggs to pancakes, and soups and salads for lunchtime.

308 A Center St. (at Matheson St.). ℭ **707/431-2719.** Pastries and breads $1.35–$5.50; breakfast and lunch main courses $7–$10. Cash only. Mon–Fri 6am–5pm; Sat 7am–5:30pm; Sun 7am-4pm.

Jimtown Store ✦✦ DELI   Full of Wine Country character, this retro-hip country store is a Sonoma County landmark. Stop by and grab a seat at the counter for a cup of strong coffee and check out their seasonal menu—it focuses on local farm fare—or take your order to go as a boxed lunch. The store, owned by cookbook author and chef Carrie Brown, sells its own brand of condiments. (Try artichoke, caper, or fig and olive spreads.) In addition, bottles of local wine share shelf space with candy, antiques, and an assortment of wares they describe as "Gifts that are Different." I puttered through aisles of patterned oilcloth (sold by the yard), metal lunchboxes, vintage Coca-Cola signs, and gift boxes teeming with homemade crostini and local cheeses, and considered purchasing the loudest whoopee cushion I've ever encountered. I resisted, choosing instead to munch my Niman ham and Brie with Mendocino Mustard Butter served on a fresh baguette out on the front porch and contemplate the rolling vineyards stretched out to the horizon.

6706 State Hwy. 128, Healdsburg. © **707/433-1212.** www.jimtown.com. Box lunches $11–$13. Breakfast and lunch only; hours vary; call ahead.

6 Where to Stock Up for a Picnic & Where to Enjoy It

See also listings above for Jimtown Store and Costeaux French Bakery.

Even if you don't make it to Napa Valley you'll be able to get a taste of one of if its greatest attributes with a stop at **Oakville Grocery Co.,** 124 Matheson St., at Healdsburg Plaza (© **707/433-3200**), which is open daily 8am to 8pm. You'll enjoy maneuvering through the isles loaded with fancy breads, spreads, meats, cheeses, sweets, and more condiments than you ever knew existed. You can also select from the ready-made gourmet items, which range from mini–crab cakes and Caesar salads to pizza, rotisserie chicken, and daily specials.

Though you can sit at one of the tables outside to feast, it's a better idea to take your edible booty to-go and head to one of the wineries where you'll get surroundings as sumptuous as the food. Try **Matanzas Creek** (p. 168), where picnic tables are surrounded by oak trees and have vineyard views. **Passalacqua** (p. 171) welcomes guests with umbrella-shaded tables on patio surrounded by Dry Creek's vineyards. **Bella Vineyards & Wine Caves** (p. 173) has patio tables inside their super cute caves. The mother of all choices is **Preston of Dry Creek** (p. 173), which welcomes guests with enough picnic tables to welcome a busload of hungry visitors within a garden surrounded by wisteria. Ahhh, the good life.

Appendix: Grape Varietals in the Wine Country

by Erika Lenkert & Matthew R. Poole

1 Major Grape Varietals

Below is a list of the most prevalent grape varietals found in California Wine Country and abroad.

CABERNET SAUVIGNON   This transplant from Bordeaux has become California's most well-known varietal. The small, deep-colored, thick-skinned berry is a complex grape, yielding medium- to full-bodied red wines that are highly tannic when young and often require a long aging period to achieve their greatest potential. Cabernet is often blended with other related red varietals, such as merlot and cabernet franc (see below), into full-flavored red table wines. Cabernet is often matched with red-meat dishes and strong cheeses. If you're looking to invest in several cases of wine, cabernet sauvignon is always a good long-term bet.

CHARDONNAY   Chardonnay is the most widely planted grape variety in the Wine Country, and it produces exceptional medium- to full-bodied dry white wines. In fact, it was a California chardonnay that revolutionized the world of wine when it won the legendary Paris tasting test of 1976, beating out France's top white burgundies. You'll find a range of chardonnays in the Wine Country, from delicate, crisp wines that are clear and light in color to buttery, fruity, and oaky (no other wine benefits more from the oak aging process) wines that tend to have deeper golden hues as they increase in richness. This highly complex and aromatic grape is one of the few grapes in the world that doesn't require blending; it's also the principal grape for making sparkling wine. Chardonnay goes well with a variety of dishes, from seafood to poultry, pork, veal, and pastas made with cream and/or butter.

MERLOT   Traditionally used as a blending wine to smooth out the rough edges of other grapes, merlot has gained popularity in California since the early 1970s—enough so that wineries such as

Sonoma's St. Francis are best known for producing masterful merlots. The merlot grape is a relative of cabernet sauvignon, but it's fruitier and softer, with a pleasant black-cherry bouquet. Merlots tend to be simpler and less tannic than most cabernets, and they are drinkable at an earlier age, though these wines, too, gain complexity with age. Serve this medium- to full-bodied red with any dish you'd normally pair with a cabernet. (It's great with pizza.)

PINOT NOIR   It has taken California vintners decades to make relatively few great wines from pinot noir grapes, which are difficult to grow and vinify. Even in their native Burgundy, the wines are excellent only a few years out of every decade, and they are a challenge for winemakers to master. Recent attempts to grow the finicky grape in the cooler climes of the Carneros District have met with promising results. During banner harvest years, California's pinot grapes produce complex, light- to medium-bodied red wines with such low tannins and such silky textures that they're comparable to the finest reds in the world. Pinots are fuller and softer than cabernets and can be drinkable at 2 to 5 years of age, though the best improve with additional aging. Pinot noir is versatile at the dinner table, but it goes best with lamb, duck, turkey, game birds, semisoft cheeses, and even fish.

SAUVIGNON BLANC   Also labeled as fumé blanc, sauvignon blanc grapes are used to make crisp, dry whites of medium to light body that vary in flavor from slightly grassy to tart or fruity. The grape grows very well in the Wine Country and has become increasingly popular due to its distinctive character and pleasant acidity; indeed, it has recently become a contender to the almighty chardonnay. Because of their acidity, sauvignon blancs pair well with shellfish, seafood, and salads.

ZINFANDEL   Zinfandel is often called the "mystery" grape because its origins are uncertain. "Zinfandel" first appeared on California labels in the late 1800s; hence, it has come to be known as California's grape. In fact, most of the world's zinfandel acreage is planted in Northern California, and some of the best zinfandel grapes grow in cool coastal locations and on century-old vines up in California's Gold Country. Zinfandel is by far the Wine Country's most versatile grape, popular as blush wine (the ever-quaffable white zinfandel: a light, fruity wine, usually served chilled); as dark, spicy, and fruity red wines; and even as a port. Premium zins, such as those crafted by Ravenswood winery in Sonoma (the Wine Country's Zeus of zins), are rich and peppery, with a lush texture and nuances of raspberries, licorice, and spice. Food-wise it's a free-for-all, although premium zins go well with beef, lamb, venison, hearty pastas, pizza, and stews.

2 Lesser-Known Grape Varietals

Here are a few lesser-known grape varietals that you may encounter as you explore the Wine Country.

CABERNET FRANC   A French black grape variety that's often blended with and overshadowed by the more widely planted cabernet sauvignon, cabernet franc was actually recently discovered to be one of the parent grape species that gave rise to cabernet sauvignon. The grape grows best in cool, damp climatic conditions and tends to be lighter in color and tannins than cabernet sauvignon; therefore, it matures earlier in the bottle. These wines have a deep purple color with an herbaceous aroma.

CHENIN BLANC   Planted mainly in France, chenin blanc runs the gamut from cheap, dry whites with little discernible character to some of the most subtle, fragrant, and complex whites in the world. In the Wine Country, the grape is mostly used to create fruity, light- to medium-bodied, and slightly sweet wines. Chenin blanc lags far behind chardonnay and sauvignon blanc in popularity in the Wine Country, though in good years it's known for developing a lovely and complex bouquet, particularly when aged in oak. It's often served with pork and poultry, Asian dishes with soy-based sauces, mild cheeses, and vegetable and fruit salads.

GEWÜRZTRAMINER   The gewürztraminer grape produces white wines with a strong floral aroma and litchi nut–like flavor. Slightly sweet yet spicy, it's somewhat similar in style to Johannisberg Riesling, and it is occasionally used to make late-harvest, dessert-style wine. The grape grows well in the cooler coastal regions of California, particularly Mendocino County. The varietal is particularly appreciated for its ability to complement Asian foods; its sweet character stands up to flavors that would diminish a drier wine's flavors and make it seem more tart.

PETITE SIRAH   Widely grown throughout the warmer regions of California, petite sirah's origins are a mystery. The grape, which produces rich red wines that are high in tannins, serves mainly as the backbone for Central Valley "jug" wines. Very old vines still exist in cooler northern regions, where the grapes are often made into a robust and well-balanced red wine of considerable popularity.

PINOT BLANC A mutation of the pinot gris vine, the pinot blanc grape is generally grown in France's Alsace region to make dry, crisp white wines. In California, pinot blanc is used to make a fruity wine similar to the simpler versions of chardonnay. It's also blended with champagne-style sparkling wines, thanks to its acid content and clean flavor.

RIESLING Also called Johannisberg Riesling or white Riesling, this is the grape from which most of the great wines of Germany are made. It was introduced to California in the mid–19th century by immigrant vintners and is now used mainly to produce floral and fruity white wines of light to medium body, ranging from dry to very sweet. (It's often used to make late-harvest dessert wine.) Well-made Rieslings, of which California has produced few, have a vivid fruitiness and lively balancing acidity, as well as a potential to age for many years. Suggested food pairings include crab, pork, sweet-and-sour foods, and anything with a strong citrus flavor. Asian-influenced foods also pair well with Riesling.

SANGIOVESE The primary grape used in Italy's Tuscany region and northern and central Italy is used to make everything from chianti and Brunello di Montalcino to "Super Tuscan" blends. As of late, it's also making a name for itself in California. Its style varies depending on where it's grown, but it's commonly described as anything from "fruity," "smooth," "spicy," "good acidity," and "medium-bodied" to "structured" and "full-bodied."

SYRAH This red varietal is best known for producing France's noble and age-worthy Rhone Valley reds such as côte-rôtie and hermitage. Syrah vines produce dark, blackish berries with thick skins, resulting in typically dark, rich, dense, medium- to full-bodied wines with distinctive pepper, spice, and fruit flavors (particularly cherry, black currant, and blackberry).

Index

See also Accommodations and Restaurant indexes, below.

RESTAURANTS

FROMMER'S® COMPLETE TRAVEL GUIDES

FROMMER'S® DAY BY DAY GUIDES

Amsterdam
Chicago
Florence & Tuscany

London
New York City
Paris

Rome
San Francisco
Venice

FROMMER'S® NATIONAL PARK GUIDES

Algonquin Provincial Park
Banff & Jasper
Grand Canyon

National Parks of the American West
Rocky Mountain
Yellowstone & Grand Teton

Yosemite and Sequoia & Kings
  Canyon
Zion & Bryce Canyon

FROMMER'S® MEMORABLE WALKS

Chicago
London

New York
Paris

Rome
San Francisco

FROMMER'S® WITH KIDS GUIDES

Chicago
Hawaii
Las Vegas
London

National Parks
New York City
San Francisco

Toronto
Walt Disney World® & Orlando
Washington, D.C.

SUZY GERSHMAN'S BORN TO SHOP GUIDES

Born to Shop: France
Born to Shop: Hong Kong, Shanghai
  & Beijing

Born to Shop: Italy
Born to Shop: London

Born to Shop: New York
Born to Shop: Paris

FROMMER'S® IRREVERENT GUIDES

Amsterdam
Boston
Chicago
Las Vegas
London

Los Angeles
Manhattan
New Orleans
Paris

Rome
San Francisco
Walt Disney World®
Washington, D.C.

FROMMER'S® BEST-LOVED DRIVING TOURS

Austria
Britain
California
France

Germany
Ireland
Italy
New England

Northern Italy
Scotland
Spain
Tuscany & Umbria

THE UNOFFICIAL GUIDES®

Adventure Travel in Alaska
Beyond Disney
California with Kids
Central Italy
Chicago
Cruises
Disneyland®
England
Florida
Florida with Kids

Hawaii
Ireland
Las Vegas
London
Maui
Mexico's Best Beach Resorts
Mini Las Vegas
Mini Mickey
New Orleans
New York City

Paris
San Francisco
South Florida including Miami &
  the Keys
Walt Disney World®
Walt Disney World® for
  Grown-ups
Walt Disney World® with Kids
Washington, D.C.

SPECIAL-INTEREST TITLES

Athens Past & Present
Cities Ranked & Rated
Frommer's Best Day Trips from London
Frommer's Best RV & Tent Campgrounds
  in the U.S.A.

Frommer's Exploring America by RV
Frommer's NYC Free & Dirt Cheap
Frommer's Road Atlas Europe
Frommer's Road Atlas Ireland
Retirement Places Rated

FROMMER'S® PHRASEFINDER DICTIONARY GUIDES

French
Italian
Spanish

IF YOU BOOK IT, IT SHOULD BE THERE.

Only Travelocity guarantees it will be, or we'll work
with our travel partners to make it right, right away.
So if you're missing a balcony or anything else
you booked, just call us 24/7, 1-888-TRAVELOCITY

travelocity
You'll never roam alone